THE SHAME FACTOR

THE
SHAME
FACTOR

Heal Your Deepest Fears
and Set Yourself Free

STEPHAN B. POULTER, PhD

Prometheus Books

59 John Glenn Drive
Amherst, New York 14228

Inquiries should be addressed to
Prometheus Books
59 John Glenn Drive
Amherst, New York 14228
VOICE: 716–691–0133 • FAX: 716–691–0137
WWW.PROMETHEUSBOOKS.COM

23 22 21 20 19   5 4 3 2 1

Library of Congress Cataloging-in-Publication Data

Names: Poulter, Stephan, author.
Title: The shame factor : heal your deepest fears and set yourself free / by Stephan B.
    Poulter, PhD
Description: Amherst, New York : Prometheus Books, 2019. | Includes bibliographical
    references.
Identifiers: LCCN 2018056212 (print) | LCCN 2018060171 (ebook) |
    ISBN 9781633885233 (ebook) | ISBN 9781633885226 (pbk.)
Subjects: LCSH: Shame. | Self-esteem.
Classification: LCC BF575.S45 (ebook) | LCC BF575.S45 P688 2019 (print) |
    DDC 152.4/4--dc23
LC record available at https://lccn.loc.gov/2018056212

Printed in the United States of America

CONTENTS

Foreword by Dr. William Carter Felts   15

Acknowledgments   17

Author's Note   19

The Preface of Shame: On a Personal Level   21

SECTION I: WHAT IS SHAME AND WHY IS IT A PROBLEM?   25

Chapter 1: The Shame Factor: What Is It, Doctor? Exposing the Big Secret   27

Shame Is Not Guilt   28
  Working Definition of Shame   28
  Real Life Victims of Shame   29
Five Emotional Elements of Shame   31
  1. Shame Is the "Emotional Cancer" of Your Heart and Soul   31
  2. The "Big Secret" of Shame   32
  3. Shame Is an Inside Job, Not Something Outside of You   32
  4. Chronic Fear of Not Feeling "Good Enough"   33
  5. Shame's Emotional Super Glue: Addiction Mixed with Shame 33
Shame Factor: The Classic Symptoms   34
  Exposure Is Really Good   35
  Your Shame Scale and Shame Checklist:
    What's My Shame Status?   36
  Your Own Shame Triggers.   38
The Cycle of Shame: Anger, Embarrassment, and Self-Loathing   40

Shame Cycle #1: No One Is Winning—Anger   42
Shame Cycle #2: Embarrassment Has No Limits   44
    No Lasting Relief   45
Shame Cycle #3: Self-Loathing Is an Underestimated Force   46
Stopping and Exposing Your Shame Cycle   47
    Letting Go of Your "Bad" Self   47
    Emotional Sobriety Exposes Shame   47
    Keeping Your Emotional Clarity via Personal Boundaries   48
Closing Thoughts   49

Chapter 2: Your Early Years and Your Personal Shame Beginnings: Five Common Shaming Parenting Styles

                                                                  52

    Family Shame Defined   54
Family Shame   54
Perfectionism Style of Parenting   58
Chaotic Parenting Style   62
Single-Parent Style of Parenting   65
Explosive Style of Parenting   69
Best-Friend Style of Parenting   73
Closing Thoughts   77

Chapter 3: How Shame Plays Out for the Sexes: Toxic Male and Female Shame

                                                                  80

Shame Is Emotional Cancer   82
    John and Road Rage   84
    Toxic Shame   90
Guns, Violence, and Men   90
    2017 Las Vegas Concert Shooter: Shame Unleashed   92
    Evidence of Male Violence   94
        Other Truths about Suicide   95
Self-Loathing, Depression, and Women: It's an Inside Job   95
    Food for Thought: Shame's Silent Weapon   98
    Why Did Kate Spade Commit Suicide?   99
Closing Thoughts   100

SECTION II: SHAME'S SECRET OPERATING SYSTEM IN YOUR LIFE 103

Chapter 4: The Daily Functioning of Shame: Seven Common Emotional Cycles 105

Mental Illness and Shame 107
Shame's Three Closest Friends: Denial, Amnesia, and Avoidance 109
    Present-Day Story of the Big Three Defenses Working 24/7 112
The Seven Classic Triggers of the Shame Cycle 112
    1. Fear of Embarrassment: Emotional Paralysis 113
    2. Feeling Angry, Invisible, or Worthless: Distorted View of Yourself 115
        Bar Room Fight 117
    3. Imposter Syndrome and Feeling like a Fraud:
        Fear of Being Revealed as Incompetent 118
    4. Feeling Isolated: Fear of Rejection 120
        My Safe Place 122
    5. Suspicious: Untrusting of People and Authority 123
        Rookie Police Officer 125
        Fast-Forward Thirty Years 126
    6. Fear of Intimacy: Feeling like Damaged Goods, Unlovable 126
        Dating Sucks: No Good Men or Women to Date in This City 129
    7. Fear of Criticism: Inability to Tolerate Feedback,
        Acting as a People Pleaser 129
Closing Thoughts 131

Chapter 5: Where Shame Hides and Terrorizes: Your Money, Your Love Life, Your Family Past and Present, Your Health/Body, and Dying 133

Six Areas of Consideration 136
    1. Money and Finances: You and Your Money 138
        Retail Therapy 140
    2. Love Relationships and Marriage 141
        Love Hurts 143
    3. Childhood Family 145
    4. Your Present-Day Family: You and Your Children 147

5. Your Health and Your Body Image   150
    Shame, Self-Loathing, and Cutting:
        A Dangerous Combination   152
    You Are Your Health   153
    Brad's Accident   156
6. Loss and Death: The Unspeakable and the Unexpressed   158
    Childhood Dog   160
Closing Thoughts   161

Chapter 6: The Big Cover Up, Super Glue: Addictions and Shame

Chapter 6: The Big Cover Up, Super Glue:
    Addictions and Shame   165

Psychology of Addiction   167
    Emotional Regression   168
Some Common Addictions   170
    Tobacco   171
    Alcohol   172
    Drugs   173
    Gambling   174
    Food   175
    Sex   177
    Video Games   179
    The Internet and Handheld Devices   181
    Risky and Reckless Behavior Addiction   182
    Shopping: Retail Therapy   184
    Work: Type A and B Personalities   186
Your Self-Reporting Shame-Addiction Stress Scale   188
Closing Thoughts   191

Chapter 7: Your Personal Brand of Shame: Fear, Avoidance, and Emotional Terrorism

Chapter 7: Your Personal Brand of Shame:
    Fear, Avoidance, and Emotional Terrorism   195

    Fifth Grade Crisis   197
Cognitive Dissonance: The First Step   201
The Endless Civil War: Your Intellect and Your Heart   204
    Your New Normal   205
    Shame's Insidious Resistance to Change at Any Age:
        Two Stories from the Valley of Despair   208

Jon, Age Sixty-Two: "I Am Never Leaving My Patio"   209
Lynn, Age Twenty-Nine, Single Female: "I Am Moving Away" 210
Exposing Your Hidden Fears, Anxiety, and Terror   211
Five Keys to Exposing Your Fear Connection to Shame and Anxiety   216
1. Expanding Your Comfort Zone   216
2. Built-In Fear Limits   216
3. Emotional Terrorism: Relentless Force   217
4. Loss of Control: Change Is in the Air   218
5. Your Full Acceptance   219
Closing Thoughts   219

Chapter 8: Shame and Relationships: You, Your Parents, Children, and Lovers—How It's All Related   221

Shame's Role in Relationships: The Big Cover-Up   221
Codependency Exposed and Defined   226
How and Where Did It Start?   228
How Codependency Looks and Works at Any Age: Four Scenarios   231
Scenario 1: Silent "Abusive" Neglect   231
Scenario 2: I Am Embarrassed   234
Scenario 3: Never Leave Me   236
Scenario 4: I Am a Good Person   238
The Game of Tennis: Player 1—
Shame/Codependent Relationship Control,
Player 2—You   240
Emotional Boundaries   242
Five Common Relationship Styles and the Shame Factor   244
Addictive Relationships   245
Noncommittal Distant Relationships   247
Placating Relationships   249
On-Again, Off-Again Relationships   250
Secure Relationships   252
Closing Thoughts   253

SECTION III: HEALING THE BIG SPLIT IN YOU
AND YOUR OTHER SELF

257

Chapter 9: No More Secrets: Your Own Healing
Exposure Process—Viewing All the Parts
of Your Life from 10,2 Feet

259

What Are Individuation, Self-Acceptance, and a Core Sense of Self?   260
    Definition of Self-Acceptance   262
    Definition of Separation-Individuation   263
    Definition of Your Core Self   265
Going from the Outside to the Inside of You: Your Journey Within   267
Your Five-Step Acceptance Process   268
    Step #1: Roadblocks within You   269
    Step #2: No Perfectionism—Life Is Messy   272
    Step #3: Accepting Change in Your Life—It's Not Personal   274
        Comfort-Shame Level of the Status Quo   275
    Step #4: Taking Personal Responsibility for Your Life   276
    Step #5: The Power of Empathy and Self-Forgiveness   278
Writing Your New Self-Accepting Narrative: Six Opportunities   281
    1. Money, Finances, Wealth, and Career   282
        Shaming Money Beliefs   282
        Self-Acceptance Beliefs   282
        Your Self-Acceptance Money Script   283
    2. Love, Romance, Marriage, and Emotional Intimacy   283
        Shaming Love and Intimacy Beliefs   283
        Self-Acceptance Love and Intimacy Beliefs   283
        Your Love-Relationship Self-Accepting Script   284
    3. Childhood Family Issues   284
        Shaming Family Issues Beliefs   284
        Self-Accepting Family Beliefs   284
        Your Self-Accepting Family Script   285
    4. Present-Day Family   285
        Shaming Current Family Beliefs   285
        Self-Accepting Current Family Beliefs   285
        Your Personal Self-Accepting Family Script   286
    5. Your Health and Your Body Issues   286
        Shaming Health and Body Beliefs   286

Self-Accepting Health and Body Beliefs 286
Your Self-Accepting Health and Body Script 287
6. Loss and Death: The Unspeakable and the Unexposed: 287
Shaming Loss and Death Beliefs 287
Self-Accepting Life Beliefs 287
Your Self-Acceptance Life Script 288
Closing Thoughts: Happiness and You 288

Chapter 10: Rewriting and Rewiring Your Emotional Triggers

290

Your Mother Factor, Father Factor, and Shame 292
Client Examples of Their Mother Factor Messages 294
Ann 294
Dave 295
Jean, age, fifty-two 295
Client Examples of Their Father Factor Messages 296
Barry, age thirty-six 296
Cindy, age forty-two. 296
John, age fifty-six 296
Mother Factor and Father Factor Impact and Insights 297
Four Cornerstones to Updating and Completing
Your Separating-Individuating Process 301
1. Emotional Boundaries: Staying on Your Side of the Court 302
2. Emotional Enmeshment: You Aren't Responsible
for Your Parent's or Anyone Else's Life
(Everyone Has Personal Responsibility) 303
3. Emotional Sobriety: Responding Rather Than Reacting 306
4. Frustration Tolerance: Understanding, Accepting,
and Developing Emotional Maturity 308
Healing and Removing Terror from Your Life:
Contrasting Shame Triggers with Your Self-Acceptance Responses 311
The Seven Shame Triggers and Seven Self-Acceptance Options 313
1. Fear of Embarrassment (Emotional Paralysis) 313
Embarrassment Shaming Inner Belief Dialogue 313
Self-Acceptance, Exposure, and Honesty Inner Dialogue 314
Your I AM Rebuttal to Fear of Embarrassment 314
Your Self-Accepting Dialogue about
Becoming Empowered Rather Than Embarrassed 315

2. Feeling Angry, Invisible, or Worthless: Distorted View of Yourself   315
    Anger and Self-Loathing Shaming Inner Belief Dialogue   315
    Self-Acceptance of Anger and Emotions Inner Dialogue   316
    Your I AM Rebuttal to Anger, Rage, and Feeling Powerless   316
    Your Self-Accepting Dialogue about Anger
       and Abusive Behavior   317
3. Imposter Syndrome: Feeling like a Fraud
  (Fear of Being Revealed or Exposed)   317
    Imposter Syndrome Shaming Inner Belief Dialogue   317
    Self-Acceptance Empowering Inner Dialogue   318
    Your I AM Rebuttal to Imposter Syndrome
       and Emotional Terrorism   318
    Your Self-Accepting Dialogue about Your
       Imposter Syndrome Fears and Fear of Exposure   319
4. Isolation: Feelings of Rejection, Defectiveness, and Inadequacy   319
    Fear of Vulnerability, Feeling Defective, and Not Being
       Good Enough Shaming Inner Belief Dialogue   319
    Self-Acceptance Feeling Competent Inner Dialogue   320
    Your I AM Rebuttal to Isolation and
       Feeling Defective in Relationships   320
    Your Self-Accepting Dialogue about Shaming Isolation   321
5. Feeling Suspicious: Untrusting of People and Authority   321
    Dread of Life, Authority, Feeling Small, and
       Powerless Shaming Inner Belief Dialogue   321
    Self-Acceptance Trusting and Embracing Inner Dialogue   322
    Your I AM Rebuttal to Paranoia, Fear of Authority,
       and Fear of Living   322
    Your Self-Accepting Dialogue about Having
       Trusting, Supportive, Caring Relationships   323
6. Fear of Intimacy: Feeling Like Damaged Goods and Unlovable   323
    Fear of Intimacy Shaming Inner Belief Dialogue   323
    Self-Acceptance Secure Relationship Inner Dialogue   324
    Your I AM Rebuttal to Fear of Intimacy   325
    Your Self-Accepting Dialogue about
       All the Relationships in Your Life   325
7. Fear of Criticism: Placating, People Pleasing,
  and the Inability to Tolerate Feedback   326
    Shaming Fear of Being Exposed, Inferior and
       Inadequate Inner Belief Dialogue   326

Self-Acceptance Feedback and Feeling
   Competent Inner Dialogue   326
   Your I AM Rebuttal to Criticism and People Pleasing   327
   Your Self-Accepting Dialogue about Fear of Criticism   327
Closing Thoughts   328

Chapter 11: Three Big-Time Changes: Acceptance, Empathy, and Understanding—It's All within You   331

Looking Inside for Your Happiness and Healing   331
   Insight into Your Healing   333
Changing of the Guard: Removing Your Psychological,
   Emotional, and Body Guards   336
   Action Belief Questions   347
Two Stories of Approach, Acceptance, and Engagement: Jon and Lynn   351
   Jon from Chapter 7: "I Am Never Leaving My Patio"   351
   Lynn from Chapter 7: "I Am Moving Away"   353
Exposing Your Secret: No More Emotional Terrorism   354
New Collective Qualities of You   357
   What Is Exposure?   358
   What Is Blending?   358
   What Is Direct Access?   359
Closing Thoughts   360

Chapter 12: Developing Your Own Eagle Mindset: Your Endless Resource   363

The Three Mindsets within Your Emotional Headquarters:
   Lizard, Owl, and Eagle   365
   Lizard Mindset   366
   Owl Mindset   366
   Eagle Mindset   367
Eagle Mindfulness Mindset: Presence of Your Mind   370
Full-Capacity Eagle Mindset Benefits   371
Your Quick Self-Check Healing Guide   374
Further Thoughts   384
When and Why Should I Get Professional Support—No Stigma   385
Closing Thoughts: My Thoughts for You   386

Notes   389

Bibliography   395

Resource Guide   399

FOREWORD

by Dr. William Carter Felts

Self-image is more important than any other factor in determining direction, success, and overall happiness in life. This "ground zero" influences all of our choices, perspectives, and perceptions.

In his seventh book, renowned psychologist Dr. Stephan Poulter explores the profound emotional experience of shame. No emotion in a man or woman's life is more confusing, debilitating, and damaging than shame.

What is shame? Its insidious nature is complicated and difficult to explain. You can live with all of the symptoms of this debilitating emotional condition and never want or be able to identify the origin. In *The Shame Factor*, Dr. Poulter exposes the secret and nonfunctional nature of this psychological malaise.

He carefully dissects the root cause of shame, how it originates, and the many ways in which it can manifest and severely damage our lives. Understanding the origin and nature of shame is the first step in bringing awareness and healing to this misunderstood emotion.

Beyond simply defining shame, Dr. Poulter provides a road map to healing using insights, techniques, and exercises that have proven successful in many years of clinical practice. Self-acceptance and a person's identity can be negatively impacted by the unseen role and harmful nature of shame.

In broader terms, the understanding and clarity Dr. Poulter provides can apply to "imposter syndrome," fear of rejection, and all kinds of insecurity and self-doubt. He shows the emotional and psychological connection between shame and the negative self-image responsible for the majority of our suffering.

When trying to develop clarity about our "deep inner self," I find it immensely helpful to expand the definition to include living a shame-free life. The day-to-day integration of psychology and the emotional insight given in this book can aid us in our understanding of self.

Dr. Poulter is unique in his credentials and perspective because of his additional training in theology and law enforcement. His inclusive and comfortable presentation style resembles a personal meeting with him. Without being overly academic or philosophical, he speaks to you in a manner that is practical, safe, and full of hope. I'm looking forward to the powerful transformation this book will have in your life.

ACKNOWLEDGMENTS

T o my family, who are powerful loving souls: Miriam, Madison Wendy, Jonathan Brett, Matthew, and Julia.

Additionally, I want to thank and extend my hands to those who have helped me discover, heal, and live a shame-free life. Many of you have no idea of the positive impact and lasting impression you made in my life. Special thanks to my editor, Steven L. Mitchell; Brad Jenkins; Christopher Casey; Erik Odom; Carter Felts; Barry Weichman; Jim Myerson; Evan C.; Dave D.; Paramahansa Yogananda; Jay Grossman; Sean Novak; Jack Levy; my late parents, Peter and Charlotte Poulter; Debbie Davis; Peter Chang; the late Grace Chang; and to all my clients over the years. Additionally, the following were instrumental in helping form me and this book within me: Paraiso Way neighborhood, Valley View, Dan Curtis, Coach Goorjian, Coach Goffredo, Paul Roberts, La Crescenta, COTW Church, CVHS, USC, GPD, Dr. Winston Gooden, Barbara Zax, Lunada Bay Little League Baseball, 11980, and the shame-factor process.

AUTHOR'S NOTE

All of the non-personal stories by the author, third-party references, names, clinical vignettes, and examples are a vast composite of many different individuals designed to protect privacy and anonymity. Therefore, any similarity between the names and the stories of individuals that the reader might recognize is inadvertent and purely coincidental in nature. All the names used in this book are for illustration purposes only. The people are fictional and have no relationship to any person known by the author. Throughout the book I will be using pronouns such as son, daughter, mom, dad, and parents to refer to the wide range of people and circumstances we will be discussing. I will alternatively be using him, her, he, she, dad, mom, father, and mother unless referring to a specific case example.

THE PREFACE OF SHAME:
ON A PERSONAL LEVEL

It always seems impossible until it is done.
—attributed to Nelson Mandela

My journey with shame started early on. I had many personal challenges. I had a speech problem, a terrible time with learning how to read, and I wore glasses when it was a stigma to have four eyes. When I was around six or seven years old, I knew something didn't feel right inside of me. I knew it wasn't mental illness because I saw plenty of that in my family and relatives. This feeling of terror and despair in my stomach was an all-too-common experience. What was it? I couldn't describe it; I could only feel it.

My reading problem became a source of personal contention with my parents. I was always in the lowest reading group during elementary school. This feeling of inadequacy was my closest and best friend. I just couldn't mentally put things together, and I struggled with reading out loud in class. I tried so hard, but my mind just didn't process it. I got Ds for reading all through elementary school, which was catastrophic for me and impacted how I felt I was viewed by my parents. I am not saying that a lot of other things weren't happening at home, but poor reading grades were the bane of my young life. Finally, in the sixth grade, my teacher had me read to her privately. I got my first A in reading. I literally, for the first time, felt I was the luckiest kid in the world as I mastered how to read. Unfortunately, the damage was done. The self-loathing of feeling stupid, defective, and odd was already set in cement. I tried to hide my emotional malaise, but it was never far away.

Growing up in the 1970s and early 1980s, no one talked about anything below the surface of life. There was an emotional gag order on expressing anything negative or remotely emotional insightful. I had figurative gray duct tape around my heart and soul. This continued through childhood and into early adulthood. It wasn't until my second major romantic breakup that I realized I had to do something. My heart felt like it was hemorrhaging emotional pain, and I chronically felt I was "defective" and "not good enough." When I would mention my emotional malaise to my closet buddies, they would look at me oddly, like my beagle does when I refuse to give her my dinner. I clearly had a problem that no one else felt or that they just didn't talk about. This realization post-college was even more upsetting. On paper my life looked fine; I just didn't feel fine.

It wasn't until my mid-twenties that I finally sought out a therapist. I had to do something because the future didn't look or feel very promising. I didn't tell anyone that I was going to get professional help because none of my friends or family had ever done that before.

Putting words to this "dis-ease" and emotional malaise seemed impossible. I didn't feel depressed, and not particularly anxious, but I just felt seriously defective. On our first visit, I said to my therapist, "I feel really messed up on the inside. What is it? Because I feel terrible and empty inside?"

My mild-mannered psychologist looked at me and said, "Stephan, you are struggling with shame!" Finally, my emotional terrorist was named and exposed. The relief I began to feel over the following months was tremendous.

Shame was now formally named. The state of not knowing what was wrong with me had been torture in itself. Not allowing shame to control my life has been a bumpy dirt road of a healing process ever since.

This book, *The Shame Factor*, is an in-depth exploration into the insidious unrecognized role shame plays in people's lives. Smart, loving men and women tell me all the time that they don't have any shame. The denial, avoidance, and emotional amnesia of trauma is the perfect setting for shame's growth and control in our lives. In this book, we will discuss childhood, family history, emotional expression, addiction, self-loathing, body image issues, career, money, love, sex, relationships, people pleasing, self-doubt, food concerns, embarrassment, imposter syndrome, and all the other factors of shame.

Shame is a very tricky psychological phenomenon, but we will look at it systematically so you can see how it has affected you and decide how you want to manage it. I know you have the courage to read this book and continue your journey to living a shame-free life. Let's start this process.

> *There is nothing in a caterpillar that tells you it's going to be a butterfly.*
>
> —R. Buckminster Fuller,
> "Everything I Know," 1975

WHAT IS SHAME AND WHY IS IT A PROBLEM?

The possibilities are numerous once we decide to act and not react.

—Gloria Anzaldúa,
Borderlands/La Frontera: The New Mestiza, 1987

All journeys have secret destinations of which the traveler is unaware.
—Martin Buber, *The Legend of the Baal-Shem*, 1955

Until you make the unconscious conscious it will direct your life, and you will call it fate.

—attributed to Carl Jung

CHAPTER 1

THE SHAME FACTOR: WHAT IS IT, DOCTOR? EXPOSING THE BIG SECRET

For reasons rooted in the values of contemporary culture, the concept of shame had until recently all but vanished from discussions of emotional disarray. Now it is regarded by many psychologists as the preeminent cause of emotional distress in our time.
—Dr. Robert Karen, "Shame," *Atlantic Monthly*, February 1992

It's like there is a hunter [shame] over your shoulder, and the hunter is always coming. And they're going to . . . find out that I am flawed and defective. They're going to find out that I am not what I look like I am.
—John Bradshaw, "Healing the Shame That Binds You," PBS Special, 1987

No mental health professional, psychologist, healer, or medical practitioner will debate that there are many different psychological and emotional issues, personality disorders, and chronic human conditions in life. None of these disorders have the deceptively negative influence and residual toxic power of shame—none! Shame is one of the most universally traumatic emotional states, fraught with irrational beliefs and paralyzing experiences for people of all ages (after about the age of five) and races, spanning all economic and educational levels. No one is immune or exempt from shame, one of the most highly underrecognized and terribly misunderstood of all human emotions and states of being. Shame is clearly a taboo topic and is rarely discussed in therapy or outside the therapy office. I have been in practice for a long time (over thirty years) and my clients look at me with an air of suspicion and mistrust when I ask, "Tell me about the role shame plays in your life?" The typical response is, "What shame? I am not guilty of anything, and I don't have shame." That response, and the professional silence on the issue, is why shame is the most common emotional or psychological condition to remain untreated, unhealed, and unexposed. My clients are dramatically more comfortable discussing more familiar topics like anxiety or depression, or verbally bashing their ex-husband or wife. Because of shame's complexity and insidious nature, it is difficult to discuss or describe. I often describe the physical experience of shame as trying to nail sand to the wall and wondering why you can't get a handle on it.

SHAME IS NOT GUILT

Guilt is directly associated with a wrong action or poor behavior that violates one's moral values. Shame is a much different beast. Before we define the inner workings of shame, let's first describe in detail the raw, dark experience of it. Both writers quoted at the beginning of the chapter are identifying the social, personal, and psychological gravity of shame in its role of creating irrational personal beliefs that separate us from the people we love—and ultimately from ourselves.

Working Definition of Shame

For our discussion purposes, I am defining shame as the following:

> a primary emotional wound, not a secondary belief, based on a partic-
> ular action; a paralyzing emotional, mental, psychological state of mind
> that distorts a person's view of themselves in their world and with others,

> preventing them from developing a loving sense of self and impairing
> the individual from developing trusting, secure, safe relationships that are
> based on mutual respect and understanding; a chronic fear state of being
> discovered as a phony, a fraud, and an imposter.

The person is emotionally incapable of feeling like a valuable and productive adult, has an underdeveloped inner sense of self, and lacks personal self-acceptance. This is further characterized by a negative inner self-portrait and an unclear perspective of relationships with self and others.

This definition is not out of a book or from a particular theory but from thousands of clients and friends (me included) who have struggled with this distorted, ugly, and blinding emotional state. The far-reaching influence of being ashamed isn't limited to any particular situation in a person's life. It is pervasive. Like physical cancer, it becomes the driving force in all of your decisions: romantic, financial, sexual, health, career, parenting, etc. There is no area of functioning, feeling, and living that isn't colored or touched by this silent shadow. Shame in psychological theory is frequently referred to as a person's "shadow" side, part of the unwanted and disowned aspects of their personality.[1] Clearly, if you feel ashamed, you don't want to expose or explore these aspects of your behavior or emotions. Concealing these feelings and beliefs from everyone can begin as early as age five. This concealment process is called the false, or public self versus the real, wounded self.[2] Throughout this book we will explore how to reconcile the false self with the true inner self. Exposure and emotional rewiring (section III) is the pathway to your transformation and inner healing. If left untreated, shame has the potential to completely and thoroughly take control of any man or woman's life (a prime example is the fact that virtually all addictive behaviors are shame-based).[3]

Real Life Victims of Shame

My client Dave, age fifty-three, is a very successful tract-home developer in the greater Southern California area who struggles with random emotional paralyzing bouts of shame. Regardless of his career accomplishments, Dave feels inadequate and inferior and is often prone to raging verbal outbursts toward his employees, wife, family, and colleagues. Dave has the reputation of having anger management issues. (I personally don't believe that there is such a thing as anger management issues—rather, anger is a symptom of untreated shame, as we will discuss.) He recently lost his emotional composure with a home loan officer and was arrested for making death threats to everyone in the bank. Dave recounts this story, along with many others, saying, "I suddenly feel this surge of embarrassment, my stomach drops, and I feel this hole inside of me open up, and I can't stop the rage from coming out. I know I don't really believe what I am screaming, but it has a life of its own." Dave explains that his rage outbursts come and go quickly and do a lot of relationship and emotional damage in his life. He feels incredibly mentally defective, emotionally damaged, and beyond help or repair. When we started to discuss the undercurrent of shame in his career, marriage, childhood, health, friendships, and his relationship with his children, Dave began to see the different emotional connections, reaction patterns, self-loathing, and chronic negative self-talk playing out in his life constantly. We will discuss Dave's story, progress, and prognosis further in section II of this book.

My client Emily presents a different storyline, but her core issue is the same as Dave's. Emily is a nineteen-year-old college freshman at a major local university in Los Angeles, who has been secretly cutting her lower stomach and pelvis area with scissors, razor blades, and thumb tacks since she was twelve years old. Whenever Emily becomes upset, ashamed, or embarrassed, or when a friend is mad at her, she impulsively engages in this self-mutilation. Emily came to see me because she is frightened that her self-hatred, perfectionism, and false social image is falling apart. In the past, she has been hospitalized for self-destructive behavior, with little or no behavioral change. During our first therapy session, I asked Emily what she was so ashamed of or was hiding from. She looked out my office window and said, "I have a lot of secrets and no one will believe me. I hate myself and my life. Yet I don't want to die. I have good days, then this rage boils up in me and I lose my shit and hurt myself." Emily paused and listened to the possibility that shame could be an emotional issue she had never considered or understood. She was very interested in the idea that her unresolved, untreated shame was a primary driving emotional force in her life. We will revisit Emily in section II of the book, when we talk about body image and shame.

FIVE EMOTIONAL ELEMENTS OF SHAME

1. Shame Is the "Emotional Cancer" of Your Heart and Soul

The best way I know how to express the power of shame is to liken it to an emotional cancer of the human heart and mind. We all know what a cancer of any type or magnitude can do to the human body by attacking a person's health and vitality. Shame functions the same way on an emotional and spiritual level. It rebels against the heart and soul of an individual in the same way that a cancerous tumor attacks the person's body. Rebellion of any sort against your healthy sense of self is never an easy issue to address or to see clearly. Emotional cancer can literally kill you (for example, through a drug overdose) or can sabotage you in its attempt to remain in control. Regardless of its insidious and intrinsic nature, shame is an issue that is treatable, but it must be addressed head on in order to move forward on your life and spiritual path.

The lasting legacy of emotional shame is that you feel you are secretly and privately defective, always hiding that you are not being good enough or that there is something "not enough" about you, which is counterintuitive to your self-acceptance process. The "hunter" in the John Bradshaw quote is your shame, always terrorizing you and threatening to emotionally blackmail you into remaining a victim, captive and psychologically repressed. Shame is an awful taskmaster, driving you into complete despair and hopelessness. This reaction is in direct opposition to having a fulfilling life journey, which is expansive, loving, caring, forgiving, and compassionate. Two entirely direct paths that have two entirely different outcomes for your life. Shame is incompatible with your divine, intuitive, and loving nature. Many religious scholars refer to shame as our sinful nature, our fallen self, or simply as evil. Clearly, shame isn't our highest self or pure nature; it's the ego's control at its worst.

2. The "Big Secret" of Shame

One of the salient features of being a victim of shame it that it leaves its victim feeling flawed, unlovable, and/or disposable or replaceable. The core belief that you are of no value to the world and the loved ones in your life impairs and sabotages any significant personal development. Another way to put this is that you have a chronic, deep-seated fear that your coworkers, romantic partner, children, neighbors, and clients will discover that you are a fraud. The nagging voice in your head keeps telling you that "You really aren't any good. You are incompetent and incapable of doing or being whom and what you pretend to be. Eventually, everyone will find out about your terrible secret." This isn't an occasional emotional state, but rather the inner emotional geography of your fragmented sense of self and stalled self-acceptance process. The feelings of shame are chronic, but their emotional intensity can vary from low to extreme.

3. Shame Is an Inside Job, Not Something Outside of You

Shame isn't alleviated by selfless actions or loving gestures. Shame doesn't decrease with any type of outward behaviors, wealth, education, love, sex, or relationships. Shame is immune to all outward treatment or healing actions directed at it via drugs or any other mind-numbing behaviors (i.e., alcoholism, gambling, sex, or any addictive behavior). Addictive behaviors can momentarily silence your inner shame critic, but never for very long or without leading to more self-loathing later. Shame can only be addressed, treated, and removed from your life with an inward approach that involves self-acceptance, self-love, and your newly acquired emotional awareness.

4. Chronic Fear of Not Feeling "Good Enough"

Shame chronically slices away at a person's sense of self-acceptance, preventing them from developing any degree of personal autonomy or sense of competence. It also prevents a person from properly developing inner confidence and the belief that their true self is lovable, acceptable, or good enough. How could anyone ever trust or believe in what you have to say or do when you are harboring the big unspoken secret that says you're a fraud (imposter syndrome)? I can't begin to describe how many of my clients over the years identify these exact feelings and yet still argue that it's their personality that is the problem, and it is their plight in life to feel deficient and like a "phony." Many of the shame-driven people that I work with are some of the greatest individuals I have ever encountered. Unfortunately, they are addicted to their shame belief system like a dog is attached to a bone (my beagle and a bone—inseparable). They don't let go of the addiction until the emotional trauma caused by the shame cycle blows up their life. The huge explosion usually occurs in their relationships, finances, career, or health, and can be brought about through the death of a loved one or a family crisis (see section II). It is only at a point of complete despair that a personal awakening begins to become possible, as the person becomes aware of the truly deceptive power of shame. Only then will he consider the possibility of healing and resolving these powerful life-long self-defeating emotions, beliefs, and actions.

5. Shame's Emotional Super Glue:
   ## Addiction Mixed with Shame

It's my professional and personal experience that the issues surrounding shame are the least understood, least diagnosed, and least discussed emotional concepts in all the various types of psychological therapy modalities, including twelve-step recovery programs and peer counseling. The powerful emotional combination of addiction and shame is a force within a person's life that has to be reconciled; otherwise, the prognosis for healing is bleak. For instance, it is much easier to discuss depressive bipolar issues than the intangible power of self-loathing, self-hatred, and addictive behaviors—which are all motivated by shame. Psychologically speaking, shame is a deep-seated belief and feeling that is part and parcel of all maladaptive, self-defeating, and self-destructive behaviors. Shame isn't an action-related feeling or event but rather an *ongoing emotional malaise* that rears its ugly head at certain times in a person's life. It is a paralyzing feeling and a negative thought process that has no regard for a person's education, intelligence, wealth, or professional position. Shame knows no boundaries or limits in our lives.

> *As painful as shame is, it does seem to be the guardian of the many secret, unexplored aspects of our being. Repressed shame must be experienced if we are to . . . come to terms with the good, the bad and the unique of what we are.*
> —Dr. Robert Karen, "Shame,"
> *Atlantic Monthly*, February 1992

SHAME FACTOR: THE CLASSIC SYMPTOMS

The following shame severity scale contains some of the more common characteristics of shame-based behaviors and feelings that you might experience. Take an honest look at how you feel about yourself, your relationships, your romances, your sexual intimacy, authority figures, and your ongoing self-doubts, which are all influenced or fueled by shame-based emotional malaise. Understanding the silent ways shame lives and operates in your daily life is critical to exposing it, healing it, and permanently removing it from your life and spiritual path.

Nothing about you or your life circumstances is unacceptable, unlovable, or worthless. Nothing! Do not lose that perspective. Shame is a learned behavior that can be changed and healed.

Exposure Is Really Good

The first step on your recovery journey is to honestly examine your shame-based feelings, actions, and personality patterns up close *and* from a distance. It's important to mention at this juncture in our discussion that most people are involved with some form of personal growth or self-improvement, such as psychotherapy, mind and body healing, or support groups. No one is perfect, and personal growth is the process of healing and of reclaiming the underdeveloped parts of your personality. Developing personal awareness is the deliberate act of accepting your shame and making a commitment to healing it. If someone isn't inclined or interested in personal growth, then they are either living shame-free or they are avoiding their painful traumatic past.

You can think about shame as being experienced on a scale from zero to ten. A zero would mean living shame-free, and a ten would mean being fully consumed and controlled by self-destructive behaviors. Your experience of shame is personal, and it is something only you can diagnosis and treat. Below, we will discuss the shame scale and the wide range of the experiences of shame. Our life journey consists of learning, expanding our self-awareness, and transforming. Shame is a psychological and emotional malaise that can be left unnoticed and untreated for many years. Most people have some type of personal challenge, an area that needs improvement, and if shame is a factor, it will impair any positive personal change.

Unfortunately, most people stop at the critical point of confronting their "shameful" beliefs on their road to positive self-awareness. Don't stop, no matter how awful you feel or how scared you are. I assure you that this confrontation is well worth all the effort. The paralyzing fear of revealing your hidden secrets and toxic feelings is absolutely necessary to get past your current shame state.

It's a paradox because the very thing you desire is within you. Your uncomfortable feelings about yourself are the roadblocks to your immediate fulfillment and purpose. Acknowledging your shame and its incredible hold on you is a major transformational phase in your life. Staring your shame in the face with the limitless power of self-love and acceptance is applying the sun to morning fog. All your shame-based personal beliefs evaporate and disappear from your consciousness and daily life. Be brave and be honest with yourself. You can and will survive your shame exposure process. You don't want any more days living as an emotional prisoner to your shame.

Your Shame Scale and Shame Checklist: What's My Shame Status?

Remember, you aren't a monster. Shame is only a shadow in your closet of secrets. Turn the light on and look within your closet of old issues, addictions, and secrets. Everyone has a closet that needs to be cleaned out and restocked with new items. Before you move on to the shame checklist, think about rating your feelings of shame from zero (healed, shame-free) to ten (completely controlled by shame). The following scale will help you focus on where your normal shame level is, and how extreme it can become when triggered by certain events, feelings, or actions. All experiences of shame—whether on a daily, weekly, monthly, or random basis—are generally triggered by a distorted personality belief system concerning feelings, actions, or relationships (family, social, love, and sexual).

Your Shame Scale

0. Not your emotional issue.
1. You understand the concept but don't feel shame.
2. You occasionally feel shame about certain issues, but the feelings quickly dissipate.

3. You notice that certain events or experiences trigger a wave of shame, but those feelings don't last.

4. Sometimes you are scared to reveal the truth about yourself or a personal feeling.

5. You experience bouts of shame-based reactions and embarrassment. You feel enraged and like a fraud at work or with friends, and you are fearful of being exposed.

6. You have many days or moments when you feel exposed, enraged, and emotionally panicked about being discovered as a fraud or reprimanded for something.

7. It is difficult not to immediately escalate when you are being accused or questioned about a problem. You feel exposed and fearful. You react with intense anger; calming down after being triggered is very difficult.

8. You are told by people that you have an anger management problem. You engage in physical and heated verbal altercations as a means to protect your inner feelings. You are aggressive toward others when feeling shamed.

9. Your relationships are influenced and shaped by your powerful negative feelings, beliefs, and self-defeating shame-driven actions. Your life is controlled by your shame reactions. You struggle with addiction and thoughts of death or suicide. You cannot tolerate any conflict without extreme inappropriate reactions.

10. Your life is consumed with shame-based addictions and behaviors. You are incapable of functioning at your potential. You consider death as an escape plan or murder as an option. You are a danger to yourself and others, and you are resistant to seeking any type of assistance. These extreme reactions may be a result of severe drug abuse. Professional mental or medical help is necessary.

Your Own Shame Triggers

The above shame scale is a barometer for your range and cycles of feeling shame as it flows through your heart, soul, body, and mind. This self-reflective, personal inventory of shame is critical to explore and consider as you answer the following questions. The statements below are examples of how you might react, what triggers your shame, and how you feel about yourself. The shame scale illustrates how far you allow your shame at times to control your relationships—including your relationship with yourself and with your close family and friends. It is important to restate that any degree of shame can be healed within you. Nothing is ever beyond your innate ability for change and healing within your heart and soul. Nothing! Changing your belief system surrounding your shame begins to allow you to experience peace of mind. Your personal emotional transformation is the way out of the shame-cycle maze. In section III we will explore some direct ways of removing your shame reactions, beliefs, and unresolved rage. Now consider the following traits, behaviors, beliefs, and triggers concerning how your personal version of shame operates in your day-to-day life.

What Are Your Shame Beliefs, Feelings, and Actions?

- You have an irrational fear of being exposed as a fraud/phony (imposter syndrome) in your career, job, and/or role as a manager.
- You cannot allow anyone to be too emotionally close for fear they might see your awful secrets and constant failings (your true "bad" self).
- You constantly worry what other people think or know about you and you believe that their opinion can't be positive.
- You experience terrifying emotions about being embarrassed.
- You privately belief that you are an "angry" man/woman.
- When you experience intense feelings of rage or anger, afterward you experience intense feelings of regret and shame.

- Your emotional cycle of shame and regret is nonstop.
- You feel that there is a secret inside of you that can't ever come out or be seen by anyone you know or love.
- You tend to do things that are self-defeating.
- Sometimes you purposefully try to physically hurt yourself.
- You are privately convinced that people think you are a bad and worthless individual and a fraud or a phony.
- You blame yourself for anything that happens negatively in your life (because you deserve it).
- You have an explosive temper and/or anger management and self-acceptance issues.
- You have a history of physical violence and/or domestic violence.
- You become emotionally overwhelmed and feel "crazy" when you express any of your anger, frustration, or aggression.
- You experience emotional blackouts with no clear memory of what you said or did (not drug or alcohol related) when you become emotionally defensive or angry.
- Your feelings of anger or rage scare you so much that you will do anything to suppress them; this causes you to feel depressed and hopeless.
- You have strong shameful feelings about sex, your sexual orientation, and/or your sexuality.
- You have feelings of rage and wanting to physically hurt or punish others when you feel dismissed, discredited, or disrespected.
- You are secretly waiting for bad things to happen to you as punishment from God and/or the universe (because you feel that you deserve them).
- You really don't like yourself and secretly feel like a "loser."
- You sincerely believe that no one can truly care for you or love you because you're "damaged goods."
- You fantasize about dying when you experience intense feelings of shame.

- You can't accept compliments but only criticism.
- You feel this awful shame about yourself most of the time to a greater or lesser degree. It is always a part of your life.

What's your shame trigger? Which statement above hits your primary raw nerve and floods you with shame-based feelings? Think about your operating core beliefs that are part of your feelings of shame on a daily basis. Many issues surrounding shame are valuable sources of insight for your healing and resolution. One of the most commonly misunderstood elements of shame, for example, is how it is expressed when an individual is feeling it surge through her mind and heart. The response shame cycle is typically fueled by anger toward people or yourself or by extreme embarrassment. Anger and embarrassment are typical emotions to be triggered by feeling shameful.

These primary emotional responses have layers upon layers of collateral issues, feelings, and reactions attached to them (see section II for further explanations). For instance, no one would argue that a person who is expressing their shame-driven anger with violence or deadly force is in control. The person who cannot constructively express her anger and rage feels embarrassed and humiliated that she reacts the way she does. The problem is compounded emotionally because she tries to suppress this nonproductive automatic behavioral response. The inevitable failed attempt at not feeling mortified cycles into deeper feelings of self-loathing and hatred or, in the worst case, self-destructive actions. The cycle of shame is endless until you finally go beyond its reach. The ending of your shame-controlled life is the focus of the discussion in section III.

THE CYCLE OF SHAME: ANGER, EMBARRASSMENT, AND SELF-LOATHING

The shame scale and shame personal inventory list have these three parts of the shame cycle fueling your reactions, feelings, and thoughts. Shame is the gasoline, and your triggers ignite the internal fire. Your reactions might be immediate, or they might take days or weeks to play out in your particular circumstances. During this repetitive shaming cycle, one of the five common issues (i.e., finances, romance, family, parenting, and health) in a person's life is adversely affected. Given years of experiencing this emotionally crippling cycle of feeling and suppressing shame, an individual ultimately feels emotionally drained and powerless. The low self-esteem energy causes daily life to be extremely painful, disappointing, and filled with chronic feelings of hopelessness. The shame cycle is relentless, and it is the primary cause for developing many serious personal problems, life-threatening challenges, and despair and suicide.

It is important to mention that any degree of shame-based anger is dangerous for both the holder and the people at whom it is directed. Many psychologists call this type of anger narcissistic or infantile anger expression.[4] Rather than differentiate anger with many different subtypes, I am referring to any type of anger expression that is being generated from a shaming feeling or emotional defense as toxic and deadly for all parties involved.

Shame is usually expressed in one of three classic ways: anger, embarrassment/self-blame, or self-defeating choices. Which one of these three responses is your typical reaction to feelings of shame? We are going to explore all three reactions throughout the book, so you are no longer a prisoner to this damaging emotional cycle. This may seem obvious, but it needs to be said: No amount of personal, professional, social, or romantic shame-induced suffering is ever warranted or needed in your life. Shame tends to be a primary roadblock within a person's mind for moving forward in their life. Shame and personal change, self-acceptance, and inner transformation are incompatible. Shame is the emotional and psychological root cause of any type of self-doubt, self-loathing, anger management issues, and all degrees of self-hatred. It is why addressing these lifelong feelings and reactions is one of the pathways to emotionally freeing and liberating your inner true self.

Shame Cycle #1: No One Is Winning—Anger

If a man loses his temper and "goes off" verbally, he is considered dangerous, violent, or a bad guy. If a woman does the same and engages her shame-driven anger, she is considered a "bitch" or a very mean-spirited person. The truth is that neither individual is mean or inherently dangerous, but rather deeply hurt, misunderstood, and feeling powerless to stop their raw-nerve response to their long-standing wounds. These labels only intensify the anger, embarrassment, and self-loathing that a person feels when his or her shame cycles are triggered and come to the surface in any challenging encounter.

Going beyond your anger issues, emotional fears, and self-doubts are all critical parts to your life and journey. One of the goals for you in this book is this: *You no longer have to be defined by how your emotional needs and wounds control your life.* From this point and time on, you choose to define your adult life without your shame vetoing your choices. One of the challenges to healing your shame is learning to manage your angry impulses and random bouts of rage. Many times, men (in particular) are labeled as rage-a-holics when really it is their unresolved childhood emotional wounds being triggered. The primary root of all types of abuse in a relationship (be it physical, verbal, mental, sexual, or deadly violence) is unresolved shame fueled by years and years of anger. To sincerely address and heal your anger issues, the process must include insight into your neglected and ashamed inner-child. It's not enough to acknowledge your anger issues—you need to go a step further and pull out the emotional roots by dismantling (meaning to explore how and why you feel shameful) your inner shame cycle.

For instance, I have an example of out of control anger and shame. This last fall, early on a Saturday morning, I was walking with a client to get some coffee. My client is a fourteen-year-old boy, who suffers from being chronically bullied at school. We walked into a local, family coffee shop, and a well-dressed, professional-looking man, approximately fifty years old, was dragging the clerk (male, slim twenty-year-old college student) across the counter by his shirt. The clerk looked terrified, and everyone in the coffee shop looked stunned. Because I do animal comfort therapy for most of my teenager clients (they love the pooches), I had my two young beagles with me. This was a scary scene in the making. I spontaneously yelled at the male aggressor in a deep authoritative voice, "Hey, let go of the kid. You are scaring him." Everyone was shocked (myself included), and the man released his two-handed death grip from the clerk's shirt and walked out of the shop without saying a word. Of course, he was waiting for me outside the coffee shop, where he aggressively approached me and said, in a very hostile and threatening tone, "I am going to f— you up."

I looked at my young client and told him to keep walking away. The hostile guy got within twenty-feet of us, and my two beagles became enraged and leapt to attack him. I have had both dogs since they were born, and I have never seen either of them react so violently. The guy stopped walking toward us, and screamed, "You f— ing a—hole, you pussy come back here!" My client and I walked back to the office, where he calmly said to me, "You know, Samantha and Stella (the dogs' names) knew that guy was crazy, and they were protecting us. You could see the craziness in his eyes."

Anytime an adult "goes off," that person is immediately flooded with paralyzing shame-based emotions. Insight, understanding, and the ability to connect to emotional reason is lost. The present circumstances of feeling emotionally rejected, misunderstood, powerless, or dismissed are all replays of the past.

The benign circumstances of getting the wrong cup of coffee on a lazy Saturday morning can trigger an overwhelming rage response as the person feels emotionally misunderstood and that he has been treated as someone without value or importance. This might sound overly simple or psychologically elementary, but, unfortunately, the perception of being disregarded or dismissed is a match to a bucket of highly flammable irrational reactions. The man's unresolved emotional pain is instantly triggered by a seemingly harmless event. These volatile reactions can lead, in the worst cases, to physical harm or death. To be perfectly clear, the power of shame is the driving force behind all crimes of passion.[5] The person who is full of anger turning into resentment doesn't understand that the feelings of being dismissed or disregarded aren't a personality flaw but rather an untreated shame-based emotional wound. The volume and intensity of emotional energy that comes out of the individual who is carrying such a wound is dangerous at best and lethal at worst for him and his world.

Shame Cycle #2: Embarrassment Has No Limits

After the extreme feelings of anger, rage, and frustration have cooled off, the next piece of the cycle kicks in: paralyzing embarrassment. When the wave of emotional embarrassment is triggered, it is like a hundred-foot wall of water crashing into the victim. The triggers again are generally centered on personal themes of not being good enough, of being a bad person, an awful parent, a horrible partner, and/or a disappointing son or daughter.[6] This very strong emotional response is an internally driven private experience.

The victim of such shame-driven embarrassment is psychologically vulnerable to any type of circumstances where they feel their world is judging them or discovering their secret. The shaming incident can be triggered by something as simple as looking at a coworker in a sexual way or having angry feelings toward their newborn child. The triggers are highly personal and private. The unconscious or conscious events always reinforce the irrational feelings of being an awful, fraudulent, and phony individual. The victim feels that they are containing, hiding, and concealing a monster within their heart and soul.

This inner monster, or the "hunter" that John Bradshaw referred to at the beginning of the chapter, is always alive and well within you. This dark force, this secret about you, is always on the periphery of your thoughts and feelings. No matter what the personal cost, these awful embarrassing emotions have to be kept undercover at all times. The long-term damaging effect on your personality, caused by repressing your natural feelings of wanting to be understood, can develop into many different types of mental illness and/or severe personality disorders.

No Lasting Relief

The secondary crisis for the horribly embarrassed man or woman is they don't know how to relieve themselves of their awful feelings. Any avoidant behavior is acceptable (the endless list ranges from sleeping to drugs, eating, sex, work, etc.), but unfortunately these behaviors are only a quick fix to a long-term problem. The incredible inner emotional pressures of these absolutely intolerable feelings of inadequacy are so painful to experience that they have learned to rid themself of shaming feelings at any personal expense, starting at a young age, and this can often lead to an addictive or compulsive personality in adulthood. Feeling this paralyzing shaming embarrassment is to be avoided at all costs and becomes the doorway to any type of addictive numbing behaviors. The spectrum of mind-numbing behaviors is as varied as the people experiencing shame. Triggering their sense of inner embarrassment is an experience so painful and crippling that their life is controlled by trying to avoid that feeling.

It is very critical to understand that the cycle of shaming embarrassment is your automatic emotional and psychological response to your preconceived notions of good and bad behaviors. Often your shame-based belief system is irrational but you have left it unquestioned. Your inner belief system is based on a foundation of feeling inadequate—not an accurate base for your future. Shame-based beliefs are the primary cause and theme of many present-day relationship problems (personal, romantic, professional). It's almost impossible to feel good about yourself and have a loving sense of self, when you have an underlying chronic sense of inadequacy. *Experiencing self-acceptance and feeling shameful, inadequate, and awful are like oil and water: they don't mix, and they naturally repel each other.* One of the most productive ways out of the emotional shame maze is to focus on your inner desires and passions for your life. Beginning to understand and see your cycle of shame allows for new personal self-accepting information to begin to transform, embrace, and heal your wounded and neglected inner self. No amount of knowledge will replace or be a substitute for your ability to feel and experience positive, loving emotions for yourself and others. Experiencing a different response to your relationships is a major step toward removing the roots of your old shaming cycle.

Shame Cycle #3: Self-Loathing Is an Underestimated Force

When the circumstances surrounding a blowup or volatile argument with, for example, an ex-partner have ended, the wave of self-loathing begins. All the shame roadblocks—personal, romantic, and professional—that you might struggle with are related to an underlying belief of self-loathing. *Self-loathing is your shame feelings in action.* It is the active ingredient of shame in your day-to-day life. Your self-acceptance process has been aborted, undeveloped, and stalled. Various degrees and feelings of shame are played out in many painful life detours, poor choices, and regret (self-loathing). Developing any degree of self-acceptance in your life will immediately benefit you by exposing this insidious cycle. Slowing down your shame cycle can and will reduce at least 80 percent of your self-loathing choices.

Self-loathing, low self-esteem, self-hatred, and self-destruction all come from the same well of the shame-driven personality. The emotional poison in your well is your shame, not you. Your personal well of goodness, empathy, passion, and compassion might feel contaminated by your current choices and circumstances, but it isn't. One of the biggest surprises in life is that all our happiness, acceptance, love, and purpose are still within our inner self. Any action, feeling, or belief that comes from a sense of disliking, hating, or punishing yourself, regardless of its significance, is a classic symptom of your shame. The range of punitive behaviors is endless, and they are all directly connected to your shame-driven belief system. Yes, it's all related.

STOPPING AND EXPOSING YOUR SHAME CYCLE

Letting Go of Your "Bad" Self

If your well of shame is full to the brim with sensitive self-accusations, distorted personal information, recriminations, and distorted beliefs, then the well needs to be drained, emptied out, and refilled with your own positive self-accepting feelings. Any degree of self-rejection is a ball and chain holding you back. Emotionally, your bad-self speaking, denying, or dismissing that ball and chain of shame that you carry around every day is a difficult pattern to acknowledge. Shame over time becomes a very ingrained belief, emotion, and state of mind. The saddest and most extreme expression of self-loathing is self-destruction resulting in suicide. Suicide is an extreme reaction to rejecting one's life. Suicidal thoughts, feelings, and wishes all come from the untreated reservoir of your shame. The cure for your insidious bad feelings about yourself is correlated to the degree that you allow your self-acceptance process to take place. What is clear is that when you detox your heart, your well of shame, and all of its paralyzing side effects, you can pursue your inner passions and dreams with courage and confidence.

Emotional Sobriety Exposes Shame

Developing a loving and nonreactive inner-self is the ultimate antidote and cure for healing a shame-based personality. When you consider a new positive approach to your life and develop a loving sense of self, you slow the shame cycle down considerably, if not completely. This is emotional sobriety. In section III we will discuss at great length how to implement all of your new life-purpose skills, tools, dreams, and desires for your journey forward. It is important to clearly define what exactly emotional sobriety is and how it is a cornerstone to your healing life journey.

> Emotional sobriety is the ability to respond, ponder, and consider the multiple issues when you're confronted with an emotionally charged situation, relationship, or crisis. Sobriety is allowing for new insights, new information, and a new perspective to influence and guide your relationships, emotional connections, decisions, responses, and self-perception. It's the absence of familiar automatic emotional defensive reactions, yelling, and abusive behavior. It's the absence of needing to conceal or hide your true feelings and thoughts in any situation.

Your evolving emotional clarity and self-acceptance allows you to better understand what you genuinely think and feel about all the things in your life. You will start responding to your inner feelings without the hunter or monster of shame lingering around your heart and soul. Instead, you will begin to experience an emotionally balanced, nonreactive, non-approval-seeking, fearless, and empowered point of view about old issues and old challenges. You will view life events with a fresh perspective and with new insights. The need for validation, acceptance, and approval from others will no longer be important factors or unspoken forces in your emotional and life decisions. You will find yourself feeling good about yourself regardless of the circumstances.

Keeping Your Emotional Clarity via Personal Boundaries

When someone triggers one of your shame issues—such as trying to make you responsible for their feelings—rather than automatically starting the painful, crippling shame cycle, you will pause and consider that maybe there are other options in your particular situation or circumstances. The ability to pause and breathe allows for new information to filter into your emotions and feelings. New behaviors and positive responses are evidence of living shame-free. When people are drunk or under the influence of a mind-altering drug, they aren't remotely capable of responding to any situation with 100 percent physical or mental capacity. That simply isn't a possible option when you're psychologically numb or checked-out. The analogy holds true for your emotions, feelings, and psychological capacity: you can't respond or clearly understand any of your life challenges with a foggy personal shaming perspective.

Your emotional clarity is directly correlated and connected to your emotional and mental ability to not react to things that trigger your shaming cycle. We are going to go into great detail throughout this book about how to unplug from these old patterns. The higher your degree of emotional and psychological clarity, the clearer your life and responses to your shaming triggers will be. The "hotter" your feelings of shame, the less clarity and inner peace and perspective you will have in your life.

Emotional sobriety allows you to consider other points of view and new possibilities that you had never imagined and that had never even been part of your previous worldview. You develop the capacity to see, through your awakening self-realization, that part of your life that is going in the right direction regardless of the emotional or physical pain and crisis surrounding you. When you are confronted with your old triggers, you no longer find yourself automatically anxious and reacting with the old shame-cycle symptoms, the powerful debilitating beliefs, feelings, and thoughts you previously experienced. You have a sense of comfort in your own emotional and psychological skin.

CLOSING THOUGHTS

The right way to wholeness is made up, unfortunately, of fateful detours and wrong turnings.
—C. G. Jung, *Psychology and Alchemy*, 1944

Having depression and anxiety is like being scared and tired at
the same time.
It's the fear of failure yet having no urge to be productive.
It's wanting friends but hating socializing.
It's wanting to be alone but not wanting to be lonely.
It's caring about everything and nothing at the same time.
Having depression and anxiety is feeling everything at once and
then being completely paralyzed and numb.
—Justin Kruger, Project Helping, 2018

The two quotes above underline the life journey that you are currently embarking on and that you will move forward along as you grow in your self-discovery and increase your emotional shame-free life. You are making your way and trying to avoid as many detours as possible. Shame is one of the toughest roadblocks to remove and one of the strongest depressed elements on your journey. Success seems impossible only because of how distorted your thinking gets from the constant recycling of shame throughout your daily life. Increased emotional sobriety and clear emotional boundaries allow you to begin feeling and experiencing your relationships without the rapid undercurrent of shame, anxiety, and psychological terror. The black inner cloud of impending doom that lingers in your heart and soul will begin to dissipate. Healing your heart, soul, and mind is a lifelong task, but it is worth every ounce of effort to reduce or eliminate the symptoms and beliefs of shame.

Think about how shame did or does play a role in creating emotional pain, psychological and physical suffering, and panic in your life? How do your feelings of shame about your life choices, big or small, influence and shape your decisions and experiences? Regardless of your answers, nothing is beyond change or impossible to heal. As your shameful feelings decrease, you will open a new chapter in your life, form deeper relationships, and develop more and more loving self-acceptance.

> *Life is the most difficult exam. Many people fail because they try to copy others, not realizing that everyone has a different question to answer and different projects to complete.*
>
> —Unknown

Finally, this quote reinforces the fact that all of us have many personal lessons to learn on the path of discovery. Developing your own life purpose and passion will always have challenges and tests, not to mention a steep learning curve. Removing the emotional roadblock of shame allows your inward education to continue and evolve. The road-trip experience through your valley of shame is all part and parcel of connecting with all the different parts of your life. Your self-healing and acceptance process is a lifelong project aimed at healing your inner self. Nothing is ever lost and everything can become learning material for the bigger plan in your life. Your shame experiences can't compare to someone else's because their "life exam" is entirely different than yours. Your only concern is to focus on your inner nature and what you need to heal in your relationships. The next chapter is going to explore your early formative years with new insights and perspective.

CHAPTER 2

YOUR EARLY YEARS AND YOUR PERSONAL SHAME BEGINNINGS: FIVE COMMON SHAMING PARENTING STYLES

The influence, importance and impact of their family on a young child isn't a question but rather how does that child experience their family.
—Dr. Benjamin Spock, *Baby and Child Care*, 1946

Defenses are put up around weakness, not around strength and adequacy.
—Dr. Dorothy Corkille Briggs,
Your Child's Self-Esteem: The Key to Life, 1958

Family is the single most important influence in a child's life.
—attributed to Sigmund Freud

The quotes above are from some of the heaviest hitters in the field of childhood psychology in the last 150 years. Their message is centered on the incredible influence families have on children of all ages (we are all children regardless of our age). Freud began the public discussion about the influence, positive and negative, parents will have on their young child. Many of Freud's writings focused on his research into the mother/child emotional bond that is the genesis of a child's mental health or mental illness. In Freud's pre-World War I Europe, emotionally uninvolved parenting was normal, and children were viewed as accessories rather than treasures. His writings began to make people aware that infants and young children are much more aware of their surroundings than previously had been considered. In fact, Freud believed that by age five a child has emotionally incorporated her parents' neurosis (shame—my opinion).[1]

American pediatrician Benjamin Spock later expanded on Freud's mother/child emotional dynamic. He was considered the leading expert and major influencer of the baby boom generation and beyond (1947 to the present). He made child development an everyday discussion. Regardless of the mother's ability, Dr. Spock made the process of having a positive impact on her baby, infant, and child less sterile and more hands on. In his classic bestseller, *Baby and Child Care*, Dr. Spock wrote about how the primary caretaker of children (the mother) has the innate ability to emotionally bond and care for her child.[2] This intuitive parenting idea shaped the country after World War II, and to some degree Spock's influence continues into the present day. In line with Dr. Spock's ideas, Dr. Dorothy Corkille Briggs, in her bestselling book *Your Child's Self-Esteem*, explains how the parent/infant relationship is based on the parents' understanding of their invaluable emotional connection with their child, and how that connection forms the child's inner self, sense of self, and ability to function in the world.[3] All three theorists brought attention to the timeless role mothers and fathers have in shaping (both positively and negatively) their child's emotional self (his feelings about himself) and psychological self (his interactions with the world).

This discussion may seem obvious and elementary, but there is a reason we are talking about the foundational parent/child bonding process. I want to underscore the power and magnitude of your childhood emotional needs, to make it clear how significant the effect can be when these needs are not met, understood, or encouraged. Your early emotional experiences are highly relevant to the formation of your core self and your shame beliefs. At the risk of being repetitive, we are going to focus on family shame, which leads to individual shame.

Family Shame Defined

Parents project their own sense of inadequacy and emotional insecurity onto their developing child, who then internalizes these feelings as her own (at around age five). The feelings of inadequacy dramatically impair the child from developing her own sense of self-esteem. The child's natural cravings for love, acceptance, and understanding aren't understood by the parents. The family relationships operate with each person avoiding their own unmet emotional, psychological, and relationship needs.

Family shame is the foundation for all forms of individual shame that emerge when someone is a child, teenager, or adult. The painful unmet emotional needs gradually begin to form an internal picture within a young child, convincing him that he must somehow be defective. There is a concept in child psychology that every adult carries around a picture in his metaphorical wallet of his scared five-year-old self. It's a picture that shame learns to cover up.

> *Growing up in my family was a series of failed attempts by my parents to make us responsible for their depression and anxiety. I didn't ever remember considering my feelings, but I always knew what my mom was feeling. Reading my mom was second nature.*
>
> —Eric, age 38

FAMILY SHAME

The family element of shame is one piece of the emotional groundwork of your early life and your experiences of frustration, disappointment, and anxiety. These powerful emotions begin to impair the natural development of feeling capable and secure in the world by about the age of five. These early corrosive feelings of inadequacy can be buried so deeply that an oil drilling rig would be needed to locate them. The wounded, neglected, and scared parts of your five-year-old self are all buried within you. I remember the first time I heard the idea that my childhood frustrations could have a lasting impact on me. I was about age twenty and sitting in a college anthropology lecture, when the professor said, "It doesn't matter what culture you are raised in, emotional needs of the infant are universal and must be addressed by every family for its legacy and growth." I was stunned that I might have some repressed feelings that were negatively impacting my adult life. I remember the rush of that very familiar, yet extremely uncomfortable, feeling of inadequacy washing over me. I knew the professor was right, and then a wave of sleepiness washed over me. My sudden fatigue was an emotional and physical defensive reaction to re-experiencing my haunting sense of inadequacy.

This isn't a fact-finding exploration into your past for finger pointing, blaming, or further "hating" your mother or father. The goal of this book is solely to help you understand and heal. The deep exploration of your early childhood thoughts, feelings, and beliefs is the comprehensive psychological approach and practice of psychoanalysis. We must understand that the core primal need and desire of every infant is to be held, fed, and attended to (in other words, to be emotionally understood). If these core needs are ignored or overlooked, three things, or a combination of them, begin to happen by preschool age:

1. Erecting emotional defenses: The child develops various cover-ups for feeling inadequate; these behaviors range from self-loathing to fear of failure.
2. Resignation and acceptance: The child internalizes the idea that he is flawed and inadequate and avoids any task or experience that might reveal his lack of ability.

3. Withdrawal and development of false self: The child retreats into a fantasy world that blocks out the chronic rejections he has experienced.

The child's internal voice: "I am bad, no one loves me, and I am a failure."

Each of these early childhood responses begin the formation of a shame-based personality. The ever-present psychological pattern of feeling inadequate begins to guide the school-age child and then continues to follow her into adulthood. These unconscious defensive behaviors are attempts to cover up the deep disappointments that she experiences every day from birth to kindergarten. The core of these childhood defensive beliefs and behaviors tend to be cemented into a young, impressionable heart and mind by about age ten.

When I talk about early childhood imprinting, many people ask, "What kind of parents would tell their son or daughter that they are unlovable?" Parents don't generally look at their three-year-old or nine-year-old and say, "You are awful." Rather, parents don't communicate verbally (through tone of voice), nonverbally (through eye contact), or emotionally (through holding and physical touch) that their young child is special, capable, wanted, or noticed. These children began to feel bad about their physical, emotional, and psychological needs not being met, understood, or embraced and valued. The repeated disappointments of missed eye-to-eye emotional connections or hugging leave a major deficiency in the child's self-esteem formation. When the sense of feeling adequate, lovable, and valuable isn't fostered, the seeds of shame begin to take hold in the child's internal picture. The following five parenting styles will further elaborate these parent/child shaming themes and their shame-inducing interactions. Each style has its own similar and distinct qualities that can adversely affect a child throughout the course of his adult life. Every newborn experiences some form of emotional bonding and attachment with their primary caretaker. No one is exempt from the early development steps that everyone must take, experiment with, and live through. All parenting styles are styles of attachment and emotional connection, and we will discuss attachment theory in the context of different parenting styles. The five styles, and a child's fundamental emotional response to each, are as follows:

- Perfectionism Style: "I never feel good enough."
- Chaotic Style: "Nothing matters; I am not noticed."
- Single-Parenting Style: "I am overwhelmed; someone please help my Mom/Dad."
- Explosive Style: "I can make you happy; please don't be mad at me."
- Friendship Style: "I am responsible for my Mom/Dad."

> *As painful as shame is, it does seem to be the guardian of many of the secret, unexplored aspects of our beings. Repressed shame must be experienced if we are to . . . come to terms with the good, the bad, and the unique of what we are.*
>
> —Dr. Robert Karen, "Shame,"
> *Atlantic Monthly*, February 1992

All shame is repressed, buried, and highly resistant to exposure. Shame and exposure are incompatible emotional elements; they just can't mix together. In the above quote, Dr. Karen wonderfully describes the pathway out of the shame maze and the journey toward self-acceptance. Throughout the rest of this chapter, we are going to briefly examine five common parenting styles. One or more style might begin to awaken old thoughts and feelings within you, but don't be alarmed if you can relate to all five styles, as this is very common. Ultimately, however, there is one predominate parenting style that shaped and influenced your early developmental years (from birth to about ten years old).

PERFECTIONISM STYLE OF PARENTING

> *I have never felt good enough and deep down I always feel like a loser. I can remember feeling this way when I was preschooler in New York City before we moved to LA.*
>
> —Steve, age 28

The perfectionist parenting style can be seen through a parent's primary focus on the theme of "always look good regardless of how you feel." The early emotional interactions between the child (you) and the primary caretaker (usually the mother) are guided by the principle of "what you look like is far more important than how you feel." In the quote above, Steve, regardless of his age, financial independence, and high-powered entertainment career, still feels inwardly like an imposter. *Everything looks good, but nothing feels good.* The child learns at a very young age (approximately eighteen months) how to gain his or her parents' love and approval. This might sound extreme for a toddler, but all the interactions between parent and child are centered around getting the child to conform to the parent's underlying need for a brilliant baby girl or boy. These young kids must act and behave in a certain way to keep their parent's attention and interest. Regardless of the child's emotional, physical, or social needs, the parent sees the child as a reflection of themself.

Children reflect their parent's unconscious values, and the challenge is to foster the child's own sense of mastery and competence. Between the ages of five and ten, psychological power struggles emerge between the child and her parents. Who is going to control the child's interests, dreams, and wishes? Ideally, the child has a supportive atmosphere to explore her interests—say, for instance, bug collecting. The parent might say to their daughter, "Girls don't play with bugs; they are poisonous." The young girl then feels "wrong" for wanting to explore her interest in bugs. This same girl is constantly imprinted with what is acceptable, good enough, and proper in the eyes of her parents.

All children crave and need their parents' verbal and nonverbal approval to develop a secure sense of self in the world. A young boy might learn early on that the appearance of being good is more important than trying to succeed. Hence, for example, he might begin to avoid playing soccer because he isn't as good as the other boys and doesn't want to disappoint his parents. The child's activity choices are based on not exposing any weakness or the need for improvement. Regardless of gender, children know by ages five to ten the painful experience of feeling flawed or feeling like damaged goods due to normal life events and life lessons.

> ### The child's internal voice: "I will never be good enough, and no one likes me."

The major psychological deficiency of this parent-child relationship is the internal and external dialogue that how things look is always far more important than how a child might feel. The predominate value of appearance (perfectionism) is far more important compared to the child or teenager's feelings, fears, and unexpressed anxieties. A person's value as a teenager or young adult becomes about how she appears and looks, and what her "brand" value is. The child's ever-present need for validation and for support of her hopes and new learning is ignored. The parent's anxiety is fostered by their unspoken belief that others' opinions of themselves and their child are more important than their own opinions. The family emphasis is on outward appearance, superficial action, and people-pleasing relationships that smoother the young child's emerging self-acceptance and feelings of mastery. There is no emotional room in this family for the child to develop her own sense of self because of the hyper-focus on succeeding and looking good. This parenting style isn't limited to any particular race, creed, or nationality. The emotional approach to the children is deeply flawed and fosters early experiences of feeling inadequate, inferior, and damaged (all elements of shame).

Reflective comment by the fourteen-year-old teenage daughter of perfectionist parents: "If I look good, who I know and what others think of me makes me happy, but not for very long sometimes."

The child, teenager, or young adult can be consumed with the preoccupation of avoiding personal challenges and uncomfortable task, and with seeking another person's approval. On the parent's part, the avoidance of self-exploration is an attempt to manage their own anxiety. The problem is that the parent's fear of feeling inadequate spills onto their child. *The unspoken family belief is that nothing is ever good enough, including you.* The terrible developing cycle of never being or feeling adequate or good enough is the core driving principle of this parenting style. No matter what the child does, he never feels good enough. The child knows by about age ten that he can't meet the invisible standards of his parents. He quickly learns that unless an action can be done perfectly he should not try to do it. This may sound overly dramatic, but unfortunately it is a real problem for many people struggling with their adult shame cycle. The fear of people discovering that you aren't "perfect" is shame's emotional stronghold, built through this early emotional imprinting. *Perfectionism grows into self-loathing and in worse cases self-hatred.* The build-up of frustration, never feeling good enough, and chronically chasing the approval of others is psychologically exhausting; the child doesn't develop a sense of his own value in the world.

Male adult client, fifty-two years old, reflecting on his core sense of feeling flawed: "Whatever I do, it's never good enough or something bad will ultimately happen to mess things up. I never get a break. No good deed goes unpunished."

Shame is like super glue for a child of perfectionist parents. The adult son or daughter experiences the terror of public embarrassment (always look good) paired with the inner critical voice telling them they never measure up to some unspoken invisible standard (not good enough). The childhood combination of outward appearance mixed with super achievement is a powerful emotional blend. A person can function on outward approval until his life hits a crisis and it becomes clear that nothing is perfect (although in truth it never was) and everything looks and feels awful. Many people describe this personal awakening as a midlife crisis. I prefer to describe it as finally recognizing your shame factor. It's a process that's worth every step you take on your path to healing and evolving.

> *Parent Shaming Fact: Perfectionism is a form of a parent's self-hatred that a child believes is why they feel defective.*

Natural life-crisis situations, such as a romantic breakup, divorce, loss of a dream job, mental health issues, or a cancer diagnosis, automatically force a person to go beyond her artificial self-imposed emotional walls that she has put up against feeling inadequate, not good enough, and deeply flawed. The crisis forces a person to look within at her unresolved feelings, thoughts, and hopes, which she has resisted exploring and had buried many years before. Psychologists often label these crises as "decompensating," the psychological and emotional experience of gaining new personal insights. This process is also commonly referred to by saying a person is "having a meltdown." The meltdown, decompensating, nervous breakdown, or any type of letting go of old negative personal beliefs is very powerful emotional process. Letting go of familiar shaming core beliefs is a positive step on a person's road to healing her shame cycle. Many children who were raised with the perfectionism style of parenting grow up and develop a narcissistic personality as they attempt to avoid their paralyzing fears of inadequacy and shame. ("No one can see my wounded child; I am a superstar.") They will use limitless emotional and psychological behaviors to repress, avoid, and run from these feelings.

CHAOTIC PARENTING STYLE

> *I thought it was normal for kids to get hit, or for parents to throw things at each other. My childhood was a series of near-death experiences from all the drugs and alcohol my parents used. It was crazy, but was it really? Or am I just making it a big deal now?*
>
> —Yolanda, age 34

Chaotic parents, regardless of age, education, or wealth, create chaotic families. This parenting style is exactly what the name depicts for the child. The family is emotionally, psychologically, and physically unstable. This is the opposite of the perfectionist parenting style, in which everything looks good. Nothing looks good with the chaotic parenting style because drama, isolation, and neglect are the parent's style of relating to their child. My client Yolanda, many years later, is still recovering from the residual shaming impact of her volatile childhood. Chaos, emotional and physical instability, and dramatic events are the daily experiences in this type of family. The child, by age five, knows how to emotionally read people better than most adults. In order to feel safe, she has learned to intuitively know whether her parents are in a good mood or a bad mood, or whether they are emotionally distracted.

> ***Parent Shaming Fact: Neglect of all types breeds a core belief (shame) in children that they are damaged goods, inferior, and flawed. Parental emotional instability breeds a sense of fear within children that their world isn't a safe place.***

Emotional, physical, and psychological neglect is the recurring problem and theme in this family. The children grow up with the early influence of not being noticed or cared for, and of not feeling safe. For instance, in this type of family, a sixteen-year-old daughter might go live with her twenty-eight-year-old boyfriend, and the parents might not notice her absence for weeks, or they might ignore her absence altogether. Children in these families grow up with profound self-loathing patterns of physical, emotional, and relational abuse (for example, domestic violence). Unfortunately, many of these children feel that experiencing any attention (including physical abuse) is still better than being neglected. The children assume that their repeated traumas and neglect are a normal way of living. The parents, for various reasons (understandable or not), aren't emotionally stable, emotionally attuned, or aware of their child's emotional needs and wants. Those who parent in this style aren't emotionally equipped or psychologically capable of fostering a young child's sense of mastery (i.e., the ability to problem solve) because of all the drama and instability in the family. These children grow up to be survivors of their own families.

> *Parent Shaming Fact: Children irrationally believe and feel that they are the cause of the instability and problems in their family.*

Teachers, neighbors, and relatives are all aware of these kids coming to school with dirty clothes, no academic support, and no parental guidance. Such a child learns to be self-sufficient for emotional survival reasons. These children are orphans even though they live with one or more parent. The use of drugs or alcohol, along with physical or sexual abuse, are common features of this family style. Unfortunately, violence and deadly force are also common occurrences in this family setting. At times, the chaos can escalate to levels of severe physical danger or death. Adults who grew up in this type of family tend to be reluctant to have children, get married, or develop close emotional bonds. Nothing in their childhood felt safe or, frequently, was safe.

My family sucks, no one cares about me or what I do. F—
them. We all die anyway!
—Male client, 17-years-old, talking about his family

My office is full of angry teens and emotionally despondent adults who survived their upbringings but are trying to psychologically process the collateral damage of feeling invisible and neglected. Neglect of all types (physical, mental, emotional, relational) breeds a strong sense of shame as a defensive wall. The purpose of these early defensive mechanisms (shame and dissociation) is solely to survive the nightmarish experiences these young children have endured and witnessed. The early emotional trauma for children (under age twelve) is covered up with a strong emotional blanket of shame and self-loathing.[4] Children disassociate from repeated emotional disappointments by walling off their emotions. The children are alert and aware, but they don't let themselves think about, or have feelings about, the drunken verbal lashing they got for leaving the house a mess. Unresolved childhood trauma is a fast track to all types of addictions, abusive habits, and self-harm. Severe cases of trauma can ultimately result in suicide or homicide (see chapter 3 for further details). The primary caretaker might be struggling with untreated mental illness, such as bipolar mood disorder, and self-medicating with prescription drugs. The untreated mental health issue is exacerbated with the use and abuse of alcohol and illegal or legal drugs. The implicit and explicit parental message to the child is that he is part of the problem in the family. Many times these children in adolescence will become runaways to escape the emotional insanity and family abuse.[5]

Female adult client, twenty-four-years-old, survivor of her
family abuse: "I always have chaos around me; it's normal and
sort of makes me feel safe. My mother is on her fourth marriage,
and I haven't seen my father since I was a child. Two of my
stepfathers sexually abused me, and my mother didn't believe
me. No one cares about me anyway!"

The chaotic parenting style is one of the most nonfunctional of the styles, as there is no communication and no desire to resolve major conflicts or physical or sexual abuse. The emotional glue in this family is the numerous unspoken secrets. Parents never discuss or acknowledge the inappropriate behavior that is part of the family's daily life. What is really happening in the family is shoved under the carpet and kept a secret. One of the major problems in this style of family is that children are often exposed to all types of abuse, including sexual. Sexual abuse occurs in a chaotic family environment more than with any other type of parenting and family style. The chaos and craziness of the parents distract from the criminal abuse that the child experiences. Children growing up in these families are predisposed to develop addictive personalities to help avoid the emotional pain and devastation of their early years. Shame is the fabric of this family, and the child learns it along with learning how to read and write.[6] Growing up in this type of family is emotionally terrifying for the child, who carries the shame into adulthood. The amount of trauma, violence, and abuse a child witnesses and experiences is directly correlated to how strong their psychological bond is to shame, denial, and avoidance. High degrees of shame in the survivor are a result of high degrees of abuse, terror, and emotional instability on the part of the parents. Shame serves the purpose of helping the children to repress and emotionally hide from their consciousness what they saw and experienced. In order to survive and emotionally manage the family chaos, shame becomes a tool (denial, avoidance, and amnesia) for maintaining a "normal" childhood.

SINGLE-PARENT STYLE OF PARENTING

My mom never stopped verbally bashing my father after they separated. She was always complaining about all his girlfriends and how she had no money. I loved my dad, and my mom never accepted that idea.

—Frank, age 23

The single-parenting style feels like the Dead Sea compared to the chronic emotional insanity of the chaotic family. The single-parenting style is the most common style because of divorce, child custody issues, and the inherent conflict that is associated with co-parenting with a former partner. Generally, one parent becomes emotionally and/or physically absent from the child's day-to-day life while the other parent becomes the primary caretaker. The absent parent typically ignites an emotional, mental, and psychological challenge in the developing child. The experience of an absent parent becomes a sense of "rejection" for the child. Regardless of which parent the child, teenager, or young adult lives with, the absence is emotionally felt within the family.

The primary parent reacts to their own relationship loss and often resents the heavy lifting of being solely responsible for raising the children. Typically, mothers become the primary caretakers after a divorce.[7] Frank, quoted above, tells me that even though it has been twelve years since his parents' divorce, his mom still talks negatively about his dad. Because of the tension between his parents, Frank rarely saw his father from the time he was fifteen years old until his college graduation when he was twenty-two. The arguing and chronic tension between their parents kept all of Frank's siblings emotionally distant from their mother and father. Frank felt, and still feels, that both of his parents are depressed and not capable of being supportive parents.

There are many uncontrollable reasons, such as death caused by accidents or illness, that a mother or father becomes the sole parent. These types of situations, however, aren't emotionally charged with the rage, resentment, betrayal, and fear that occurs in a conflicted parental relationship. The death of a parent typically breeds anxiety and grief within the child, which is very different from feeling defective.[8]

Negative emotions and hostile energy are the core long-term problems of this parenting style. The negative beliefs, opinions, and emotions are directed toward the absent or under involved parent. The child feels a heavy emotional burden to help his mother or father as a single parent. Additionally, the child feels emotionally torn because he is half of the "bad" parent. It's very difficult for a child of any age to feel emotionally secure when he is told that his mother or father is a "bad" person. Children will internalize, personalize, and accept that they are deeply flawed, just like their absent father or mother.[9] Parent alienation is a very serious problem for children and adults. The complex psychological issues that result from growing up with a critical parent (who has been left) or a rejecting parent (who has left the marriage) impact a child of any age and can be profound.

> *Parent Shaming Fact: Kids personalize a parent's dislike for the other parent as their own fault and a personal defect.*

One challenge with this parenting style is that the child often tries to become a superhero and prove to her mother or father that she is worth all the trouble she believes she has caused the family. This sounds counterintuitive, but kids personalize a parent's disdain for a partner and consider it their own fault. In some cases, kids are told in a fit of anger that if they hadn't been born they (the primary parent) wouldn't have to deal with the deadbeat father or mother. The family climate of personal exploration is never developed within the child because she is either helping one parent overcome the other or else trying to save the estranged parent.[10]

Bradley, age eight, comes to see me because his third-grade teacher has observed his aggressive verbal and physical tendencies on the playground when he is upset or disappointed. Brad's mother, Sandy, is recently divorced and has three other children under the age of ten. Sandy is emotionally overwhelmed with having the primary responsibility for four children. It's difficult to imagine the emotional stress of managing four young children's schedules plus an ex-husband whom she financially supports. Brad tells me in our first therapy session, "Dr. P, you know my dad hates my mom. He tells me if it wasn't for my mother he would be a successful actor. I feel bad for my dad and it makes me sad that he isn't happy. I worry about both of my parents. They both aren't happy. I tell my dad that Mom loves him, and he tells me it's not true." I try not to fall out of my chair or immediately correct Brad about his dad's aggressive psychological alienation of his mother.

> *Parent Shaming Fact: Children love both parents intuitively. They feel flawed when they are told not to love or to accept the other parent. Children know that they are a combination of both parents, and they don't understand their parents' conflict.*

A further challenge of the single-parenting style is that the child can become an emotional container for his parents' displaced negativity, resentment, or rage. Unresolved parental tension can be likened to exposing a child to mental radiation and then wondering why they are emotionally unstable as adults. The child becomes a negative object for at least one of his parents and develops his core sense of self around feeling responsible for his parents' emotional well-being. When a young child feels flawed and powerless to change his parents, this is the foundation for a shame-based personality. Children are like a video camera, recording everything their parents say and do, but also what their parents don't say or express. Kids, especially teenagers, know exactly what their parents think and feel about each other. Trust me, adolescents know their parents' deep unspoken secrets like they know their best friend. That is why this very common parenting style gets dismissed as harmless compared to other styles because of its benign public appearance. The hatred of parents for each other doesn't do well with children because the children's natural default psychological position is to take on and internalize the displaced rage, leaving them infused with large doses of shame for something they simply have no control over.

EXPLOSIVE STYLE OF PARENTING

Me and my siblings knew within five seconds whether my mom or dad were going to fight or argue. It was like walking over landmines; things would explode unexpectedly, and we were ultimately always scared.

—Linda, age 27

Children who grow up with an explosive style of parenting learn from an early age that their emotional well-being is based on their ability to manage their parent's mood swings. Emotional safety is a natural desire of all humans. Children will create elaborate psychological systems to ensure their inherent safe place, which is a combination of their home (emotionally, psychologically, and physically) and their parents. The complexity of a child's defense mechanism is in direct proportion to the level of terror in her household. The explosive parent creates a household that lives with dread and fear of another unexpected emotional outburst. The free-floating sense of danger and terror will automatically create a wall of psychological shame to protect the vulnerable boy/girl on the inside. Young children *always* (I mean literally *always*) internalize, personalize, and blame themselves for the raging parent's unhappiness and mood swings.

This parenting style is very different from the chaotic style. The primary difference is that the explosive parent can be extremely wealthy, occupationally and socially high functioning, and a wonderful person outside of the home. The home is where this parent's own unresolved inner child shame issues are unleashed on his or her children. The addiction in this family is rage.

In this family, the children, whether quite young or even older adolescents, tend not to question the family status quo and learn intuitively how to manage the emotional instability of their parents. Kids are very resilient, and they will adopt any type of psychological coping mechanisms to stay out of harm's way (in this case, from a parent's rage). These psychological coping mechanisms can range from simple denial of the situation to severe depersonalization, in which the child feels like he is outside of his body, to the extreme of multiple personality disorder, in which the child develops different personalities to cope with the trauma. All of these compensating self-preservation behaviors serve to help the child live in an unsafe home. The extreme end of the trauma disorder spectrum, in which mental illness becomes a survival tool, shows the child's inability to properly process the level of fear and terror in the home.

> *Parent Shaming Fact: Children can only thrive in a safe emotional environment; in any other environment children will only learn how to survive.*

Usually the rage-a-holic father or mother (for whom rage outbursts are a regular mode of communication) uses yelling, threats, violence, and intimidation as an iron fist of control over the family. Children in these families don't have the luxury of trying to meet their need to feel safe and loved. Rather, life becomes only about emotional and physical survival. In order to survive, children will do whatever it takes, they will placate, lie, and emotionally hide. Kids who grow up in this type of family assume that children in all families live in constant fear and anticipation of violent outbursts, physical abuse, or emotional abuse.

> *It never occurred to me growing up that not every family has constant physical beatings, fighting, and sexual abuse. I didn't even know that this wasn't normal until I was about fifteen years old.*
>
> —Travis, age 44 (unmarried)

The explosive parenting style is based almost entirely on fear, intimidation, and emotional instability. No one is exempt from the tyranny of this parent, including the other parent. Often, the father of such a family is the one commonly known as the "screamer" and is prone to random angry outbursts. These mood swings might occur, for example, while driving a car full of children; the situations that can trigger an outburst are as varied as the parents involved. The long-term effect on children who have been exposed to this chronic angry energy is that they become very secretive and private. Shame, like an infection, needs an emotional opening in a child's developing personality in order to take root. Vulnerability and openness offer such an opening, letting in the negative energy given off by explosive parents. As a result, this parenting style breeds secrets. Children in these families fear embarrassment and fear being exposed as "bad."

Kids who grow up under an explosive parenting style, however, are often very polite adolescents and become placating (people-pleasing) adults. Since being open and vulnerable was not something that was encouraged in their family, but was rather seen as something to be avoided, these adults consciously or unconsciously avoid being emotionally or psychologically forthcoming in order to avoid triggering anger or conflict. When these individuals were growing up, the emotional climate of their family was driven by their parent's mood swings and rage. By around the age of five, they had usually become experts in emotionally reading people and their surroundings. They likely never reported any type of abuse because they were too scared to take such a step. If they had, their entire life would have been in jeopardy.

The explosive parent is also suffering from his or her own shame-driven personality. The anger that is regularly loosed on the family is extreme and dangerous to all parties involved. The rage that is incited by alcohol use, recreational drugs, medical marijuana, and/or prescription drugs (usually opiate based) is a symptom of the parent's own unresolved shame feelings and identity. When drugs or alcohol play a role in the explosive parent's life, this fact is usually minimized by the family and dismissed as trivial by the user. Shame, anger, and addiction form a very tight emotional circle that is resistant to outside interventions and input. The children in this family will do whatever it takes to avoid being the direct target of the hostile parent's rant, which can mean ignoring or minimizing that parent's addictions or dangerous behaviors. Eventually, this parenting style breaks down when the child gets free from the controlling parent, either through reaching adolescence, running away, or as the result of some crisis or self-created exit strategy.

> *Parent Shaming Fact: Children's self-esteem must be developed, nurtured, and fostered in a safe and secure parent/child relationship. The alternative results in a highly anxiously and shame-dependent child.*

The long-term effect of the explosive parenting style is fear of vulnerability, embarrassment, self-inflicted anger (e.g., cutting oneself, eating disorders, or suicide). This toxic emotional buildup in a teenager or young adult is expressed in nonproductive ways that all become functioning components of her shame-driven life. Those who have grown up with this parenting style have an emotional terror of ever being "exposed." The fear of vulnerability is a very strong deterrent to developing intimate romantic adult relationships, having their own children, and building meaningful social and professional relationships. The survivors of this parenting style often struggle with anxiety and deep feelings of shame, and they frequently try to avoid any type of emotional confrontation or expression. In my clinical practice, I have repeatedly observed that those who have grown up with an explosive parent have difficulty tolerating someone being upset or mad at them because this can trigger a cycle of repressed fear and terror.

BEST-FRIEND STYLE OF PARENTING

> *My mother insisted on getting breast implants with me when I was twenty-four years old. My mother always called me her best friend, and I didn't feel that way. All my girlfriends have mothers; I have an older sister called my mother. I hate that Mom can't be a mom.*
> —Tina, age 39

> *My dad became very needy after my mother divorced him when I was nine years old. He was always asking me for my opinion and would tell me all his problems. I feel like I raised my dad and was his emotional crutch. I stayed local when I went to college because I couldn't handle leaving my dad alone. My dad still calls me or texts me every day, and I am married and have three children and live 2,500 miles away from him.*
> —Brett, age 37

The mothers and fathers of the best-friend style of parenting are usually very well-meaning; they just don't want to be in the role of the parent. For as many reasons as there are best-friend style parents, the underlying motive is self-driven not child-driven. Being a parent who is actively involved in their children's lives is a full-time, often thankless job. The rewards are priceless, but parents must sometimes make a conscious choice to be the bad guy and not the cool parent.

Another term for the best-friend parenting style could also be the dependent parenting style. The parent befriends his child for his own emotional support, but he doesn't consider his child's needs. To the outside world, this style can seem like the new twenty-first-century child empowerment approach, but when it is experienced on a day-to-day basis it becomes insidiously harmful. The lack of a parental model for children in such families creates a myriad of long-term psychological, social, and emotional challenges. The void created within a child's psyche by having a "friend" instead of a parent is often filled in with shame-based beliefs and actions.

In such a family system the parent is ultimately parented by her child. This unnatural process for the child will, over time, develop into a powerful shame-driven relationship. The child is emotionally conflicted between resenting her parent(s) and feeling guilty if she doesn't support them. By between the ages of five and seven, the young child knows that she is emotionally responsible for one or both of her parents. Psychology would describe her as a *parentified child*, which means that she acts and functions, both emotionally and psychologically, in the role of the parent. The child skips her childhood developmental milestones and becomes the emotional caretaker of the caretaker(s) in the family. These adult-behaving children are raised to become the parent's parent at a very early age and for the rest of the parent's life. This parenting style extends way past the legal age of eighteen, past high school and college graduation. Looking after her parent becomes a lifetime job and duty for such a child. The psychological burden of caring for a parent indefinitely is overwhelming and frightening. What if she (the child) can't help and emotionally care for her mom or dad? This nagging question will be part of the emotional tension within this parent/child relationship.

A young child or teenager in such a family feels a sense of neglect, but he pushes it down and suppresses it. The child receives positive reinforcement for being his parent's own personal emotional support system. Often a parentified child will essentially raise his younger siblings because this is part of the role he has taken on within the family. The parent's approval of such a child is centered around his ability to act as the emotional glue that holds the family together. The child's own desires, wants, and dreams are ignored, or else used only to support the parent.

The two quotes from Tina and Brett at the beginning of this discussion typify the negative long-term consequences of the best-friend parenting model for adult children. Neither Tina nor Brett view their parent as a friend, yet their parent views them as their "bestie." The situation is psychologically paradoxical because the parent's attempt to be their child's best friend has created exactly the

opposite result. Rather than viewing their parents as friends or con-
fidants, these adult children see them merely as emotional burdens.
The child's shame (from her feelings of inadequacy) and guilt (for
failing to help her parent) are an essential element of this type of
parent/child relationship. While the child attempts to follow the
unspoken command to fulfill her role as emotional caretaker of her
parent(s), no child is equipped to meet her parent's adult emotional
and psychological needs.

> ### Parent Shaming Fact: Adult children still
> ### need a parent's approval, regardless of their
> ### age or position in life.

Later in life this same parent may become a financial burden on
their son or daughter because of this long-standing dependent relationship. The slippery slope of shame for a child in this situation is
that he will unconsciously seek (naturally crave) his parent's love and
support, regardless of the personal consequences. All children, despite
their age, want to please their parent(s), even at their own personal
psychological expense. Parental approval is the gold standard for children as they develop a sense of competence and self-acceptance and
set out on a self-directed life. The fear of not receiving, or of losing,
their parent's love and approval is emotionally devastating for children
of any age, and they view that loss as a fate worse than death. The
chronic uncertainty as to whether they could lose their parent's affec-
tions creates a deep sense of inferiority (shame and self-loathing) and
the feeling of being unlovable. By about age ten, and continuing into
adulthood, the unspoken fear of losing a parent's approval begins to
create a powerful cycle of self-defeating behaviors and self-hatred (possibly even resulting in violence—see chapter 3).[11]

It can't be stressed enough that the best-friend parenting style
is complicated by the emotional and psychological use of love and
acceptance versus rejection of the child if he doesn't meet the needs
of the parent. Unlike the other four parenting styles, in this situation

the fear of losing a mother's or father's love is unspoken, but it is felt by everyone. *The parental power of withholding emotional support and love from children is very dangerous and damaging to all parties involved.* Neither the parent nor child feels secure or emotionally safe. This unspoken psychological burden starts by around age five and continues throughout the child's entire life. The parent holds tremendous power in the relationship for either being loving and accepting or punitive and rejecting. Sometimes, parents use their power to grant approval and love as a means to keep the child as their own emotional security blanket. The implied threat of emotional abandonment is the cornerstone of this parent/child dynamic. The child intuitively fears being rejected or emotionally abandoned by his parent(s) if he doesn't please them.

> **Parent Shaming Fact: Children, *regardless of age, crave and desire their parents' approval and love. Without positive unconditional acceptance, children can suffer a lifetime of self-doubt and shame.***

The parent is suffering from her own childhood history and unconsciously looks to her child to heal her own wounded inner child. The unconscious desire of the parent to have her unmet emotional needs and wounds resolved by her child is a very common phenomena, one that I see play out in my therapy practice all the time. The strong emotional force the parent projects toward her child, looking for that child to heal and love her, is scary and difficult to address. The parent feels abandoned when their ten, twelve, or eighteen-year-old desires normal emotional space from them. The parent feels rejected by her child spending time with friends, and reacts by saying something like, "He hates me! What's wrong with me that my child doesn't want to spend time with me?" My stoic answer—"Your child isn't your romantic partner"—is given with the hope of showing the parent that she is the problem and the solution to her own sense of abandonment.

Parent Shaming Fact: Children crave the support of a loving parent so they can securely explore their world. Children deeply resent when they must become a parent to their parent.

Over time, as the child enters pre-adolescence, the problems with this parenting style become glaringly obvious. Being an actively involved parent and being a best-friend parent are distinctly different and each parenting style creates a completely different emotional outcome within the child. The former style creates self-confidence and mastery within the child, while the latter style creates rage, resentment, and a sense of neglect and shame. Why? The best-friend parent has abdicated his role and is more focused on his child liking him rather than on being a parental role model, disciplinarian, and an emotionally supportive adult who will say no when necessary. Emotional support systems develop within a teen-ager's life depending on how authority and the word *no* operate within the family. Whether or not these emotional support systems are secure is determined by the parenting style within the household. A parent decides early in his child's life if he is going to act predominantly as a parent or a friend. This isn't, of course, a black or white linear approach, but rather an emotional path that a child and their parents walk together. Staying true to that path breeds emotional security, courage, and happi-ness within the child, while straying from it leads to emotional instability, shameful feelings of inadequacy, and a sense of emptiness.

CLOSING THOUGHTS

Shame can't survive being spoken.
—Brené Brown, *Rising Strong*, 2015

We have covered a lot of information in this chapter. Additionally, the five parenting styles we have discussed can also be viewed as styles of attachment within yourself and in all your relationships. The goal in this section is to begin to recognize the insidious nature of shame and its highly sophisticated operating system in your life. The quote by Brené Brown shows exactly the right step to take toward recognizing and minimizing the role shame currently plays in your day-to-day life—shame can't survive when you expose it. A cave can be dark for hundreds of years, but when it's opened suddenly the light illuminates it. The cave instantly changes, and, in the same way, you are changed when the light of awareness floods into you and your shame begins to be exposed. Regardless of how you grew up and whether your mother or father treated you horribly or depended on you for their emotional support (situations that are perhaps ongoing today), this is your starting point not your finish line. Your life is much bigger than your past. Shame makes a person believe they are doomed and hopeless because of their difficult childhood. These negative beliefs are irrational, however, and they will be exposed as myths during your journey toward self-acceptance and out of the valley of despair and shame.

The primary building blocks of shame start in early childhood. We discussed at the beginning of the chapter how a young child internalizes the thousands and thousands of their unmet emotional needs. All children try to engage their primary caretaker, with mixed results. The emotional misses begin to be associated with feeling bad, unlovable, and inferior. By age five, children will innocently tell you that they are either good or bad. A negative parent/child experience becomes the emotional injury that shame starts to evolve from, becoming part of their developing personality. Understanding what and how shame began in your life is the start of a very powerful internal healing process that will transform every area of your life.

It's important to mention that a secure parenting style does breed a shame-free parent/child relationship. We can all strive to create a safe and secure emotional environment for ourselves, our children, and others in our life. What was the primary parenting style you grew up with? A negative style of parenting is part of the shame foundation that is associated with feeling less than, ignored, abused, and that you have many secret problems (i.e., that you are damaged goods). Understanding and processing these core feelings allows the powerful expression of shame to be dramatically reduced in your life. In the next chapter, we are going to explore what can happen when a man's or a woman's shame is left untreated and ignored.

CHAPTER 3

HOW SHAME PLAYS OUT
FOR THE SEXES:
TOXIC MALE AND FEMALE SHAME

I assume my life will not add up to anything, and it seems no one really cares about me. I smoke marijuana because it makes me happy so I can get through the day. If I couldn't smoke, I think I would kill myself.

—Todd, age 17

I hate my body. I hate my legs. I hate how I look in shorts. Why can't I be slim like my girlfriends? I can only relax after having several vodka shooters. I am so fat!

—Jane, age 22

Todd and Jane represent a high percentage of young adults who don't understand why they feel emotionally defective, inferior, and unlikeable. They experience a chronic, crippling sense of embarrassment and self-loathing. Their profound hopelessness grew out of an early childhood disappointment and is now part of their core shame-driven self-image. Shame creates relentless personal problems, and those affected feel they have no hope of ever resolving the issues. Todd and Jane are academically excellent students (underachieving for their ability), very attractive, and quite popular among their friends, yet they both struggle with unprocessed shame. Their psychological degree of self-loathing and dislike is extreme for their developmental age and emotional insight. Todd and Jane's emotional malaise isn't a generational issue but rather the result of their early sense of feeling inferior.

The shame factor for them is that life seems to be just a series of dead-end events with no prospect of a bright future. Todd and Jane are both my clients and previously they were both diagnosed with anxiety and depressive disorders. Neither of them responded well to the typical therapeutic approaches and treatments for these types of disorders. When we started discussing the psychology of shame and their personal experience with it, Todd and Jane both reported feeling like their emotional life was beginning to make more sense and they didn't feel so emotionally disconnected. With their new understanding, their shame-based feelings and distorted self-image didn't continue to develop or escalate. Todd and Jane were able to begin the healing and self-acceptance process before their shame became toxic and deadly.

> *I lose my cool when someone disrespects me. I can't stand to be pushed around by anyone. It's important to stand up for yourself, even though it might mean a yelling match. I own my own company, and no one will f— with me. Can't let anyone get the upper hand on you.*
> —Dave, age 53 (see chapter 1 for Dave's backstory)

> *I have had an eating disorder for over twenty years. I cope with my body image and fear of being fat. Men want a good-looking slim woman. I can't allow myself to gain weight. It's unacceptable.*
> —Laurie, age 48, divorced three times

Dave and Laurie are older, untreated versions of Todd and Jane. We discussed in the first two chapters what shame is and how it develops in a young child and progresses into adolescence and adulthood. It's never too early or too late to explore the personal power and the emotional grip of shame in your day-to-day life. Dave and Laurie are adults who live their daily lives controlled by shame's big three puzzle pieces: anger, embarrassment, and self-defeating choices. Their shame emotionally escalates as they resist addressing the underlying issues. Untreated shame has serious side effects and long-term consequences, which we will discuss in its various different emotional permutations.

SHAME IS EMOTIONAL CANCER

Considering shame as a kind of emotional cancer allows us to look at and discuss its seriousness more clearly. Cancer is a very frightening and life-threatening illness that needs no introduction. The big "C" has no regard for a person's brilliance or their family or social status. Cancer is a terrible, life-changing disease. While no one argues that either depression or chronic anxiety is harmless or benign to sufferers, shame, unfortunately, is generally considered a secondary problem when it comes to mental health treatment. My personal and professional experience is that shame issues are viewed as minor guilt problems by counselors, psychologists, medical professionals, and academic researchers. The lack of awareness about the true destructive power of shame is why its toxicity is so prevalent and lethal. Cancer awareness is designed to help the public sector properly understand this potentially fatal illness. For our discussion purposes, let's view shame as an overlooked and lethal form of emotion cancer. The possible lethal consequences of misdiagnosing shame (e.g., as simply a bad mood) and leaving it untreated are a great starting discussion to raise people's awareness. It's extremely difficult, if not nearly impossible, to treat a psychological disorder without understanding its genesis and pathology. This lack of serious understanding is why diagnosing shame is so difficult.

The first step in gaining awareness of shame is to accept its potential for a deadly outcome if it is not properly understood, treated, and resolved. Shame isn't a seasonal allergy or something that will pass with time, rest, or a vacation in the south of France. Shame is a toxic emotional tumor that will ultimately consume a person's entire life, relationships, and future. Shame is to the soul what cancer is to the physical body—deadly.

Cancer Is Physical Rebellion against the Body.

Shame Is Emotional Rebellion against the Self.

Shame is emotional rebellion against a person's true potential and authentic loving self. This emotionally malignant tumor must be removed from the inside of a person's soul, belief system, emotions, and heart. When someone has a cancerous tumor, we understand that it should never be ignored or left untreated. Typically, the cancerous cell mass is surgically removed. Allowing a tumor to grow freely in a person's body is never a plausible way to heal it or shrink it. In the same way, the exposure, healing, and resolution of emotional shame should never be ignored or avoided. Shame must be removed, or at least dramatically reduced in psychological size. Cancer, whether physical or emotional, needs to be taken out. Neither shame nor cancer have any value or productive role in the sufferer's life.

The popular, superficial approach to shame issues is to argue that external events—such as accomplishments, charitable gifts, and wealth—will cure and resolve the problems. Helping other people and adopting lost animals are wonderful acts of kindness, but such things don't mitigate the shame cycle, which begins when one of the shame triggers is activated inside a person's emotional system. A core problem for anyone working to address their shame issues, triggers, and beliefs is the recurring psychological trauma and the attempts to avoid shameful feelings. (In chapter 4 we will discuss seven common emotional shame triggers.) The primary goal for someone trying to deal with shame is to deactivate the response cycle within their core belief paradigm so that their reaction doesn't escalate to a dangerous personal and social level. The psychological treatment process for shame is an inside healing journey, anything else is to minimize its toxicity and long-term seriousness.

John and Road Rage

If you live in Los Angeles, you likely drive a car and spend a lot of time sitting in traffic. Naturally, tempers and emotions can get amplified when people are stuck in gridlock. Bumper-to-bumper traffic that only moves ten feet in ten minutes can frustrate the best of us. When illustrating the different ways shame is expressed, road rage comes to mind as a classic example. The following vignette is of a high school boy (my client John) and an older man (early forties): John is driving on a residential street at approximately 4:00 p.m. on a sunny spring afternoon. John and his passenger are taking a shortcut through the residential streets to avoid the traffic congestion on the freeway. While driving past a very expensive mansion a guy yells, "Slow down A–hole," at John. (John said he wasn't speeding.) The guy then proceeds to get in his exotic car and chase John down to the next stop sign. The guy gets out of his car, runs up to John's car, opens the door, and pulls John out of his small vehicle. The guy pulls a handgun out of his waistband, shoves it in John's face, and says, "You rich entitled punks speed past my house all the time and you better not anymore. Got it?"

The guy then pushes John to the ground and walks back to his car. John's passenger calls 911-and tells the dispatcher his buddy is being held at gun point. The guy drives away, and the police arrive within minutes of the incident. John explains the circumstances, and the police officer taking John's statement tells him that he knows who the guy is. John is stunned. The police call for approximately twelve to fifteen more officers and they go to the guy's house. The guy is confronted in his driveway. His gun is still under his dress shirt, and he proceeds to get in a physical altercation with the police. He screams at John as he is handcuffed, "I should have killed your sorry ass!"

Ultimately, the road rage incident resulted in the man going to state prison for violating his domestic violence parole (as illegal gun incident). The assailant was feeling powerless and resorted to violence to offset those feelings. Shame can erupt anytime the victim perceives an emotional slight, as in this case. The extreme response of jamming a gun in someone's face is the outward expression of shame wrapped around prior unresolved personal issues (e.g., losing his family). John told me in one of our sessions after the case was settled, "I knew the guy was going to kill me; I could see it in his eyes. All I did was drive past his house." John continued working in therapy on his emotional trauma (from the violent assault) and shame (from thinking that he had caused the incident and was responsible for the assailant going to prison). He learned from the district attorney handling his case that the guy had a long history of violence and gun-related encounters. His wife had divorced him two years prior for repeated domestic violence issues. She now lives on the East Coast with their two teenage children. John knew he was very fortunate to not have been killed, but was only thrown to the ground.

Shame Is a Progressive Emotional Dis-ease Condition.

Shame isn't static; it's always either increasing (as anger) or decreasing (as calmness) in a person's world. For example, an increase in angry outbursts, avoidance of anticipated vulnerable situations, and a sense of self-loathing are all signs of deep distress. John's story points to the mental instability that can come from feeling powerless. The dangerous expression of shame shown in this vignette is all too common. Fortunately, all the parties in this incident are alive and things ended peacefully. Generally, when guns and untreated shamed-based men are united the outcome is grave (as we will discuss later in this chapter). When they are ignored for years, the three components of shame (anger, avoidance, and self-loathing) will eventually grow to toxic and lethal levels. The man who impulsively assaulted John for a minor event is now in prison.

Men who externalize their toxic shame can psychologically ter-rorize the people in their world. This has led to the idea of anger management education, emotional self-control skills, and psycho-logical training to deal with anger and outbursts, which are popular disguised versions of shame healing and management. Any type of class, court-ordered counseling, or program that addresses shame (such as anger management) is a positive step forward in the detoxing process. Considering their youth, Todd and Jane are very courageous to examine their shame cycle before it can become toxic and lethal. Dave and Laura have ongoing episodes and reactions to their unresolved and unbridled shame. Regrettably, John's dan-gerous encounter with a "raging" man is the kind of all-too-common event that is often ignored by family and friends. It is important to remember that no one is ever immune or untreatable when it comes to resolving their deep emotional malaise and fragmented inner self (their shame).

***Shame Healing Fact: Your past is a lesson,
not a life prison sentence. Your present-day
choices are your keys to emotional freedom.***

We all know that when love is expressed it creates positive emo-tional energy. Shame has its own emotional energy expression. For example, a person's shame might be expressed as self-defeating, humiliating energy. Their body language and word selection can contain the energy of the embarrassing inner personal experience (their inner wounded child—see section III). The intensity of a shaming moment is directly related to the level of anger, fear, and self-loathing that is consciously and unconsciously expressed. The term "raging" is a perfect example of the energy of shame in a per-son's life. Just like cancer, shame is either resolved and healed or it will be expressed in more and more counterproductive ways. The legal/ court system is trying to address the toxic male shame epidemic with mandated classes, restraining orders (for the public safety), and anger (i.e., shame) management training. These emotional and psychological exposure techniques are extremely important for raising awareness in individuals about their untreated emotional cancer. The gun encounter example points to the ever-increasing potential of shame turning lethal.

In chapter 1, we discussed the shame scale, which ranged from zero (no shame) to ten (deadly shame, with the intention to do harm to self and others)—see chapter 1 for the complete scale explanations. For the sake of review, let's look at the top end of the shame scale, starting with number six. This scale is a self-reported barometer for shame-directed actions and reactions, offering a series of escalating actions, thoughts, distorted rationales, and shrewd perceptions. It shows the progression of negative outcomes for men and women of any age. At the higher levels on the scale, shame is toxic to increasing degrees because of the ways it is expressed inappropriately, the violent reactions it can cause, and the loss of cognitive balance available to the individual to offset the emotional chaos.

Your Shame Scale: 6–10: Entering into Toxic Areas.

6. You have more and more days or moments when you feel exposed (causing embarrassment), enraged, and emotionally terrified about being discovered as a fraud or an imposter and reprimanded (disrespected) for something you did or didn't do. Your days might be consumed with feelings of impending doom with no specific cause; you feel an invisible sense of dread on a regular basis. You might be afraid that your intimate partner is having an affair but you're scared to confront the issue; you feel too powerless and worthless to do anything for yourself; you are convinced that your life is a big lie and that everyone knows it.

7. It's difficult to prevent your emotions from immediately escalating when you are being accused or questioned about a problem. When you feel emotionally exposed and fearful,

you react with intense anger or with feelings of despair. Your cooling-off period takes more and more time, and you experience a higher frequency of rage episodes. Afterward you feel awful about your reaction. You feel increasingly depressed and ashamed of your life; you have tremendous regret for your abusive behavior and consider suicide an option. You may have been arrested for fighting in public or for illegal drug possession. You may have been terminated from work for fighting or for threatening violence. You could be either a victim of domestic violence or a perpetrator.

8. You have likely been told by your romantic partner or your close circle of friends that you have anger management (i.e., shame) issues. You frequently threaten physical violence against strangers or engage in hostile, emotionally charged verbal disagreements. You have some cognitive insight that your verbal rants are triggered when you feel embarrassed or that you're being unfairly blamed for something (real or imagined). You ignore the frequency and the emotional intensity of your explosive rage even though restraining orders have been issued against you. You may currently struggle with an eating disorder, self-mutilation, or sexual abuse secrets. Your recent romantic relationship is likely physically violent and emotionally dangerous. You feel depressed, and you have strong feelings of shame daily.

9. Your entire relationship world is shaped and controlled by powerful negative beliefs, feelings of resentment, and self-defeating shame-driven choices. Your life is controlled by your aggressive verbal or physical reactions, and you may struggle with active addiction behaviors (e.g., alcoholism or prescription drug abuse) and thoughts of suicide (worthlessness). You feel hopeless and see little that is positive in your future. You are unable to cope with or tolerate any type of personal conflict without resorting to aggressive means (such as rage) or emotional withdrawal (due to shame). Your emo-

tional default is rage, violence, or despondency, and you may be frequently told that your outbursts scare your family, intimate partner, or children. Alternatively, your partner may scare you and you may feel trapped in the relationship with no foreseeable exit strategy.

10. Your life is likely an ongoing series of violent encounters, shame-based reactions, addictive use of drugs or alcohol, and self-defeating behaviors and choices. You are emotionally withdrawn from your family and friends, and you may consider suicidal or homicidal actions as a solution to your problems. You may even have made plans for carrying out your suicidal or homicidal ideas. You feel cheated or taken advantage of by people in your past. You may hate a particular group of people, whether your ex-partners or groups based on a characteristic such as race or gender. You consider violence as a solution to your emotional suffering, and you resist any type of professional care for your addictions and your feelings of rage. You harbor secret plans, thoughts, and fantasies of seeking revenge against yourself, others, or the world at large. You have access to deadly means and plans for carrying out your revenge.

The shame scale illustrates the frightening downhill spiral toward self-destruction via emotional denial and avoidance. The concentrated lethal energy of shame must go somewhere. The more firmly the shame is bonded and connected to a person's damaged self-esteem, the stronger the inward (suicidal) or outward (homicidal) expression will become. Typically, men will eventually externalize their shame in acts of homicide and suicide, while women more frequently internalize their shame with physical illness, eating disorders, depression, and dangerous abusive relationships.[1] The emotional toxicity of shame must be addressed because its outlets are highly maladaptive and dangerous for both men and women.

Toxic Shame

Our working definition of shame from the beginning of chapter 1 still applies, with an addendum for the term *toxic shame*:

> An emotional, psychological, or behavioral reaction that is consciously intended to cause oneself or others physical harm. The experience and primary expression of toxic shame involves violent and dangerous acts against one's self or others. That expression can be personal (as with suicide) or public (as with homicide). The primary intention of toxic shame is to cause physical or psychological harm, and it comes out of the inability to manage one's feelings in a constructive, nonviolent manner.[2]

Before we can go any further in our exploration of shame, the element of extreme (toxic) shame in men and women needs to be discussed. The four people discussed at the beginning of this chapter illustrate the serious need to treat unexamined shame. It's important to understand the significance of shame so we can then work on avoiding the emotionally fatal outcome of extreme, toxic shame. Male expressions of toxic shame are usually very different from those of women. Understanding the ways each gender expresses shame can shed some light on the perplexing behaviors that can arise. It is important to understand, however, that the differences don't minimize the severity to the individual sufferer or the level of danger to self and others.

GUNS, VIOLENCE, AND MEN

This is neither a political discussion nor a debate about guns or gun control. This is about the emotional distortion of the men who resort to these deadly weapons for personal power and social revenge. *The psychological undercurrent of all acts of violence, whether suicidal or homicidal, is toxic shame.* Whether violence is self-inflicted, domestic, in the workplace, or occurs somewhere else, it's the ultimate male expression of self-hatred (shame's best friend). Society, cultural norms, and personal beliefs about manhood all get mixed together to create either appropriate or lethal expressions of rage, resentment, revenge, and blame. The old boys' club myth that men don't feel, cry, or show emotion is the psychological breeding ground for the highest levels of pathological and toxic shame. Volatile emotions and beliefs become the jet fuel that propels some people into taking assault rifles to school, to a concert, or to a neighbor's house and carrying out violent atrocities. These seemingly unthinkable acts aren't committed in a vacuum or without warning by these toxic boys and men.

> *The male gag order insisting that men and boys* **never** *express their feelings is an outdated masculine model that does nothing to heal toxic shame.*

The gun violence debate must include the behind-the-scenes role toxic shame plays. The emotional role of toxic male shame is one of the primary lethal elements in murder, crimes of passion, and all acts of violence men carry out against themselves and others. It's critical to widen our understanding of the social gag order placed on men preventing them from expressing their deepest wounds and traumas. When men are encouraged to express their distressing feelings, actions, and beliefs, they go a long way toward defusing their potential for violence. Understanding the psychology of shame is a major component of finding solutions for male violence, and it can no longer be ignored as a nonfactor. Men externalize their rage, revenge, and inappropriate sexual behaviors. The evidence for this is staggering, as incidents continue to happen. Later in the book, we will discuss healing methods and many different therapeutic approaches offering real-time solutions for this male crisis. Every adult man (myself included) knows deep within his heart that the warning signs of toxic shame had been ignored in the perpetrator when they hear about random acts of deadly force (using guns or other destructive means), violence against women and children, and general mayhem.

> *Men externalize their toxic shame. Women internalize their toxic shame.*

Toxic shame is too often a dismissed critical element in the escalation of male gun violence, suicide, and homicide. Unfortunately, the research points to a preponderance of men becoming violent when their shame issues aren't treated.[3] Toxic shame has no regard for race, creed, education, wealth, success, or personal opportunities. Both the man driven by toxic shame and his friends, family, and acquaintances generally have a strong emotional denial about how serious and dangerous shame can be. The paralyzing experience of toxic shame is a long-standing problem for violent men, who didn't start out as dangerous. All these aggressors, sexual predators, and dangerous men were, at one time, adorable, lovable little boys. Their severe levels of shame-based beliefs and actions have roots in their childhood, adolescence, relationships, and present-day life. Their lack of psychological insight into their feelings and the causes of their shame is unfortunate. All we know as psychologists is that something went very wrong in these young boys lives prior to the age of ten.

2017 Las Vegas Concert Shooter: Shame Unleashed

Stephen Paddock, aged sixty-four, opened fire with semi-automatic weapons on concert-goers in Las Vegas on Sunday night, October 1, 2017, at approximately 10:00 p.m. Paddock fired more than 1,100 rounds of high-impact bullets into the crowd, ammunition that was designed to explode inside a victim's body. The massacre left 58 people dead (Paddock committed suicide, bringing the total to 59 deaths) and injured over 850 people in about a ten-minute period. This tragic event had been planned and designed by Paddock over the preceding months. The opinion of the investigators into this shooting is that the possible reason more people weren't killed or injured is that Paddock's high-powered rifle overheated and jammed during the deadly assault. About one hour after the last bullet was fired into the crowd, Paddock was found dead in his thirty-second-floor hotel room from a self-inflicted gunshot wound. According to the police, his motive remains unknown.[4]

Based on our earlier discussion of how shame develops, we can infer that Paddock's issues with shame probably began at about age seven, when his father was arrested by the FBI for bank robbery. Paddock and his other three siblings were soon displaced from their suburban home in Los Angeles, California, and reportedly Paddock only saw his father once after his arrest and incarceration. The humiliation and embarrassment of losing your home life because your father was a bank robber who was doing time in prison and your family finances had been lost as a result can be a formula for creating a monster. Paddock's emotional shame development could be its own book. He is an extreme example of toxic male shame going beyond any known standard or means of understanding. This incident truly started sixty years earlier when Paddock's father was an active violent criminal (leading to a chaotic family life), who was then removed from his son's life when Stephen was seven years old. Paddock serves as a reminder that shame-induced actions have no time limits, expiration dates, or boundaries.

The purpose of this example is to show that men and women from all walks of life dismiss, minimize, and consider their toxic shame issues to be merely "psychobabble." Shame isn't a psychological issue that responds well to avoidance or denial. These types of nonproductive male "gag order" behaviors can result in a Stephen Paddock–like outcome.[5]

Men who begin to engage and talk about their fears, regrets, losses, and heartbreaks are men who are becoming civilized. The exposure of shame in men is a major deterrent to the use of violence as a means of revenge. Toxic men are walking emotional time bombs who are one step or one incident away from violently exploding and destroying their lives and the lives of those around them.

Men are four times more likely than women
to die by suicide.

Evidence of Male Violence

The Centers for Disease Control and Prevention, in their 2016 annual report, stated that more than 57,000 persons died annually in the United States because of violence-induced injuries.[6] Suicide was the tenth overall leading cause of death in the United States, and especially affected young and middle-aged populations. Suicide was among the top three leading causes of death for those between ten and thirty-four years of age and among the top five for those between the ages of thirty-five to fifty-four years old. The majority of violent deaths in these particular age groups (66.2 percent) were suicide, followed by homicide deaths (23.8 percent) and the deaths of undetermined intent (8.8 percent). As these statistics show, 90 percent of all deaths that are violent in nature are from these two age groups. Suicides occurred at a rate four times higher among males than females. The contributing factors for male suicide were mental health issues, intimate partner issues, and physical health problems. Homicides were primarily precipitated by arguments and interpersonal conflicts (domestic violence) or were related to intimate partner violence (crimes of passion). It is most common for the victim and the perpetrator to know each other (e.g., violence sparked by divorce or relationship breakups). Most homicides (93 percent) were committed by a known acquaintance, friend, or intimate partner.

The conclusion from the CDC is that data collected over the last twenty-five years indicates that violent deaths resulting from self-inflicted or interpersonal violence (i.e., suicide or homicide) affects people under the age of sixty-five of all races, creeds, and education levels more than any other cause or reason. This statistic is staggering, and shame has a big of role in this crisis, as do guns.

Misleading Myths and Truths about Suicide:

- Suicidal people are unwilling to seek help. (Myth)
- Suicidal acts mean that a person is seeking sympathy and attention. (Myth)
- Fifty-four percent of people who die from suicide do not have a previously diagnosed mental disorder (shame isn't diagnosed as an emotional factor). (True)
- Suicide rates have increased more than 25 percent since 1996. (True)
- Suicide is now considered a major public health issue. (True)
- Suicide is no longer considered a selfish act but rather a psychological disturbance (i.e., toxic shame) leading to death. (True)[7]

Other Truths about Suicide

Suicide is generally the last resort after sufferers have tried to find help from family, friends, counselors, and doctors. Studies (CDC 2013–15 research) have shown that approximately 50 percent of the victims of suicide have sought help within six months prior to their death. There are tangible psychological warnings to help detect and treat suicidal feelings and thoughts. At the end of this chapter we will talk about some common shame-induced mental and emotional distortions that can lead to suicide or homicide.

SELF-LOATHING, DEPRESSION, AND WOMEN: IT'S AN INSIDE JOB

> *Depressive illnesses are serious medical condition that affect more than 19 million American adults every year.*
> —*The Numbers Count: Mental Illness in America*, 1999

Approximately 12 million women in the United States experi-
ence clinical depression each year.
—National Institute of Mental Health
(Unpublished Epidemiological
Catchment Area Analyses, 1999)

Women tend to internalize their deep sense of toxic shame. Women account for approximately 66 percent of all reported cases of depression. The psychological foundation of depression, shame, and self-loathing develops in a negative internal belief system. Depression and toxic shame are impossible to separate. Which came first, depression or shame? The answer is they coexist together in a sealed, airtight vacuum of despair and self-blaming. The emotional connection between feeling sad, unloved, and hopeless took years to build and is a terrible cycle to break. Hormonal levels, menopause, post-partum childbirth challenges, and menstrual cycle swings are some of the biological factors that influence paralyzing shame.[8] Properly prescribed psychiatric medications for any type of depressive disorder can help to alleviate the physical elements of depression and shame. Psychotherapy along with the medication is a powerful tool for addressing the role of toxic shame.

In her early years, a young girl's soul is like wet cement that gets imprinted by the world around her. Girls are socialized to behave quite differently than boys. The early development of the toxic shame process in young girls happens with exposure to family trauma, sexual abuse, and parental emotional instability. The lack of proper emotional outlets for girls, and the social pressure against them expressing anger, are the cement walls that surround their emotional growth. These psychological walls can help a young girl survive the horrors of physical abuse, sexual abuse, and related traumatic events. The problem is that when the young girl becomes an adult woman, her early defense mechanisms are no longer needed in the same way. What worked for her in childhood isn't as useful at twenty-four, thirty-eight, or sixty-six years of age. Women who haven't psychologically treated their early childhood traumas (those that occurred between birth and approximately age twelve) carry those shameful events into their adult life.

The lethal emotional effect on women of toxic shame caused by sexual abuse is only comparable to the use of deadly violence by men toward others. For both genders, toxic shame is life altering.

Trying to emotionally digest of shame for the female victim is like drinking poison and wondering why it hasn't killed the other person, the abuser. The victim of shame is always the sufferer, regardless of the circumstances or the family's denial of its shaming behaviors. Women with toxic shame blame themselves for their trauma (often struggling with hopelessness and despair), unlike men, who blame everyone else for theirs (and can lash out in homicidal rage). Women have been socialized to personalize their suffering as a naturally occurring consequence of what they deserve. The shame scale earlier in the chapter shows the mental and emotional trauma of the day-to-day experiences for women who live with a toxic partner. Like men, women tend not to express their extreme levels of shame in a productive or healing manner.

The compounded effect of the embarrassment of shame and its associated self-defeating behaviors leaves women vulnerable to personal and relationship abuse. Relationship abuse can come in many different forms, such as, for example, marrying a physically violent man, personal neglect of pleasing your partner to your own detriment, or supporting a drug addict.[9] Some women resort to punishing their bodies with life-threatening eating disorders as a means of suppressing their paralyzing feelings of self-hatred. The use and misuse of food by women is as dangerous as guns are to men. In both cases, those experiencing shame are victims of their own negative self-distortion and fear of being discovered.

Food for Thought: Shame's Silent Weapon

According to an ongoing study (2013–18 CDC) in Minnesota, the incidence of anorexia has increased over 200 percent over the last fifty years in women aged fifteen to twenty-four. All other demographics of women have remained stable and level during the same time period. The symptoms of eating disorders, however, are beginning earlier and earlier in women (girls as young as ten years old are being treated).

The following facts demonstrate the seriousness of this silent yet toxic shame-driven self-care and food-related behavior:

- Anorexia is the third most common chronic illness among young females after asthma and type 1 diabetes.
- Women between the ages of fifteen and twenty-four years old who suffer from anorexia have ten times the risk of dying compared to their peers of the same age.[10]

For young women, these facts are similar to the way deadly violence and guns negatively impact young men in the same age group (fifteen to twenty-four years old). Food is a necessity of life, however, unlike violence and guns. The female role of nurturing, motherhood, and female self-acceptance is wiped out with a shame-driven food relationship. Toxic shames makes it very difficult for women to fully experience an emotional sense of self-love, healthy motherhood, and romantic intimacy.

> **The misuse and abuse of food by women is as deadly to them as guns are to men.**

Women throughout history have been defined by their ability to nurture their family, others, and themselves with food. The ability to nurture yourself and others is lost in the toxic shame cycle. I live in the entertainment capital of the world (Los Angeles, California), where eating disorders and body image are a serious problem for everyone, and especially for women. Body dysmorphia/distortion is developed throughout childhood and into adolescence as a form of chronic self-loathing.[11] For instance, in chapter 1 we met Emily, a college freshman who has struggled with food issues and self-mutilation (cutting) since age twelve. Emily feels ugly, fat, and wants major facial plastic surgery (i.e., having her nose, chin, and eyes structurally changed) to feel good about herself. Emily tells me she has no self-worth when she gains four or five pounds. She hates seeing a nutritionist because they will tell her that she isn't overweight for her height and body type. Emily said to me recently, "Dr. Poulter, those bitches (the female nutritionists) are a size 4 and I am a size 6. They tell me the medical chart stuff, so I think they are right, that I am not fat. My parents made me see a nutritionist or I would have to move home." (Her parents live in Chicago.) Emily is addressing her core emotional belief that she is defective (fat), ugly (has a big nose), and unlovable (shame). Many times, the self-rejection not only includes food but also body mutilation or cutting, as in Emily's case. The expressions of toxic shame can be as varied as the men and women who struggle with it.

Why Did Kate Spade Commit Suicide?

The surprising and shocking events surrounding the "unexplainable" suicide of the well-known fashion designer Kate Spade again underscore the way that toxic shame has no regard for a person's position, responsibilities, wealth, or life accomplishments. To the outside world, Kate Spade looked to have everything working for her. She had created one of the most successful designer accessory businesses in the fashion industry. The Kate Spade fashion brand was world renowned. Despite this, she secretly felt flawed and inferior.[12] Her chronic fear that people might discover that she struggled with emotional issues prevented any positive change from happening. Shame's grip on the fear of emotional exposure is frightening and can be deadly. The prolonged avoidance of these classic shame issues (secrets, self-loathing, and feeling like an imposter) eventually evolved into a severe case of toxic shame. Kate's shame escalated to a point where she was living apart from her husband and family. She had begun to withdraw from her close girlfriends and her world-famous fashion line in the twelve months prior to her suicide. All of her symptoms were covered up by shame's greatest friend: secrets without exposure.

Kate's psychological decline was very well disguised and kept private from her inner circle of friends. Despair, self-loathing, and hopelessness distort a person's ability to ask for help; the embarrassment of seeking help becomes its own problem and an emotional roadblock to healing. People often wonder why the victims of suicide didn't get help. Over time, toxic shame isolates a person from her inner strengths, cognitive abilities, and available resources. The emotional impairment caused by feeling depressed, defective, and hopeless is a dangerous sign of major psychological distress.

The tragic outcome for women who suffer silently is that their family and close friends never truly know the severity or depth of their isolation, depression, and shame. Unfortunately, this was true in Kate's tragic ending; no one knew.

CLOSING THOUGHTS

> *Life is like riding a bicycle, to keep your balance you must keep moving.*
>
> —Albert Einstein, letter to his son Eduard,
> February 5, 1930

> *Everything you've ever wanted is sitting on the other side of fear."*
>
> —George Addair, George Addair Foundation

Fear is shame's best ally, friend, and emotional watchdog. Fear and all its emotional components impair a person's cognitive growth and their psychological awareness that would allow them to understand their personal crisis. Dave and Laurie's ongoing shame-healing processes will continue in the next section along with their personal shame-healing journey. Our discussion of extreme toxic levels of shame might seem overwhelming and fatalistic, but it is important to accept and acknowledge is that shame truly is an emotional cancer. The toxic qualities and powerful long-term effects of untreated shame have been illustrated in this chapter. Shame left untreated over time can result in the suffering man or woman committing suicide or homicide. This is evident in Stephen Paddock's mass homicide and suicide and in Kate Spade's suicide.

Paddock's horrendous mass murder in Las Vegas can't be ignored any more than the tragic millions of men and women who suffer from depression and shame. Untreated shame destroys the sufferer's life. Kate Spade's suicide is another reminder that shame can't be buried, ignored, or avoided. All the variables in a man's or woman's life that lead them to the brink of destruction can be healed. If you wonder or fear that you or someone you love might be heading toward a serious shame crisis, consider the following warning signs.

These thirteen warning signs of suicide due to increasing levels of toxic shame aren't listed in order of importance but rather as points on a spectrum of increasing emotional distress that could lead to a fatal outcome.

The Classic Signs of Suicide

- Negative view of self.
- A sense of hopelessness and having no hope for the future.
- Isolation and/or feeling alone.
- Increasing levels of aggression and irritability.
- Feeling like a burden to others.
- Drastic changes in mood and behaviors.

- Frequently talking about death.
- Self-harm such as cutting behaviors.
- Engaging in risky behaviors.
- Giving things away.
- Chronic substance abuse.
- Making suicidal threats.
- Possessing lethal means.

Shame is a primary psychological driving force in a person's decline and cycle of despair. If you feel or believe that you or someone close to you has these symptoms, immediately contact a mental health professional. There is hope, healing, and a bright future if you address the roots of your shame. The two quotes above, by Albert Einstein and George Addair, remind us to take the next step in our life. It's possible to change what feels impossible, and inner peace is within in our reach. In the next section, we are going to discuss how to recognize your emotional shame triggers and your internal shame cycle, and we will talk about the ways your shame shapes all of your relationships (past, present, and future). By amending your toxic shame reactions and uncovering the task master of shame, your emotional suffering and torture can be ended.

SHAME'S SECRET OPERATING SYSTEM IN YOUR LIFE

Shame is a soul eating emotion.

—attributed to Carl Jung

Whatever is begun in anger ends in shame.
—Benjamin Franklin, *Poor Richard's Almanack*, 1914

Shame is the most powerful, master emotion. It's the fear that we're not good enough.
—Brené Brown, "Brené Brown on Shame—
The Most Powerful Master Emotion,"
The Coaching Room, blog, January 9, 2017

CHAPTER 4

THE DAILY FUNCTIONING OF SHAME: SEVEN COMMON EMOTIONAL CYCLES

Many people live under the burden of guilt and shame. Guilt says, "I did something bad" and Shame says, "I am bad."
—attributed to Albert Ellis

Your shame hides in many places—in anger, blame, denial, workaholism, perfectionism, drinking, and anything else you compulsively engage in to make yourself feel better.
—Adam Appleson

What is good shame? This may seem like an odd question to ask at this point in our shame discussion. Considering we have begun to uncover the insidious nature of shame, the idea of good shame versus bad shame is important to clarify. The term "good shame" can be understood in the context of a person's moral character, their integrity, honesty, and emotional self-control. Good shame can be viewed as a moral motivator, as inspiration to change and bring one's actions back in line with one's code of behavior. Many times, men or women will say, "I am so ashamed of my behavior." Good shame is a person's inner conscious mind and moral compass. Without it, they are lost on their road of life. When a person ignores their internal moral guide, values, and wisdom, the uncomfortable emotional reaction begins. Good shame can also be viewed as your intuitive voice to empower and guide you through the maze of your daily life and myriad decisions and choices. Good shame and guilt help you to be emotionally conscious of when you are violating your own morals or making self-defeating choices (not sleepwalking through life). It's difficult to consider shame as being anything positive or productive. Understanding good shame, though, means understanding the invaluable role the emotions and feelings of guilt have in a person's life. Good shame and guilt are very important in helping us lead a productive and peaceful life.

Good shame is closely related to guilt because they have a cause–and-effect reaction. Guilt and good shame are emotional barometers, offering an emotional feedback loop for one's actions, and behaviors. In stark contrast, bad shame is a chronic emotional state that is completely immune to outward benevolent acts, good Samaritan actions, and loving gestures. The quotes at the beginning of this section and chapter are all painful reminders that shame can be dangerous and deadly. Ignoring the role shame plays in your life is like ignoring a sudden black cell mass growing in your lungs and wondering why you aren't feeling healthy. As I said earlier, shame is kind of emotional cancer.

> *Good shame is purposeful and empowering. Toxic shame isn't a moral guide; it disempowers and is cancer to the soul.*

The bottom of the slippery slope of good shame is when it transforms into emotionally paralyzing shame. The positive moral influence and the positive behavioral changing feedback loop are both lost and become nonfunctional by this inner transformation. How does good shame become toxic shame? The transition starts between the ages of five and twelve years old. In chapter 2, we discussed different families and parenting styles that unfortunately can contribute to the development and growth of shame. School-age children begin developing their inner emotional "software," which includes moral character, self-image, and sense of their place in their world. The balancing act between the two contrasting types of shame is established during the school-age years. The first signs of childhood shame are feelings such as inadequacy and incompetence ("I am a failure"). Positive self-development creates feelings of courage, mastery, and trust within the child. An imbalance between these two emerging parts of the "self" cause a child to feel emotionally fragmented, unstable, insecure, and scared of life. The emotional imbalance is the start of the psychological cancer (shame) growth within the child. Just like physical cancer, the growth within a person can take many years to fully impact their life. Shame takes a very long time to fully control and direct a person's life choices, relationships, career, and emotional and mental health.

> *Ignoring and avoiding one's guilt over time will develop into a shame-based life. Guilt (good shame) is a warning, and shame is the avoidance of it.*

Mental Illness and Shame

In chapter 3, we explored the escalating nature of shame that can lead to despair, isolation, suicide, and homicide if ignored and dismissed over time. The role of mental illness in the shame cycle is an important ingredient to consider. Mental illness and shame have a complicated relationship, and each element needs to be evaluated separately. Our purpose is to explore the insidious nature of shame, with its emotional layers of fear, embarrassment, and insecurity. We will not ignore or dismiss the mental illness component in our discussion, but we will, rather, view it through the shame perspective. What role does shame play when a homicidal man kills his ex-wife and children? Did this man act out of his insidious rage for feeling abandoned? Does the emotion of being abandoned trigger a shame-based belief and feeling like he is "damaged goods?" Or did he act out of his distorted view of reality caused by mental illness? After many years, shame can lead to profound mental disorders (e.g., delusional and narcissistic personality disorders) and distorted views of one's self and the world. As we move toward understanding and healing, we will continue to explore all these facets in our shame montage, looking first at the seven common emotional triggers. Let's begin by revisiting the shame scale from chapter 1 and looking at how it operates from zero to five (zero meaning not dealing with shame at all and five meaning having moderate feelings of shame).

The Shame Reaction Scale Zero to Five

0. You have no emotional reaction to critical feedback, no sense of self-loathing, and no fear of being emotionally close or intimate. Shame isn't a controlling psychological issue for you. You feel secure in who you are and what you do. You are living a shame-free life.

1. You cognitively understand the concept of shame (feeling defective, not good enough), but you don't allow it to control your life in regards to your career, relationships, money, family, health, and moral choices. You feel guilty at times regarding a poor choice or action but not inwardly damaged as a result.

2. You occasionally feel bad about yourself, internally defective, and fearful of being discovered as a fraud or imposter. These uncomfortable feelings don't last very long, though, and happen only randomly. You wonder about why you even feel such negative emotions.

3. You notice that certain events, people, and behaviors trigger an emotional wave of shame. You try to avoid these triggers and you deny the underlying and unresolved issues within you. You have emotional amnesia and quickly forget the uncomfortable feelings and experience of your shame after they have passed.

4. You seldom reveal personal truths about yourself or voice unpopular opinions. You choose to be very private for fear

of being embarrassed, emotionally exposed, or discovered to be a fraud. You don't allow people to get emotionally close to you for fear of being emotionally trapped or mentally paralyzed. You don't have close intimate friends because of your uncomfortable feelings about yourself.

5. You have unexplainable random bouts of shame-based reactions. You chronically fear being embarrassed. You experience the fear of being exposed as a bad person and you hold the irrational belief that any minor or major relationship issue is fatal. Your automatic people-pleasing behaviors keep you from feeling like dying; your expressed or repressed rage reactions are completely disproportional to the event or circumstances surrounding the incident.

SHAME'S THREE CLOSEST FRIENDS: DENIAL, AMNESIA, AND AVOIDANCE

The shame reaction scale is an escalating cycle of shame-driven feelings and actions. This scale is based on self-diagnosis, which can be very informative as well as a method of avoidance. My professional experience is that people are either at a zero response (denial or healed) or at four or five, trying to keep their uncomfortable feelings under control (avoidance) and keep them from negatively impacting their life (amnesia). Exploring the subject of shame is a clue that a person might be struggling with these uncomfortable feelings listed above. The shame scale is designed for people wanting to uncover and heal the unconscious influence of unresolved shame on their daily life. The gift of amnesia allows all of us to live our lives without re-experiencing every single disappointment we have ever experienced as if it had just occurred. If our minds and souls didn't have the useful tool of emotional amnesia, none of us would ever be able get out of bed or leave the house each day. Ultimately, amnesia helps us to fade and dull our emotional memory for positive and negative purposes. The problematic role of amnesia is the creation of emotional defenses concerning our personal issues that will cause personal and relational problems later in our life. Another feature of amnesia is it can cause us to forget what we should remember. When old shame issues gets triggered, amnesia can then turn into unexplainable rage and frustration. You aren't aware of the underlying reason for the old emotional wound, but you experience the emotional flood of despair and fear.

The daily use of defensive denial, amnesia, and avoidance allows shame to grow in the shadows of your fears, unspoken secrets, and emotional terror. For many years, psychologists have viewed the emotional defense mechanism of denial as the cement wall surrounding the injured and unexplored parts of our life. Conscious and unconscious avoidance behaviors mixed with amnesia are a very powerful defense against experiencing any degree of shaming feelings or childhood trauma. Unfortunately, shame, like cancer, can spread regardless of the sophisticated, elaborate, and brilliant cognitive structures built around the wounded and scared child within. Shame is like a rebellious dictator that rules and controls for his own personal gain. Shame wants full control of its victim's life.

Denial, avoidance, and amnesia start developing in a child by age five and are in full force by age ten. These three tools are a means of survival for a powerless child who might be sexually abused or emotionally neglected by the parents. A chaotic family, poverty, death of a parent, and endless other traumas can all contribute to the creation and use of these three powerful psychological tools. The child needs these basic methods of psychological survival to go to school every day, for example, as if nothing is wrong at home. The problem is that these three tools are time limited and their usefulness ends in adolescence. What happens many times in adolescence is that addictive behaviors become the self-soothing emotional escape from the unresolved psychological terror. The addictive behaviors develop alongside the teenagers' denial, anger, and avoidance of their emotional trauma.

Denial, avoidance, and amnesia are short-term solutions to unresolved long-term shame issues.

The power of shame is only contained to the extent that a young boy or girl can avoid, deny, and forget about the horrors of their life at home. Kids naturally assume all families have physical abuse, emotional blackmail relationships, outbursts of rage, screaming arguments, or an emotional dread surrounding one's family life. The normal childhood of a shame-based adult was formed in the daily uncertainty of his or her parent's behaviors and unpredictable emotional reactions. The purpose of all the different types of psychological therapy is to expose the reason for the defensive personality structures. The therapeutic focus is on assisting the adult in removing their emotional cement walls and amending their shame-based beliefs and behaviors. Addressing these three psychological roadblocks is a life-changing experience and will be further explored throughout the rest of the book.

Among the many challenges involved with deconstructing our inner defense system is navigating the emotional triggers that activate the automatic defense response. The paralyzing terror of experiencing shame is what makes people destroy their relationships and sabotage their careers, families, and lives in an attempt to avoid their shame factor. In a moment, we will talk about the seven emotional triggers of shame that must be understood as the primary operating system that protects the wounded soul, child, and vulnerable man or woman within. These three facets are within all adults and need to be recognized as important parts of our whole personality. All psychological healing approaches and methods are designed to reduce the endless power and psychological force of denial, avoidance, and emotional amnesia. These three coping skills can cause a person's core sense of self to be fragmented and emotionally disconnected.

Present-Day Story of the Big Three Defenses Working 24/7

Dave, whom we met in chapter 1, offers a classic example of these defense shame mechanisms in full operation, with a myriad of emotional triggers starting the cycle. Dave's life and childhood are an example of how and why such denial, avoidance, and amnesia are created. Dave's childhood was extremely chaotic, emotionally unstable, and very scary. During one of our therapy sessions recently, Dave told me, "Dr. P, my mom would lie in her bed for weeks at a time. She wouldn't come out of her room for months at a time. My dad would pretend that nothing was wrong, that nothing was happening. They would argue about my dad's family and how it was killing my mom. My mom had an affair with my dad's brother when I was about ten years old. My uncle told me at Thanksgiving dinner. Neither of my parents ever acknowledge this crazy f—ing event. After that holiday, we never saw or even mentioned my dad's brother, my uncle, again. I remember being so angry that my parents had disowned my uncle. He was great to me and my siblings." Dave and I discussed the idea that there could be an emotional connection between Dave's outbursts of rage, his family secret, and his fear of being exposed. We will discussion this more in chapter 5.

THE SEVEN CLASSIC TRIGGERS OF THE SHAME CYCLE

The following emotional triggers are all a part of the inner wall of denial, avoidance, and amnesia of a shame-based life. These seven emotional states are the fast lane to feeling shamed and psychologically paralyzed. Each of these ingrained automatic responses come with layer upon layer of conflicting feelings and beliefs. Each of these triggers is the hard evidence of the power shame holds in a person's adult life. Peeling away the walls of denial, avoidance, emotional reflexes, and amnesia about your secret self-doubts are necessary for disconnecting your shame triggers. Healing and peace of mind will only be possible when the initial triggers of shame are understood and exposed. Revealing these powerful beliefs and reactions can help you understand how shame controls your life and drives it down a series of dead-end streets. Each trigger can function both independently and interdependently with the other triggers, keeping shame's psychological confusion in place.

1. Fear of Embarrassment: Emotional Paralysis
2. Feeling Angry, Invisible, or Worthless: Distorted View of Yourself
3. Imposter Syndrome and Feeling like a Fraud: Fear of Being Revealed as Incompetent
4. Feeling Isolated: Fear of Rejection
5. Suspicious: Untrusting of People and Authority
6. Fear of Intimacy: Feeling like Damaged Goods, Unlovable
7. Fear of Criticism: Inability to Tolerate Feedback, Acting as a People Pleaser

1. Fear of Embarrassment: Emotional Paralysis

The humiliation of being laughed at and seen as incompetent, while you feel psychologically vulnerable and completely exposed, is the kind of thing nightmares are made of. People often have dreams about being naked in front of a crowd, forgetting what they are saying while public speaking, or doing something that isn't appropriate sexually. A person might feel embarrassed, for example, when they experience a sexual attraction for a married friend, coworker, teacher, personal yoga instructor, or a younger person. The immediate physical reaction might be a wave of heat and blushing, which can be a fight or flight response to your shame. The emotional response is a paralysis in thinking and functioning and a lack of mental clarity. The sense of dread around feeling vulnerable creates many avoidant, emotionally numbing behaviors (e.g., impulsive drinking, binge eating, smoking, abusing drugs, or any compulsive behavior) designed to minimize these crippling shame episodes. This cycle of embarrassment can last a few minutes, hours, days, or weeks, ultimately becoming an avoidant personality disorder. The driving force with any type of shame-based embarrassment is the deep sense that you are defective, inadequate, and exposed. Three areas of life that can be sensitive areas for triggering a shaming embarrassment are:

- Social: Feeling inferior, inadequate, and projecting a false image of yourself and self-importance; being divorced, single, gay, unpopular, or estranged from family and children; having a criminal record or no close friends.
- Career: Not having an important job, not making enough money, not working at the "right" company, or having a boring job; being fired or laid off from work, financially dependent on your family, or unemployed; feeling lost in your career.
- Personal: Wanting no one to know about your emotional issues, challenges, traumatic background, or recovery issues; being uncomfortable about your appearance; dealing with eating issues, body image fears, or secret sexual orientation concerns; struggling with addictive behavior such as a shopping addiction or being in debt; feeling inadequate; or having a secret life (e.g., concerning sex, food, affairs, embezzling money, sexual abuse, etc.).

These three areas of a person's life can be an unlimited source of paralyzing shame. That hundred-foot wave of embarrassment can be triggered by any of these perceived areas of personal inadequacies. The development of this sense of embarrassment has its early roots in childhood. Often, the first time you were caught doing something wrong, people witnessed you having a tantrum, you were beat up on the school playground, or your best friend told someone your secrets was emotionally traumatic. You don't ever want to expose that psychological wound or let it be publicly seen again. There is no lasting relief from the fear of embarrassment, and it is a full-time job to keep yourself heavily defended against this perceived weakness.

2. Feeling Angry, Invisible, or Worthless: Distorted View of Yourself

Anger is a secondary emotion, coming out of a deep sense of feeling powerless, inadequate, worthless, and unseen in your family and world. Men and women both experience rage, anger, and disappointment, although they face different social shaming guidelines for expressing them. The male expression of anger is part of the cultural "gag order" that insists men never show or express any emotion except anger. The stoic man is an angry male with no socially approved outlet for his traumatic life experiences and his range of emotions and feelings. The social bias is against men verbalizing their feelings of doubt, grief, sorrow, depression, and fear, and viewing such feelings as signs of shame-inducing male weakness. This narrow perception of the non-expressive masculine psychology is an outdated model, and this is a big piece of male rage and anger issues. *The lack of psychological understanding and insight into the shame cycle for men is a major barrier to their healing process.* Men who aren't emotionally insightful only feel safe expressing their thoughts and emotions through aggression. These men are considered dangerous and violent and seen as having anger management issues.

Dangerous, violent, and physically abusive men are all shame-driven men.

Many professional football players in the NFL, and no doubt other professional athletes as well, have been shown to be prime examples of the results of the male gag order in this country. The implied social standard of masculinity is that men should express themselves through aggression and by beating the other man down. Please don't misunderstand me; I love football, but I know the sport can be the symptom of a much deeper male shame issue. Too many of these athletes illustrate the dangers of the aggressive male model through chronic levels of violence (off the field), domestic violence, and drug abuse, and fans can be caught in this vicious shame cycle as well. Anger management theory is another way to describe the power of male shame expressed through rage and violence. Any degree of psychological therapy and insights toward healing for the men who rage, abuse themselves and others, and sexually victimize women is a positive step toward exposing shame. Rage and shame coexist inseparably. There is no emotional relief from raging, fighting, and aggressiveness. Male anger and violence is reduced to the extent that these elements of the shame factor are exposed to the healing process. The sense of personal humiliation that comes from allowing a rage outburst only reinforces the wounded inner child's fear of exposure. The shame of exposure must then be buried even deeper in the psyche so that such humiliation never happens again—that is, until the next outburst occurs.

Female anger is dangerous when it's avoided, ignored, and dismissed for fear of expressing it.

Women are also constrained by an emotional strait jacket, as evidenced by the social view that any type of angry expression by a woman in the workplace, the home, or a relationship is bad and unacceptable. Women who express their anger are frequently considered a "bitch," or at least a mean-spirited individual. Women who suppress their rage, however, ultimately turn it on themselves with a myriad of self-destructive choices and behaviors. The pressure to withhold, ignore, and suppress any unpleasant thought or emotion is shame's controlling influence.

Suppressing anger is very dangerous physically because of the stress hormones it creates. Neither gender has much social room or emotional air space to adequately express their deep-seated sense of powerlessness and frustration, which can lead to choosing inappropriate option such as violence to self or others. The wave of shame that is activated by both men and women when they experience an explosion of anger is paralyzing. The wounded inner child is screaming for attention, understanding, and nurturing. Anger is a cover-up for the deeply rooted psychological trauma concealed in the raging adult. The fear of feeling powerless, inadequate, dismissed, disrespected, and ignored are all symptoms of deeper unresolved trauma. Shame keeps the unexpressed trauma concealed and buried deep within the raging man and the angry woman.

Bar Room Fight

Mark, at twenty-seven years old, is a handsome, career-driven young man who is a vodka wholesale district manager for a major liquor company. He came to see me concerning his work suspension for recently punching a coworker in the face at a happy hour event. I asked Mark, "What gets you feeling so angry or rageful?" Mark told me the following:

> When I feel like someone is disrespecting me or my friends, I lose my cool sometimes. I can feel this energy exploding in my gut when I feel like someone is f—ing with me. The anger moves up into my chest and head. Then I feel this adrenaline flush over my entire body. My hands start to shake, and my mouth gets dry. Then I sometimes just lose my cool and get verbally aggressive and if needed I will throw punches. I have been this way since I was a little kid in elementary school.

Mark looked very embarrassed telling his story, and I asked what he feels like during or after the explosion. I asked him what had triggered his rage in this case. Mark said, "This other manager was making fun of me for not meeting our sales quota. I kind of felt like he was my dad lecturing me, and I snapped and punched him in the face. Afterwards, I was so embarrassed for hitting a colleague, I felt like dying!" This is a classic example of unresolved male shame being expressed in a violent and nonproductive manner. Mark wasn't aware of the connection between his childhood shame and his present-day anger, but he was very aware of his chronic emotional dis-ease whenever he perceived himself as a powerless little boy. He began, during the course of therapy, to understand his unre-solved psychological connection between feeling powerless and his inappropriate rageful responses.

3. Imposter Syndrome and Feeling like a Fraud: Fear of Being Revealed as Incompetent

Linda is a thirty-eight-year-old high-powered entertainment attorney for a major movie studio in Hollywood. She was recently up for pro-motion to become the head of the legal department. Linda came to see me for her sudden onset of severe panic attacks. Denying the connection between her paralyzing anxiety and the shame triggered by her sincere belief that she would be discovered as an imposter and a fraud caused her to abruptly quit her job. Linda told me, "I just couldn't take the pressure of my colleagues seeing me as a failure and imposter. I don't want to be responsible for the legal department and have twenty people looking closely at me and my work. My boss wouldn't accept my resignation last week. He told me to take a two-week vacation and calm down." I asked Linda how she had been able to manage her shame-based imposter syndrome after becoming an attorney? Linda laughed and said, "That's easy, I always stay away from the big movie deals, defer to my colleagues even when I know how to manage a particular deal. I am always hiding while working to keep everyone impressed with my work ethic and abili-ties. There is absolutely no way I can manage the department and keep everyone from seeing through me as a fraud. No way. I'd rather work by myself than do that."

Shame sustains and fuels the imposter syndrome much the way water sustains our health and well-being. One element needs the other for survival. Shame uses the threat of exposure to make a person keep hiding their real or imagined weaknesses, shortcom-ings, and mistakes. Shame has emotional leverage over a person who fears their personal and professional world will find out how "bad" and inadequate they are. In Linda's case, self-sabotaging her career was much easier than facing her terror that she would be exposed as deficient. The chronic, relentless fear of being unmasked as incompetent, unable to lead, or unable to do the task at hand (personally or professionally) is how shame blackmails a person. Physical symptoms such as heart palpitations, hot flashes, stomach problems, and other stress-related physical issues are all signs of a severe shame episode.

The imposter shame cycle is a major deterrent to personal and professional growth and change.

The imposter syndrome is a popular workplace term that implies you are secretly scared of being exposed as inadequate regardless of your career, responsibilities, abilities, and prior accomplishments. The deep paralyzing fear of taking professional risks is a prison that keeps you professionally isolated and unstable. Once Linda realized that her chronic unspoken fear of being exposed as a fraud was shame, and had nothing to do with her actual real-life abilities, she went back to work and postponed her promotion for two more months. Prior to Linda's shame "meltdown," she truly believed that she had been fooling everyone since elementary school into believing that she was smart and capable while, in her mind, she was actually neither of those things. Once Linda saw her shame as a symptom of her outdated childhood sense of inadequacy, which wasn't a proper present-day gauge of her abilities, she was finally able to accept her new professional promotion.

The imposter emotional shame cycle can be triggered with a simple email request from a client, question from a coworker, missed phone call from a supervisor, quality control issue, or subordinate employee asking for assistance. The best kept secret of a victim of the imposter shame syndrome is that they are inadequate, not good enough, and damaged goods. The secondary shame issue tells them that everyone else is smarter, faster, and much more capable, regardless of their own past and present performance. The fear of being professionally or personally discovered to have no talent or ability is shame's ten-thousand-pound ball and chain that the person is hobbled with in his or her professional, personal, and social world. The chronic and relentless self-doubt is emotionally exhausting and psychologically shaming.

4. Feeling Isolated: Fear of Rejection

The emotional power and belief surrounding the fear of rejection is underestimated by the casual observer. How many times has a person who is suffering from the shaming fear of rejection unconsciously created the undesired outcome of feeling rejected and isolated? The person can't seem to stop their repetitive self-isolating shaming cycle. Rejection is a very subjective experience and a major cornerstone to the shame mosaic of isolation and fear. The emotional resistance to approaching any type of new relationship (e.g., business, personal, romantic, family, or parenting) or situation where a person will be emotionally and psychologically vulnerable is shame's sweet spot. There is a situational opportunity for a paralyzing rush of feelings of rejection and defectiveness—"I am bad" and "I am unworthy"— which is shame's ultimate control. Highly capable men and women will avoid situations and potential opportunities to stay away from their dread of feeling rejected.

The ingrained automatic response to feeling rejected is isolation and withdrawing from the painful experience. The major emotional disappointments in a person's childhood (from about ages five to nine) came from the early painful experiences of believing they were defective and "bad" and that if they had been better things would be positive. Children automatically assume that if something doesn't work out or feels negative, it's because they are the cause and reason. These early life experiences create the inner monologue of isolation as being the only safe place when a person feels emotionally threatened. Isolation grows into psychological avoidance and denial of present facts (such as personal strength and obvious individual success).

Emotional isolation along with physical isolation only reinforces the insidious nature of shame and feeling defective. The cycle of shaming isolation is an emotional sanctuary from experiencing the fear of failure. The perception of fear (the person's distorted view of reality) is deeply rooted in the core belief of feeling defective. The paralyzing sense of feeling flawed is only reduced by isolating and withdrawing from those around you. Prolonged isolation can lead to severe psychological issues (e.g., major depressive disorder, feeling life has purpose, or suicidal thoughts) and can ultimately be damaging to oneself and all of his or her relationships. Isolating oneself for fear of people discovering one is flawed, damaged, and bad causes a downward emotional spiral into despair. The perception of rejection can be a psychological distortion of a person's role and responsibility in any type of relationship. Many times the other person in a relationship—whether business, personal, or romantic—might have personal issues that you are completely unaware of. Those issues could be the reason for the relationship ending, which isn't rejection but rather a personal matter.

Shame, anxiety, and isolation all comfortably coexist in a closed vacuum of fear.

It's important to mention that rejection can be a personal myth. No one can reject you unless you allow that belief to control you. The objective point of view about any relationship or friendship is the fact that the other person has their own set of projections and beliefs that pre-date you. Your behavior, actions, and emotional connection can very easily trigger a shame cycle in your new boyfriend, girlfriend, or other friends. Shame never considers that the other person has his own set of challenges and wounds; it makes you feel that any situation is always your fault. The fear of rejection can evolve into an anxious personality. The anxious shame-driven man or women is unable to emotionally or psychologically tolerate any type of vulnerability or risk-taking behavior. All anxiety disorders, if not properly addressed and resolved, will eventually lead a person to physical and psychological isolation. The shame and anxiety isolation can ultimately become agoraphobia, which is a shame-based anxiety disorder manifesting itself as extreme and irrational fear of crowded spaces, public places, and feeling emotionally vulnerable when in those places. Isolation is the salient feature of rejection and feeling vulnerable.

My Safe Place

Judy is a twenty-two-year-old college senior. She attends a major university and is in a sorority. During her sophomore year of college Judy fell in love with an upperclassman. They dated for approximately two years, up until the time he graduated, broke up with her, and moved away. The break up was so emotionally painful and devastating that Judy didn't leave her apartment for the entire summer and the fall semester other than to attend class. When we met to explore her extreme isolation (in the spring semester, eight months after the breakup), Judy told me, "I felt so rejected and useless. I started binge drinking and blacking out in my apartment. Then I started cutting my lower stomach and inner thighs. I felt so rejected and hurt that my heart literally hurt. I thought I was going to die from heartbreak. It sounds corny but it's scary and serious. I finally told my older sister about my drinking and cutting, and she forced me to come and see you. I hate Matt [her ex-boyfriend], I hope he dies and burns in hell." Judy became increasingly more and more agitated as she recounted her heartbreak and her deep sense of feeling flawed, damaged, and romantically rejected.

Judy committed to coming to therapy, and she stopped cutting herself and drinking herself into unconsciousness. Her only request was that she didn't want to socialize or see her friends. Judy felt that she could keep her shame-based feelings under control by isolating herself. Interacting or emotionally connecting with her friends was too emotionally upsetting and psychologically overwhelming for her.

5. Suspicious: Untrusting of People and Authority

The suspicious shame trigger is very different from the other six dynamics. The lack of trust and the fear of life is covered up with shame, defensiveness, and suspicion of everyone and everything. Many times, adults affected by this are described as hard, bitter, loners, outcasts, and mistrusting of everyone. The pop-psychology view of a suspicious person is to say they are mysterious, secretive, and hiding their dark side (their unresolved trauma). A person who feels suspicious and untrusting of their world is a person who lives in a daily survival mode full of fear. Their negativity and bitterness about how unfair life is began with early traumatic events many years earlier. The underlying truth is that the wounded, scared inner child is trying to conceal his deep, insidious sense of shame and inadequacy. The wounded inner child has a distorted view of how their life works and progresses, based on their outdated childhood perceptions. The outdated inner picture of authority (their parents or caretakers), mistrust (due to family instability), and feeling defective (shame) creates a very non-trusting adult.

A person's lack of trust, understanding, and appreciation for the positive role of authority in the present day is a serious problem for any degree of long-term fulfillment and peace of mind. Trusting authority breeds emotional safety, courage, and psychological stability. Suspicion, paranoia, and emotional defensiveness against the positive parts of life only breeds more fear and distrust. A person's shame cycle combined with fear and mistrust is a very lonely, painful, and alienating relationship style.

> *Mistrust is the emotional guardian against ever feeling like a powerless child again, in adult life.*

The mental energy needed to constantly question, second guess, and distrust authority figures is endless and psychologically exhausting (as it manifests itself in depression and hopelessness). The fear of being controlled, exploited, abused (in any way), and taken advantage of is very powerful shaming trigger. Regardless of the distortion of the reality of a given situation, shame keeps the adult imprisoned in fear. When a person re-experiences the loss of their sense of personal power as occurred during a shaming childhood trauma, they come up against a psychological wall that is resistant to trust, love, and safety. There is no psychological, emotional, or cognitive openness that would lead to feeling vulnerable and to healing. Victims of sexual abuse, incest, parental neglect, and emotional or physical abuse simply can't trust their world or anyone in it. Their early worldview was formed by terror, survival, and powerlessness. They never want to re-experience those early imprinting events or allow them to ever happen again. The only thing people who view the world through a lens of suspicion trust is their own ability to survive while they deny and try to forget the past. The problem is that often the barriers to healing (such as avoidance) prevent the victim from letting go of their past traumas, their shame, and their fear of vulnerability.

The emotional connection between shame, mistrust, and authority figures has its genesis in an unprocessed traumatic childhood. The emotional, psychological, and physical violation of a young child creates a non-trusting suspicious persona as a defense mechanism for survival. Children who survive a chaotic, violent, abusive family background have tremendous feelings of fear, inadequacy, and trauma surrounding their well-being. The terror of re-experiencing powerlessness and hopelessness is intolerable and adults with this type of childhood history want to avoid it at all cost. They are automatically resistant to trusting someone on a deep intimate level, but they avoid the cause of their resistance, ignore it, and dismiss the disconnect as the other person's problem. Their sense of shame and feeling defective is kept out of their consciousness because of its insidious painful nature. Seeing the world as only an unsafe place is emotionally paralyzing and psychologically terrifying.

All forms and types of trauma create a suspicious, distant, and emotionally avoidant person who is controlled by shame.

Rookie Police Officer

I (the author) was a police officer from the ages of twenty-three to thirty-one. The real-life experiences I had surpassed anything I was learning while going to graduate school and working as a police officer. This story is about Linda, who at the time was seventeen years old, while I was just out of college. Linda was very transparent with me about how her childhood trauma (filled with shame and fear) was driving all her present-day decisions and choices. She was being detained by the Department of Child Services because she was a runaway from New York State (we were in Los Angeles, California). I arrived at her twenty-eight-year-old boyfriend's house because Child Services had requested a police investigation into Linda and her adult boyfriend.

When I walked into the house with my partner, Linda was sitting on the couch in the living room. Linda leaped up and bit the social worker on the arm. I had to tackle her to get her off the social worker, and when Linda finally relented and let go of the woman's arm, blood sprayed everywhere. Over the next few hours with Linda, I heard how she hated all authority, teachers, and the police. I understood the disdain for the police, but the hatred for all authority and any type of teacher, nurse, counselor, or foster parent was mindboggling to me. I sat with Linda until her new foster parents arrived. I remember, as though it were yesterday, Linda telling me this secret about herself: "You know why I don't trust anyone and especially adults? Because my parents gave me away, at age two my grandmother died, my foster parents molested me, and no one ever believed me. Do you believe me?" I was stunned by both her disclosure and her question. I said, "I believe you and don't know what to say." I felt her deep fear of authority (me) and her sense of feeling powerless. The negative energy, fear, and shame resulting from her sexual abuse was palpable as I sat across from her. Linda embodied the complete picture of a traumatic past, a present-day struggle, and a future ahead as a solo adult on the path of her life. Ultimately, Linda's new foster parents arrived at the house, and the boyfriend was arrested for having sex with a minor and harboring a runaway.

Fast-Forward Thirty Years

I was contacted by a friend of a friend about seeing a woman in her late forties concerning her shame issues. During our first therapy session, the new client began describing her early childhood story as a runaway from New York coming to California and all the circumstances surrounding her past. I didn't recognize the woman, but she asked me, "Were you ever a police officer like thirty years ago in Los Angeles? Do you remember a teenage girl biting a social worker's arm?" While she was talking, I suddenly recognized Linda and remembered her story clearly. I literally said, "No way, how did you find me?"

Linda explained, "After that incident, I was placed in a great foster family who sent me to college and helped me mend my life. They hired attorneys to find and criminally file charges against my two previous foster dads who molested me. I saw your books and wanted to come see you. I am still trying to be less resentful of authority figures, men, and people in general."

I told her, "You always stood out to me as a very hard, strong, and courageous young lady. Your mistrust of authority was your only defense against your traumatic childhood, and it is a miracle to reconnect and help heal your past trauma."

6. Fear of Intimacy: Feeling like Damaged Goods, Unlovable

The strongest and most common explosion of shame is within the arena of intimacy with a romantic partner, friends, family, and/or colleagues. Shame and intimacy are a very lethal combination for psychologically paralyzed adults. The natural combination of being exposed and feeling inadequate is terrifying within the context of close friendship or a romantic or marriage relationship. Frequently, people are not consciously aware of their built-in intimacy barriers. In relationships, all the emotional shame issues we carry are triggered. Why? Intimacy pushes all of us to explore our ability to like, love, and accept others and ourselves. The problem with shame is that there is a clear glass wall between you and your true self (you can see it, but you can't touch it). Psychology refers to the outside part of you as your false self (shamed self) and the private part of you as your true self (core self). The false self is a very powerful psychological force and keeps everyone in your life believing something about you that you don't truly believe or trust. An extreme degree of a false self can evolve into a narcissist personality disorder. The daily functioning of the narcissist is that they unconsciously hide their scared little boy or girl inside. The person puts in place elaborate barriers (avoidance), sophisticated defense mechanisms (denial), devaluation of others (fear of intimacy), and anger/rage (amnesia) as a means of helping with their nonstop task of keeping everyone away from their inner private self.[1]

> *Intimacy and shame are a lethal combination for emotionally fragmenting all your relationships (with yourself and others).*

Shame has no intention of ever revealing or exposing your private self to anyone. Married couples can spend decades together and never break through their partner's glass shame wall. Superficial intimacy (without ever exposing one's true, scared self) keeps the wounded child isolated from self-love and all the other contexts of love. When we embrace and accept our true self, our false, public self is no longer necessary. Hence, shame loses its power base and loses its emotional control of you and your relationships. Intimacy has the natural power to force some people to resolve their shame factor issues in order to maintain their marriage or other type of relationship. This concept will be further elaborated in section III when we talk about reconciling the fragmented pieces of your sense of self.

Many people will become serial daters, remarry repeatedly, or avoid any degree of emotional and psychological intimacy altogether. For some, loneliness feels much safer and wiser, given the terrible prospect of being revealed as defective and damaged goods to someone else. The downside of intimacy is that you are chronically scared of being exposed and feeling defective. The natural repulsion from this degree of psychological closeness starts in childhood if you experience difficulty safely bonding with your mother or father. The miscues or poor emotional connection in these relationships leaves a young child feeling very scared and mistrusting of their world.

Feeling unlovable is shame's intimacy block and hindrance to self-acceptance.

The natural barriers put up against being emotionally connected and psychologically vulnerable become a shame-driven behavior. The interruption in a child's attachment process from birth to about five or six years old is experienced within the child as a failure. The disappointment of a failed maternal or caretaking bond creates a very distant and guarded adult man or woman. The bonding process exists on a continuum ranging from no bonding to secure and safe bonding. Shame develops on the poor bonding end of the spectrum, and can be further complicated by early childhood losses such as the death of a parent. A very important takeaway from this section is that shame can't tolerate intimacy or exposure. For many, the unconscious need to keep people at a safe emotional distance allows shame and fear of intimacy to grow untouched. The net result of this built-in relationship cancer is the distorted view of feeling unlovable and unacceptable. Feeling loved, however, is one of the cornerstones to having a fulfilled and meaningful life.

Dating Sucks: No Good Men or Women to Date in This City

Many of my single, divorced, or widowed clients feel hopeless, cursed, or not good enough to meet a great man or woman and have a healthy romantic relationship. This despair only accelerates as my female clients feel their window of opportunity for having children closing (between the ages of twenty-nine to forty-two years). My male clients (twenty-eight to forty-five years old) feel that as they get older they need to have a high-power career, big house, and financial independence. Neither the men nor the women feel that their core self is good enough to attract or maintain a long-term relationship that could lead to something special. When it comes to intimacy and love, the fundamental shame belief issue of a damaged or inadequate core self can be a very challenging dynamic to expose. Dating, romantic relationships, and marriage (regardless of sexual orientation) require emotional vulnerability, psychological openness, and intimate communication. Shame is opposed to any type of formal exposure beyond a predetermined level. This natural detour (unconscious avoidance) away from a basic core emotional need to love and be loved is the insidious character of shame. The denial of a person's shame cycle is evident when that person blames outside circumstances (such as being too old or too young), the lack of available good men or women to date, or a stated belief that love is not in their future.

7. Fear of Criticism: Inability to Tolerate Feedback, Acting as a People Pleaser

Fear of being criticized makes any relationship tenuous and inherently unstable regardless of its type (i.e., personal, professional, family, etc.). The unconscious need to avoid certain situations, prevent unpleasant conflicts, and do whatever it takes to keep the peace is a dangerous short-term relationship strategy. The unexamined goal of feeling good enough and emotionally safe is solely based

on making everyone "happy." Many people can maintain this jug-
gling act of people pleasing, but ultimately it's impossible to sustain
without huge personal costs (e.g., an underdeveloped sense of self).
The wife, husband, best friend, son, or daughter who tries to avoid
the insidious experience of feeling "bad" will jump over buildings
to keep everyone happy. No one is exempt, regardless of their level
of selflessness, from becoming enraged, bitter, or resentful of those
whom they placate to their own detriment.

The adult who secretly fears someone is upset, critical, or threatening their comfort zone is confined by an ongoing paralyzing belief.
Constantly avoiding being criticized keeps the wounded inner child
trapped inside an adult body and mind. The adult who was traumatized as a child (between the ages of about three and twelve years old)
never feels safe or secure when they are criticized and their relationship world is upset. They have built up enormous resistance to any
degree of perceived negative feedback. Yet the chronic need to keep
everyone happy is an impossible goal to achieve and maintain. The
shame cycle of criticism has its roots in a volatile, verbally abusive
childhood. Children learn by four or five years old how to please
their parents and avoid the verbal chaos that occurs when anyone
is displeased. At times, these children function as young but mature
adults in a seven-year-old body. The child's emotional, psychological, and physical safety hinges on her ability to placate the adults
in her life. Such children become adults who ignore their core self
and focus only on everyone else. In the relationship paradigm, such
people have no ability to process any degree of conflict, confrontation, or disagreement.

The adult operates psychologically in their relationship out of
their deeply rooted childhood fear of being verbally criticized for
being "bad." The inability to accept negative feedback or constructive teaching is based in the adult's attempts to preserve their fragile
sense of self. The fragile young child within a shame sufferer is desperate to stay away from any degree of exposure. Shame and criticism are an emotional shackle that keeps men and women from

expressing their true thoughts and feelings. The unspoken fear of conflict is the ten-foot wall of defense against being viewed as defective and disposable. The damaging effect of having an intolerance for feedback or emotional conflict with other people is a narrow life experience pathed with despair. This relationship style is commonly described as a codependent or placating relationship.

CLOSING THOUGHTS

> *Sometimes letting things go is an act of far greater power than defending or hanging on.*
>
> —Eckhart Tolle, *A New Earth: Awakening to Your Life's Purpose*, 2005

The big three friends of shame—denial, avoidance, and amnesia— have highly sophisticated operating systems within each of the seven common shame triggers. Consider the following questions as a quick guide to your embedded shame triggers. These emotional hot spots are critical to understand so you can begin chipping away and exposing your psychological denial, behavioral avoidance, and emotional amnesia. Recognizing and beginning to let go of your automatic shame response cycle frees you from the hunter within. Recognizing the ways your shame can be triggered in a variety of settings and circumstances are steps toward changing and healing your daily routine.

Questions to Ask Yourself (Again and Again)

- What role does good shame play in my life?
- What is my primary emotional trigger that will activate any degree or feeling of shame?
- What terrifies me most that people might think, know, or feel about me?

- What don't I want people to know or see about me?
- What act or action have I taken that feels unforgivable?
- What event, circumstance, or situation is your shame trigger?
- Does anyone in my world know about my painful experiences of shame?
- Do I trust authority?
- For women: Do I trust men?
- For men: Do I trust women?
- How often do I experience a shaming moment?
- What roles do avoidance, denial, and amnesia play in my day-to-day life?

All these questions are cues to stop and question your inner critical voice, your reactions, and the beliefs that you hold in your head and your heart. What question is the most insightful about your shame cycle? Everyone has at least one of the seven shame triggers if not more. Recognizing your trigger(s) can help you to disconnect and change your outdated self-statements. Questioning and emotionally pausing the cycle of despair and shame is a major step toward changing your life. In the next chapter, we are going to discuss how six common life settings can activate your deep-seated fears and shame. The adult circumstances of your life can frequently be a natural setting and a breeding ground for all your self-doubts, self-loathing, and shame. The courage to look inside your heart and soul is truly an act of bravery. Emotional freedom and personal choices are on the other side of your shame barrier.

> *Your mind is a powerful thing. When you fill it with positive thoughts, your life will start to change.*
>
> —Unknown

CHAPTER 5

WHERE SHAME HIDES AND TERRORIZES: YOUR MONEY, YOUR LOVE LIFE, YOUR FAMILY PAST AND PRESENT, YOUR HEALTH/BODY, AND DYING

In a world of tension and breakdown it is necessary for there to be men who seek to integrate their inner lives not by avoiding anguish and running away from problems, but by facing them.
—Thomas Merton, *Come to the Mountain*, 1964

We are continuing our journey of uncovering, exposing, and eliminating the control shame has in any area of your life. The quote above by Thomas Merton is an important reminder that the only lasting solution and relief from the emotional terrorism of shame is *confrontation*. Direct exposure is challenging as it reveals the most feared and avoided pieces of our emotional trauma. Other approaches to healing your shame cycle and strengthening your core self are often an avoidance of the deeper problem. In chapter 4, we explored how shame operates in your moment-to-moment emotional life. The seven emotional triggers all function within six common areas of life. The triggers can be seen as the electrical wiring in your psychological home or building, while the six different areas in this chapter can be viewed as the different floors within that building. Each floor (i.e., area) has its own set of unique shaming issues and challenges for you. These six areas are ways that shame hides in and terrorizes your life, relationships, and soul. The floor you are currently living on will determine what areas of personal growth and shame issues you are addressing. Your phase of life is important to consider when looking at each of the six areas. Depending on your age and what else is going on in your life (e.g., whether you are a college student, newly married, the parent of a newborn or adolescent children, whether you are divorced, an empty nester, retired, have grandchildren, etc.,) the situations in which shame can attack and terrorize you and your wellbeing may be slightly different.

No phase of life issue or individual external circumstance can resolve or minimize the cancerous nature of your shame factor. The insidious inward operation and emotional malaise of shame can sometimes change the outward appearances of a person's life. For instance, the various forms of material wealth or a new house will never heal the core trauma or wound. Cancer attacks the physical body in many different forms, but all forms are a rebellion against the body. Shame attacks your emotional and psychological body through the six life circumstances we have mentioned. Shame rebels against your core self, soul growth, and healing. Consider the idea that seen and unseen shame could have an impact in your emotional, psychological, and physical functioning as you face your present-day challenges.

Emotional bonding with self and others is a natural biological drive and need.

Relationships matter. Relationships are the lifeblood and oxygen of your life, destiny, and fulfillment. In the absence of important meaningful relationships, life can be very bleak and empty. The wartime punishment of solitary confinement is evidence that relationships have a great deal of power for the basic well-being of any individual. Our biology is designed to form strong emotional bonds with ourselves and others. We simple can't live without our intrinsically valuable emotional connections and bonds. When psychologists are diagnosing and treating any emotional or mental health condition, they always consider the invaluable role of strong emotional bonds. The most important relationship in your life is the one with yourself, and how you manage that relationship dictates your sense of well-being, sense of belonging, and personal empowerment. Our entire life path is directed by our important and meaningful relationships. *Shame interrupts the natural biological, psychological, and physical human drive to bond and form lasting secure relationships.* Our whole life is a series of relationships, and shame interferes with them; shame hinders and distorts the value and importance of your relationships to yourself, your family, and everyone around you. But shame can't exist in a loving, supportive, and caring emotional relational environment.

My client Adam, age twenty-eight, told me the following story about how he has never liked himself or his sexual orientation: "I remember walking past the mirror at home around age twelve and seeing myself and flipping myself off. I couldn't stand seeing myself or my reflection in a window then and barely can now. I used to say to myself in the mirror f— you! I would go weeks without looking at myself in the mirror. I used to abuse myself with binge drinking and random anonymous sexual partners. I am trying to accept myself and my world. Now when I feel anxious I try not to over drink." Adam has tremendous shame around his family of origin concerning his sexual orientation. His conservative parents reject the notion of alternative lifestyles as acceptable and appropriate. Adam is thoroughly convinced he is going to hell, and he hides his lifestyle from his family and relatives. Any degree of rejecting, resisting, and avoiding relationships with others is a chronic source of paralyzing emotional shame and psychological suffering, however, and we will talk more to Adam later in this chapter about his family and his romantic shame.

> **Shame fights against close supportive emotional bonds because of its destructive nature.**

In this chapter, we are going to start with the most important relationship in your adult life: *your relationship with yourself.* Your emotional bond to your core self is the barometer for the rest of the relationships in your life. The degree to which we accept and like ourselves is the same degree to which we will like and accept others. Self-acceptance and shame are at opposite ends of your fulfillment of life spectrum, but shame derails the self-acceptance process with any of the six areas we will be talking about in this chapter. It is critical to understand and explore your personal relationship to all six areas of your life, in order to reveal shame's subtle poisonous influence. How you navigate each area determines your happiness, fulfillment, and well-being in life. Each relationship (area) is a piece of your history, your present-day interactions, and your relationship pattern of shame or emotional freedom. This Cherokee proverb illustrates the timeless struggle of shame versus self-acceptance within us.

> *There is a battle of two wolves inside of us. One is evil. It is anger, jealousy, greed, resentment, lies, inferiority, and ego. The other is good. It is joy, peace, love, hope, humility, kindness, empathy and truth. The wolf that wins is the one you feed.*
> —Cherokee Proverb

SIX AREAS OF CONSIDERATION

Any one, any combination, or all six of these areas of life can be a chronic shame trigger, stirring up your past or present stress or fear of the future. The Cherokee proverb about the wolves is fitting, as it parallels our discussion of focusing on either giving in to your shame or else on developing your core sense of self-acceptance. You can't starve your shame factor out of existence without first understanding the role it plays in your present life. It's imperative to know how and where your shame secretly operates below the surface of your life. There is usually one area of your life that will demand your full attention and energy to manage your emotional shame and despair. Your life, relationships, and psychology is comprised of these six areas:

1. Money and Finances
2. Love Relationships/Marriage
3. Childhood Family
4. Present-Day Family (Your Own Children)
5. Your Health/Body Image
6. Loss/Death

Many times, people will say to me out of frustration and despair, "My issues never change; I am always struggling with money issues; I am always having issues with my mother and family; my health has always been poor; I am no good at relationships." These types of self-statements are all coming from an emotional place of frustration, despair, and feeling psychologically lost. Why does it seem that the same personal issues, challenges, and problems never get resolved?

Shame has us believing that we are the only ones who have any recurring significant personal issues to resolve. It seems that no one else has the same degree of nagging dread that they are not good enough. It's the lie of the ages that you are the only person to have issues to learn from, change, resolve, and overcome. No one is exempt from these life challenges and life lessons. Shame helps people maintain their denial of their own issues until those same issues bring them back to the same unresolved problems. The repetition of relationship themes is an emotional warning sign that something is out of balance in you. Let's look at the six areas of your life to uncover the insidious role shame plays in creating confusion, despair, and hopelessness in your heart and soul.

1. Money and Finances: You and Your Money

Shame and money matters are complicated. Acquiring and spending money can be a very empowering experience. For centuries, money, wealth, and possessions have been the standard measurement of success and self-worth in life for men. In more recent decades, women have also been dragged into this shame-based belief system telling them that their self-worth is only equal to their net worth.

Emotional deprivation is the classic symptom of all shame and money matters. Emotional deprivation is the sense of never having enough money, houses, watches, jewelry, designer clothes, exotic cars, or anything else. This sense comes out of a very powerful and relentless desire. The feeling of needing more love, emotional empathy, and comfort starts in childhood at around age three.[1] When a young child lacks parental nurturing, she feels the beginnings of emptiness, emotional neediness, and psychological neglect. These core feelings of neglect impact a child's ability to develop and feel competent and capable. In adulthood, she pursues the social status of wealth, money, fast cars, and power as a compensation for her deep sense of childhood neglect and deprivation. Shame's power, by way of emotional deprivation, moves a person away from discovering and connecting to their core self and heart. Psychological neediness is a powerful force that can't be resolved with money and accomplishments. The surface level of a person's life can often feel to them like the only safe place to live. The problem with this type of avoidance, however, is that your core self needs your inward attention and time.

> *Emotional deprivation is never resolved or healed with acquiring or owning material possessions.*

Emotional deprivation can lead to serious addictive behaviors unless it's exposed and healed. The psychological power of trying to heal deprivation with money is a self-destructive force. The feeling of being deprived, less than others, or ripped off by life can be silenced momentarily with the many faces of money and its power, but this is only a short-term relief. In fact, the sense of emotional and mental emptiness is exaggerated by the chronic focus on money. Because of this, avoiding shame through money and possessions is a fast track to chronic despair. Places like Las Vegas, with their lure of money, wealth, and importance, would be unnecessary if emotional deprivation and addiction were not part of our human shame malaise.

Shame and money are mean taskmasters that don't treat their followers very well or with any lasting peace of mind. Money has an emotional energy that is either shame based or involves calm nonattachment. When self-worth is wrapped up with wealth, the emotional energy becomes a restless, chronic cycle of despair based around never having enough. Money concerns about cash flow, business deals, country club memberships, prestigious jobs, huge savings accounts, and living in the right neighborhood are all temporary distractions from the lurking fear and despair within. The psychological money shame triggers are very sophisticated, and many times manifest as fiscally reckless behaviors. Such behaviors include, but are not limited to, worry, anger, greed, entitlement, deception, embezzlement, fraud, stealing, withholding, and denying the consequences of actions. People will sometimes even commit suicide or homicide when they feel threatened or betrayed by their financial ups and downs. The psychological security and healing that people seek to offset their nagging shame is never found in their bank accounts or their retirement portfolios. The healing and peace of mind they long for is always found within.

> ### *Self-worth and net worth must never be confused, mixed up, or connected.*

Shame keeps a person's sense of deprivation alive and always grasping. The feeling that the next hottest item will fulfill and completely satisfy the deep emptiness is just an illusion. The short-lived emotional rush of buying, spending, and acquiring is a very slippery shame slope. Attempting to use money to try and solve the nagging self-doubt and feelings of being defective is like running on a treadmill and wondering why you haven't gone anywhere, and multiple personal and financial problems can arise as a result. You might have done the shopping equivalent of running seven miles and feel exhausted, but nothing has changed within your empty black shame hole. Shame issues surrounding self-worth are never resolved or healed with money and its material power. As obvious as it sounds, the insecurity of self-doubt, inadequacy, self-loathing, and deprivation can't be healed with a credit card. Shame thrives with avoidance, compulsive spending, and financial debt, and all these compulsive behaviors accomplish are to reinforce your sense of feeling awful and less than others.

Retail Therapy

My client Sally is a thirty-four-year-old elementary school teacher who has a compulsive shopping and spending habit. Sally doesn't shop everyday online or at high-end department stores, but when she feels "bad" or like a "fraud or imposter" because her students' parents have been questioning or criticizing her, she immediately goes to her favorite retail therapy location, Century City Mall (a high-end mall in West Los Angeles), after school from around 4:00 p.m. until 6:00 p.m. In that two-hour window of time (her own preset time limit), Sally buys at least one new seasonal outfit. Sally's fear of being exposed when questioned by a student, her principal, or a parent (due to imposter syndrome) triggers her automatic reflex to avoid the emotional wave of painfully uncomfortable feelings. A quick two-hour shopping session on any school-day afternoon helps to immediately reduce her sense of inadequacy. Sally has accumulated two master bedroom closets full of clothes with the sales tags still on them. Sally currently has credit card debt exceeding $125,000.00. She came to therapy to start exploring her shopping addiction and denial of her limited finances and her underlying shame. Sally was sleepwalking right into credit card debt that exceeded her yearly salary by more than 30 percent.

All compulsive behaviors (e.g., spending) reinforce shame's influence on you, making you feel even more powerless.

The unresolved emotional pain and trauma from Sally's childhood, adolescence, and divorce were too painful for her to address or explore. Instead, she was in denial about the death of her mother (Sally had been only eight at the time), her own reckless drug use all through high school, and her ex-husband divorcing her to marry his business partner. Sally is smart and psychologically insightful, but she has been traumatized by her life. Whenever she was sad after her mother's death, her father would take her shopping to make her feel better. Sally's early experience of loss created an emotional longing to feel loved and secure. Spending money was a quick and very temporary fix for her deep sense of inadequacy (shame) and isolation. Sally started to see the emotional connections between her childhood traumas and her impulsive urge to shop and spend money. Exposing her hidden shame and grief dramatically reduced her desire to compulsively shop and emotionally "numb out." Her sense of feeling "defective-shameful" was a symptom of her unresolved grief and romantic loss.

2. Love Relationships and Marriage

Love and shame are a very odd couple. Love doesn't understand shame, and shame is scared of love. Loving relationships have an innate power and ability to expose all the hidden parts within each person. This exposure process is counterintuitive to shame's need to remain unseen and untouched. Intimate relationships and shame can't coexist peacefully or with any long-term success. Shame and love are like oil and water; they simply don't mix and never will. This natural incompatibility is the chronic tension that is felt in all types of love relationships.

Love and shame can't coexist!

The deep root cause of a couple's fighting, disagreements, and inability to grow together is the silent influence of shame on each partner. Shame is resistant to being seen and viewed by anyone and particularly by an intimate partner. Love relationships are based on a close emotional bond that doesn't have room for fear, secrets, and inadequacy. When a person's shame is being exposed, the defensive cover-up is often blame, finger pointing, and possibly leaving the marriage or relationship. Shame has many elaborate ways to keep a person's wounded child concealed and unseen by their intimate partner.

> *A broken heart is the worst. It's like having broken ribs. Nobody can see it, but it hurts every time you breathe.*
> —Unknown

Shame beliefs, feelings, and experiences distort the sufferer's perspective of their relationship and their partner's ability to love and support them. The power of intimate relationships comes from our unspoken wish to have our childhood wounds understood and healed. The terror of vulnerability, though, keeps couples from developing a deeper loving relationship. A person's shame is buried inside of them, and a close emotional connection opens all the doors and windows in a person's life. A person's level of comfort with emotional closeness is really their level of comfort at revealing their hidden sense of inadequacy. Shame eventually becomes a major deterrent to every stage of evolving intimacy and lasting love relationships. Why?

The natural craving for love, understanding, and emotional safety are all healing elements for a person's shame factor. The problem, however, is that often a person isn't aware of his glass wall of intimacy resistance. The wounded young child within an adult doesn't cognitively know how to be healed or loved. The inner self only knows how to stay covered up and concealed. This intrinsic battle between love and shame within a person is why love relationships are so complicated, painful, and yet desired. Feeling loved and loving another person are major mental, psychological, and emotional signs of fulfillment and peace of mind. The above quote describes one of the reasons that love relationships are so volatile and at the same time so healing. Our spoken or unspoken hope is that the marriage or romantic relationship will heal all the childhood wounds and shame within us. Unfortunately, this is not something the other person can do. We must each individually heal and resolve our own inner wounds and shame. When a person feels her relationship has failed by not healing her inner childhood wounds, she is set up for major disappointment, rage, and all forms of self and spousal abuse. We want our significant other to magically take away our shame and suffering. We have to realize that we can only do this ourselves, however. We have to come to terms with the causes of our own shame and expose shame as the source of the pain we inflict upon ourselves and others.

> *Romantic breakups and divorce are a valu-*
> *able source of information about the shame*
> *issues a person carries (as painful as they*
> *are to look at).*

Love Hurts

All breakups, and especially divorce, regardless of a person's age or life experience, have the uncanny ability to pull up every self-doubt and personal insecurity in a person's life. The overwhelming amount of shame, loss, and self-loathing characterized by the "broken rib" analogy in the earlier quote gets unearthed in emotional disconnection (such as a breakup). Breakups reveal all the dormant and current shame issues that a person is currently carrying in their present relationship. The despair of heartbreak is an internal psychological signal that it's time to change your relationship style with yourself and with romance itself. The emotional clarity gained from heartbreak comes from your shame exposing you as a fraud and as a liar about your true core self. The challenge is to get past all the emotional blame, psychological defensiveness, and the need for revenge. Engaging in any type of revenge or punitive behavior toward your ex-partner is a convenient way to keep yourself insulated and distracted from your core shame issues.

> ***Self-love and self-acceptance always prevails over a person's exposed and hidden shame issues.***

Emotional clarity, which can also be referred to as emotional sobriety, is almost impossible to achieve in an agitated emotional state of mind. Exposing shame is like waking up a sleeping bear, which is why the response is often aggressive and deadly. A vast amount of personal information about your shame issues is exposed during a breakup. Many times, the divorce, broken engagement, breakup, or betrayal exposes your deep sense of feeling alone and not belonging in your world. The deeply repressed emotions surrounding feeling unlovable, invisible, dismissed, rejected, and abandoned are all from your unresolved childhood trauma and shame. A romantic breakup brings all these lifelong lingering self-doubts and fears back up to the surface. Shame and romantic relationships can't coexist because eventually one side (i.e., one wolf inside of you, be it love or shame) will control the other. This internal battle between the two is the cause and the reason that crimes of passion, divorce, and loss of love are nuclear energy when not properly processed and understood. Even brilliant, compassionate, and professionally successful men and women can spend years fighting, blaming, and litigating with each other to keep their shame covered up.

3. Childhood Family

Three thieves: Fear, Self-Sabotage and Self-Doubt, will rob you
of your present and future if you let them; don't let them.
—Unknown

Discussing a person's childhood family can be very insightful and informative but it is never neutral. We are all sons and daughters, regardless
of our age and family history. The different family dynamics involving
blended families, step-parents, biological parents, step-siblings, and
adoption all influence our personal development. People know they have
unresolved family issues when the subject is raised and they suddenly feel
emotionally overwhelmed and angry. A hot flash of adrenaline surges
through their body like an unguided missile. This physiological response
is a person's shame factor spilling into their body with a sudden emotional overload of rage and resentment. The rush of shame is only compounded by the frustration of trying to explain how "crazy" their family
was or is. Discussing your family of origin can feel like trying to explain
a ten-volume book series about dysfunction and insanity. Considering a
chaotic, neglectful, or abusive family history, while trying to create emotional distance from it, is a powerful shame magnetic. Shame and family
trauma are like fire and gasoline—highly explosive.

Your level of psychological openness and clarity about your
childhood is directly correlated to your level of childhood and adult
shame issues. Low levels of shame come with high degrees of emotional clarity about your sense of competence and self-acceptance.
High levels of shame, denial, trauma, and defensiveness, on the other
hand, are related to low levels of feeling capable, adequate, and self-
accepting. We all know and cognitively understand the long-term
positive (self-acceptance) or negative (shame) impact of our childhood from birth to around the age of fifteen.[2]

The above quote points out the problem of resenting, blaming,
and punishing yourself or others for a problematic family background: it only causes present-day suffering and emotional pain.

The side effects of looking into your past with a critical blaming point of view are fear, self-doubt, and self-sabotaging beliefs and behaviors. Two major relationship impairments that can emerge from a problematic, traumatic, and abusive family background are codependence (approval seeking with no emotional boundaries) and emotional enmeshment (having no sense of self without another person).[3] These nonfunctional family of origin behaviors begin to develop within a young child between the ages of six and sixteen years of age, as the child learned that he could only get his parents' approval, attention, and love by acting as their parent, caretaker, and emotional support. The child received the unconscious message from his parents to never leave or become emotionally independent from them. The parent(s) and family needed the child to be the emotional hub that psychologically held everything together.

> *Codependency and emotional enmeshment*
> *are the result of an aborted developmental-*
> *individuation process for the child/adult.*

These two psychological relationship styles (codependence and emotional enmeshment) each have inherent personal challenges and emotional blind spots. These paralyzing relationship styles are a result of a child being hindered from creating her own sense of self and emotional identity. The natural childhood and adolescent process of emotionally separating and creating her own sense of self within the family isn't tolerated or encouraged. Such a child can only receive love and empathy by being whatever her parent needs and wants. As the child becomes older (twelve to eighteen), the natural psychological pull toward independence is shame laden and forbidden by the family. All attempts to become an independent and separate individual are loaded with feelings of despair, isolation, loneliness, and hopelessness. The child, and later the adult, seeks emotional relief from her paralyzing shame-based feelings by placating her family and parents.

The person who has grown up with this family relationship style carries it into his adult relationships. Shame keeps the inner wounded child imprisoned, out of fear of being unloved if he pulls away from the family or changes his dysfunctional relationship pattern. Shame is a horrible task master that constantly threatens to psychologically annihilate a person if he tries to pursue his own dreams and goals. The natural reaction in such situations is to feel trapped and fused to your childhood family, creating an endless source of frustration and disappointment that fills up your life. It's very difficult, if not nearly impossible, to create your own individual adult life when you still feel psychologically imprisoned by your birth family.

4. Your Present-Day Family: You and Your Children

> *The world we have created is a product of our thinking. It cannot be changed without changing our thinking.*
> —Albert Einstein, *The Ultimate Quotable Einstein*, 2010

Parenting is one of the most fulfilling challenges, tasks, and responsibilities in life. You can be married for years and then become divorced, but even if you are never married when you have children you're a parent for life—that fact never changes. The title of mom or dad (being a step-parent also applies) and the sense of parental concern never diminishes with your child's age or life circumstances. One of many unforeseen parenting experiences are the dormant issues our children can trigger within us as they grow up. Prior to this parenting period in your life, many of your long-forgotten personal childhood issues were simply out of sight and out of mind. Children, though, have the innate ability to touch a parent's deepest insecurities and unresolved shame beliefs. Being a parent opens doors in your heart and soul that were previously undercover and untouchable. Regardless of their age, your children, teenagers, or college-bound kids will expose your unresolved shame issues. It's at these moments of shame exposure that the parent-child relationship can become very tense and turbulent.

The above quote by Albert Einstein becomes very relevant when your children start setting off your shame triggers. The opportunity to view your childhood as different from your child's development is critical to help reduce and heal your own shame. Addressing your shame issues helps to keep your children from developing their own set of shame factor challenges. Stopping the next generation of shaming beliefs in your family, children, and grandchildren starts with you! You can stop the family cycle of passing shame down the family emotional tree like a DNA trait.

Projecting our shame onto our children is the primary cause of parent-child tension and relationship problems (especially with children twelve to seventeen years of age)—the author's professional experience.

In my professional experience as a psychologist, I have seen that when, in adolescence, a child starts to assert her own opinions that oppose a parent's shame beliefs, it can be the start of a family civil war. Additionally, my experiences as a parent to four children and my experience of being a son has taught me that ultimately 90 percent of all parent-child problems are unresolved parent-driven shame issues. Any unresolved shame conflict within a mother or father will negatively impact their young children, teenagers, or young adult children. The parent projects his avoidance, denial, and amnesia of his traumatic past, despair, and fear onto his children, which is as unhelpful as explaining the purpose of swimming lessons to a person who thinks she is drowning. Let's agree that a parent who feels disrespected or dismissed by his twelve-year-old who would rather play the newest video game isn't responding to the real problem. The challenge of parenting involves figuring out how to manage your shame crisis while still being an effective nurturing parent. It's very difficult to function as a parent when your wounded inner child is awakened and you are feeling exposed. The parent's internal shame conflict is often automatically blamed on and projected onto her child.

It's important to remember that we all have an inner child that is as much a part of our adult life as oxygen is to water—they are an inseparable combination. We have discussed our wounded inner selves in the context of our unresolved traumas and the shame-inducing past we grew up in, but now our children have become a part of our past and present. It's inevitable that being mother or father, regardless of the official title (i.e., biological, foster, adoptive, or step-parent), will bring up and reveal to us through our children any unresolved shame, self-doubt, or fear of being an imposter. Our shame factor has its foundation and beginning in our own childhood. Our early unresolved painful experiences tend to fade out of our consciousness (i.e., amnesia) but not out of our emotional memory, and these experiences still affect us whether or not we remember them. Being a parent automatically creates emotional waves of self-doubt, inadequacy, and regression (living in the past), despite the fact that, simultaneously, parents are usually very excited to have children and build a family with them.

> *Your unresolved shame will be exposed by your child; the only question is when, not if, it will happen.*

An important part of effective parenting is accepting and knowing that your children will reactivate any unresolved childhood trauma, adolescent crisis, and present-day feeling of inadequacies. It's going to happen; the only question is when. When you are experiencing unexplainable rage or having an unreasonable emotional reaction to spilled milk or the game your child's soccer team lost, these are signs that something is out of balance within you. When a minor event between you and your fourteen-year-old suddenly escalates into a screaming ordeal, or perhaps becomes physically abusive, consider the idea that your shame blind spot is being exposed.

Your shame will never tell you that these moments are a great opportunity to stop, amend, and heal your deep unspoken shame and despair. Rather, these awful parent-child encounters tend to widen the relationship gap between you and your children. Shame's primary effect is secrecy, which makes developing a strong secure emotional bond with your fifteen-year-old seem impossible. Frequently, the trauma we experienced at a certain age isn't fully activated until our children reach that particular age. The paradox of shame is feeling unlovable while having the responsibility and desire to love your children.

5. Your Health and Your Body Image

Shame, allied with silence and embarrassing secrets, is a very powerful tool for destroying a person's physical and emotional health. When shame is turned inward and operating at full capacity, a person's physical behaviors, actions, and habits can all be symptoms of untreated emotional trauma. A young woman or man may appear on the outside to be shame-free, yet psychologically nothing feels good to them. When a person's health, self-destructive habits, and physical recklessness are affected by shame, it can begin a very dangerous psychological process.

The emotional connection between the mind and the physical body is strong, and the bond can be negatively impacted by toxic self-loathing beliefs and shame-driven emotions. Good health and shame aren't friends but instead are completely incompatible. Self-care, self-acceptance, and self-liking are all healing elements that stand in contradiction to shame's insidious self-hated, body hatred, and personal recklessness. Food phobias (such as bulimia), eating disorders (such as anorexia), body dysmorphia (including excessive cosmetic surgeries), and self-mutilation (such as cutting) are all classic signs of shame manifesting and spilling into a person's body.[4]

Shame creates emotional hunger, and physical self-abuse tries to fill it.

Your body is a brilliant operating system that functions at its best when properly balanced between three areas: the psychological, the emotional, and the physical. When balanced, all three parts naturally function together in perfect harmony. The problem is when they become out of balance (e.g., through chronic sickness) or out of control (e.g., through chronic panic attacks), or when you set out to punish yourself (e.g., through dangerous, life-threatening behaviors). Your body then becomes the container for all your shame-based behaviors, beliefs, and self-loathing actions. The bodily damage, injuries, or (in the worst case) death are results of shame's physical impact on your life. The disharmony between your emotional, psychological, and physical self causes the parts to negatively affect each other. The fundamental operating philosophy of Eastern healing medicine and practices is to help an individual regain harmony (i.e., remove dis-ease) in their body that was caused by their emotional disharmony (i.e., shame).

Removing the emotional blocks connected to self-defeating beliefs helps to release the physical blocks. For instance, Judy (from chapter 4) was having many psychosomatic illnesses such as indigestion, ulcers, food allergies, and severe muscle spasms in her back as a result of her self-loathing after her breakup. Once she began to grieve and accept the end of the relationship and her prior history of feeling shame, her health issues and concerns dramatically declined. Within three months of starting therapy and addressing her unresolved shame, she was symptom-free and had begun working out again on regular basis.

The mind and body connection has been a widely accepted fact in Eastern medicine for thousands of years. The power of the mind, emotions, and their (positive or negative) impact on the body is still an evolving science in Western medicine, but is becoming more widely accepted and understood.

Your body is directly impacted by your emotions (whether you are excited and happy or fearful and scared) and your psychological outlook. How you physically live your life each day is basically directed by your feelings of self-acceptance and self-approval or by your feelings of self-loathing and self-hatred. Your psychological beliefs about yourself, along with how you feel about your body and health, strongly influence whether you live a healthy and positive lifestyle or a dangerous self-abusing and shaming lifestyle. The unresolved trauma, sexual or physical abuse, and feelings of body hatred that grew during your childhood, adolescence, and adult life, shape and form how you inwardly look at yourself (i.e., whether you see yourself as attractive and desirable or ugly and inadequate) and how you function physically in the world. The delicate balance between the three parts of your life (psychological, emotional, and physical) can be completely derailed by unresolved emotional shame, which frequently shows itself physically.

Shame, Self-Loathing, and Cutting: A Dangerous Combination

We first met Emily in chapter 1. She is a nineteen-year-old college student who has been secretly cutting herself on a regular basis (at least once a month) since age twelve. Emily's shame trigger is when she starts to feel "bad" about herself, and self-loathing for her appearance, weight, binge drinking, and chronic need for social media attention and friends. Emily continued her therapy, started attending a support group for eating disorders, and stopped drinking and using other drugs (like marijuana, valium, and cocaine). For a time, she was having a very calm and uneventful semester, but then she began feeling "dismissed" by her circle of friends. Emily, feeling very "bad," "not good enough," and "unlovable" (all words she used to describe herself), immediately again began cutting her lower stomach, binge eating, and blackout drinking.

Emily told me, "I didn't believe shame was an issue but the wave of feeling ugly, unlovable, and hopeless was terrifying. I freaked out when my girls dropped me from the group chat. I don't want to see anyone after that a week ago, unless I am drinking. I haven't cut myself in three months and started cutting my thighs and stomach again when I feel this anger and rage for being rejected by girls [her regular drinking and drugging friends]."

I asked Emily, "Do you feel like killing yourself?"

Emily looked at me, paused, and asked, "If I tell you, will you hospitalize me? I don't want to go and besides I can control myself."

After a few more hours of discussion, Emily willingly agreed to go into a thirty-day inpatient medical treatment program for eating, drinking, and psychological disorders. We will see Emily again later in the book and look at how she addressed her underlying shame beliefs and self-hatred behaviors. In Emily's case, the psychological, emotional, and physical manifestations of shame were life-threatening and self-destructive.

You Are Your Health

The idea behind psychosomatic disorders is that some of your physical illnesses, physical challenges, and malaise may have emotional causes that are affecting your physical health and well-being. When your emotional health is crippled in part by unresolved shame, many times these self-loathing beliefs spill into your physical body. (It's important to note here that not all illness, serious health issues, and physical challenges are caused by shame or by a person's psychological disposition. The purpose of our discussion is simply to expose the insidious nature and negative impact shame can have on our body and overall health.) The manifestation of physical shame in the body can take many different forms, such as aggressive self-mutilation, stress-related illnesses, and injuries. Shame can materialize in a person's life via extreme food habits, eating disorders, cutting, excessive or extreme body piercings, excessive tattoos, chronic cosmetic surgeries, or preoccupation with the body or physical appearance. Shame interrupts your body's functioning with insidious distortions and physical neglect.

An important element of your overall physical well-being involves developing your ability to care for and nurture yourself. Taking care of yourself emotionally, physically, mentally, and psychologically may sound a bit simple and elementary, but shame is directly opposed to self-care and self-preservation. The desire to nurture or punish yourself is reflected in part in your relationship to food. Weight-loss experts know that if a person feels good about themselves, they will eat less, exercise more, make better food and alcohol choices, and avoid developing eating disorders or gaining excessive weight.

Body shame is the externalizing of the personal shaming belief and feeling defective.

Body shame starts at a young age and continues into adulthood, cognitively and emotionally distorting a person's view of his appearance and physical functioning, and his sense of emotional and physical well-being. Nurturing and shame are an odd emotional couple, and their effects contradict each other. Taking care of yourself in all areas of your life is your adult style of nurturing, and has a positive influence in all your relationships. Shame-driven physical behaviors, on the other hand, will negatively impact your health, damage your body, and, in the most severe situations, lead to fatal outcomes. Nurturing means that you have the ability to make emotional and physical choices that make you feel better and do not reaction in response to old childhood shame beliefs. Becoming more self-aware of your emotional shame triggers regarding food, drug use, body image, alcohol, weight gain or loss, physical attractiveness, and physical abuse toward yourself will automatically start to expose your shame-body connection.

Consider the following list and think about the ways you may react physically to shame. Write your answers to the questions in the space provided. Answer candidly and without trying to edit your wounded inner self-expressions. There are no wrong or inappropriate answers. The goal is to expose the unseen emotional connections between your shame-driven behaviors and your physical health and body, and sense of emotional health via your body. Shame's relationship with your physical health, body image, and appearance is very important to manage and understand.

Body and Shame Questions

What are the events, relationship issues and fears, family interactions, and parts of your job that make you feel sad, not good enough, or traumatized, and that you feel too shamed or scared to express?

What is your physical reaction to feeling inadequate, angry, or dismissed?

Where in your body do you feel your shame (e.g., neck, stomach, shoulders, lower back, chest, etc.)?

What is your major criticism of your body, physical appearance, and/ or weight?

How do abuse and shame impact your health, body, and physical appearance?

How does shame manifest in your physical life (e.g., through injuries, illness, accidents, etc.)?

What is your emotional relationship to food, drugs, and sex?

If you felt no shame, embarrassment, or self-consciousness about your body, health, and appearance, what would your life be like?

Brad's Accident

This a very powerful real-life example of how our unresolved shame and emotional dis-ease can manifest in a serious accident and physical injury. Brad, who lives in Los Angeles, was thirty-two years old, had been married for three years, and worked for a major finance firm. Brad first came to see me about his marriage, which was strained over the issue of having a second child. His son was eighteen months old, and his wife wanted to have a second child.

When Brad was twelve years old, his ten-year-old sister was killed in a car accident, and he had buried the shame of having survived the accident while his sister hadn't. Even though Brad was emotionally insightful, self-aware, and empathetic, he was still traumatized by his sister's death, twenty years after it had happened. He was convinced that he should not have two children because of his shame that he had lived. Brad felt that he couldn't express his reluctance about having a second child to his wife. He felt like he "should" want to have more children. His sense of shame and self-doubt caused him to avoid objecting to his wife or questioning her wishes. Brad was terrified that if he expressed any disagreement, his wife would abandon and reject him, and expose him as a fraud. Brad's feeling that he was a "fraud" caused him to feel he should embrace with open arms anything his wife wanted. This was what good partners did for each other, after all, regardless of their own personal feelings or beliefs. Brad's wife had begun telling him she wanted a second child, and, while he had acquiesced to having their first baby, he was emotionally paralyzed by his secret terror and beliefs about children and death and by his inability to discuss his fears with his wife.

Three weeks after our first therapy session, Brad reported back that his wife was pregnant. Brad told me, "I can't believe she is pregnant. I am having chronic panic attacks. I don't think I can handle a second child and all the responsibilities. How am I going to afford private school, college, and buying a bigger house for the four of us? If I told my wife that I don't want children, even though I love and adore our son, she would leave me. I will find a way to accept this new child."

Two days later, I got an emergency phone call from Brad's wife, saying that Brad was in the hospital after a serious accident. Brad had been walking on Wilshire Boulevard near UCLA in Westwood Village and had walked into the crosswalk without looking. He had been hit by a car, and the impact had thrown him approximately twenty feet. His right leg, ankle, and hip were broken, and Brad spent the next three months at home in bed.

I visited Brad at his home for our therapy sessions while he was convalescing. Brad began to realize that the accident was symbolic of his fear of moving forward in life with his wife and children while holding onto the past. Having to stay lie in bed for so long forced Brad to psychologically process his unresolved grief, his fear of the future, and his inability to express his feelings. He knew the accident wasn't random, and that he had secretly wanted to escape his life (avoiding facing his shame). Getting hit by the car forced him to look at his unspoken beliefs and his feeling of "not being worthy" and

not deserving to have a good life or to have survived the car accident twenty years earlier. Brad ultimately regained his strength, his
broken bones healed, and he embraced his newborn daughter. Brad
knew that he had unconsciously created a situation with his mind
and body to rid himself of his shame and his despair for living. Brad
told me, "I wish I hadn't avoided my childhood agony and had to
have a near-death car accident again to realize I wasn't dealing with
my trauma and shame. This has been a very physically and emotionally painful process."

6. Loss and Death: The Unspeakable and the Unexpressed

Loss, suicide, homicide, and passively self-inflicted death (i.e., through
food issues, alcoholism, cocaine use, etc.) are shame's end result and
the final stopping point of control. There are many different ways
and methods that shame slowly deteriorates a person's emotional
capacity, mental clarity, and well-being. The previous five topics in
this chapter, along with the seven emotional shame triggers discussed
in chapter 4, can lead to a fatal outcome if ignored and avoided.
Unresolved toxic shame can, in the long term, manifest in a myriad
of self-destructive behaviors that can ultimately destroy someone's
life and purpose. Recognizing the insidious nature of shame with
regard to feeling hopeless can begin the exposure process of this
emotional cancer. The endless list of self-defeating behaviors are all
symptoms of shame's death wish for your life and relationships.

Passive behaviors of physical neglect, such as eating disorders,
and self-abusive addictions, such as chronic recreational drug use,
are all shame-based behaviors disguised as unhappiness and depression. Escapism choices, avoidance, and emotional numbing actions
all serve to keep a person's shame out of sight. When shame is recognized, a person's self-loathing beliefs, actions, and choices are
exposed and can begin to be resolved and eliminated. Self-loathing
isn't a self-esteem issue; it's a shame issue. Low self-esteem, self-doubt,
and self-hatred are all symptoms of the core functioning of shame.

Being mentally preoccupied with dying, being killed, or killing are symptoms of a person's internal disconnection from themselves and their world. In chapter 3, we discussed the outcomes of toxic shame for men and women, with their possible deadly expressions and fatal results. Before someone reaches the point of becoming enraged, resentful, and hopeless, their feelings and beliefs involved a fear of living. Death, loss, and grief can all trigger feelings of being helpless and hopeless, which, if left untreated, can evolve into a fear of living. Unresolved grief is a dangerous emotion to ignore because of its paralyzing psychological nature. Grief and the fear of living become part of a person's shame cycle and his distorted outlook on life. These personal psychological distortions can keep a person in an endless cycle of shame and fear.

> ### The fear of living is the beginning of a shame-based life perspective.

Early childhood emotional losses, disappointments, and neglect can create a challenging fear of living. The sense of feeling inadequate, inferior, and not good enough leaves a young child grasping for security. These early self-doubts grow into self-defeating behaviors and actions. The foundation of emotional insecurity leaves a person unable to appropriately process major losses in her adult life.

Fear of living is one of shame's strongest weapons when it comes to keeping a young child, teenager, or adult from exploring his desires, pursuing his dreams, and fulfilling his wishes. Avoiding and denying your inner motivations begins to produce a deep sense of hopelessness, sadness, and despair. We know from our discussion thus far that shame left untouched and untreated can lead a well-meaning person down a terrible, self-destructive life path. We must keep increasing our awareness of how shame silently hides and develops in our fear of life, fear of loss, and our wanting to escape from life's challenges. All of these psychological factors can create a deep sense of hopelessness that only seems manageable through self-destructive choices.

Sadness and shame are bookends that keep you in perpetual fear.

Childhood Dog

The loss of a beloved pet in childhood, or at any time in life, can become a catalyst for overwhelming grief, fear of death, and/or despair of living. For many people, their first experience of loss and feeling emotionally sad comes with the death of their dog, cat, or other childhood pet. These early childhood experiences of loss, death, and sadness help shape our emotional capacity for change.

A divorce or the tragic loss of a child, parent, or romantic partner is a significant, psychologically traumatizing, and life changing event. These major losses, echoing an earlier loss of a beloved pet, can be overwhelming beyond words or expression. The feelings of sadness, loss, and lack of safety when someone you love dies can trigger a sense of shame. The experience of grieving often makes a person feel bad, defective, or odd because she believes she should "get over it" more quickly. Grief, however, has no timetable or schedule for its process. The problem with the grief process is that it can be derailed by underlying insidious shame beliefs. Death or loss of someone or something very special to you opens you up psychologically to a degree that you normally wouldn't be. The shock and trauma of someone dying or leaving, regardless of how prepared you were for their departure, causes you to re-evaluate your life, priorities, and relationships. You may feel defective, inadequate, like an imposter or fraud, or responsible for the loss. Blaming yourself and having feelings of inadequacy for grieving are shaming roadblocks to healing and resolution after the loss.

Shame and sadness are a lethal combination that can cloud your judgment and disrupt your hope of recovery and of resuming living your life. The poem below accurately depicts a person struggling with loss, a sense of inadequacy, and shame for feeling of sad. The author of this poem is my client, and she wrote it to let me know how sad and scared of life she felt. Her mother had suddenly died from breast cancer when my client was eight years old, and she believed she was a "loser" for crying everyday about her mother's death.

Sadness

When the inside of you feels like it's put out,
And there is too much to cry about
You don't know what to put your tears into first,
Your rain of happiness feels like it's in a drought
All your passions slip through your fingers just like the sand and dust
You wish there was someone there to trust
But all your hope is covered with rust
You just want to disappear and never come back
And hide away
To no one's dismay
You feel like you're an insignificant speck on the sidewalk
Just waiting to be swept away.

—Eleven-year-old female

CLOSING THOUGHTS

The strongest principle of growth lies in human choice.
—George Eliot, *Daniel Deronda*, 1876

Below are some questions to ponder and consider as you move to uncover the deep dark shame monster hiding in your emotional closet. The truth is, when you open your psychological closet door and turn the light on, the shadow of your monster is really an old raincoat hanging there. Money, relationships, childhood family, present-day family, your health and body, and loss and death are all places shame hides in your life. Shame hides someplace in everyone's life, whether seen or unseen. Each of these six different pieces of your life can be a current challenge that is a chronic source of despair, hopelessness, and fear. Shame can disguise itself as a lifelong struggle, a character flaw, or an emotional weakness that has no resolution or possibility of change. The above quote by George Eliot reinforces the fact that it is your choice to expose, resolve, and heal your shame, not shame's choice. One of the myths concerning shame is that it's incurable rather than amenable to healing and change once it's exposed. The pain and terror of the exposure process is the explanation surrounding why certain personal issues never seem to abate or resolve with time and age. The following questions are designed to help you further expose any unseen, untouched, or unnoticed areas of shame in your life.

Shame Inventory Questions

Mark the answers to the questions below as either yes or no:

YES NO

❏ ❏ Do you value relationships and people as much as you value money?

❏ ❏ Do you sometimes use money to offset your uncomfortable feelings about your scared core self?

❏ ❏ Do you believe people only like you for your money?

❏ ❏ Do you use money and/or your position of power to cover up your unspoken shame?

❏ ❏ Do your emotional struggles with your romantic relationship or marriage reveal anything about your unresolved grief?

❏ ❏ Do you avoid being emotionally open and transparent with your romantic partner?

❏ ❏ Do you use money or wealth to control people?

❏ ❏ Are you hesitant to tell your partner about your past trauma and struggles?

❏ ❏ Do your children emotionally trigger your self-doubt?

❏ ❏ Do you frequently ask yourself, "Why don't my children love me?"

❑   ❑ Do you seek people's approval in your relationships?

❑   ❑ Do you like your physical appearance?

❑   ❑ Do you use food or substances to numb yourself, regardless of the emotional or physical consequences?

❑   ❑ Do you currently feel ripped off or enraged about your life?

❑   ❑ Do you blame your family for your present-day challenges?

❑   ❑ Do you resent how your family, children, and life partner have treated you?

❑ . ❑ Are you concerned about how you treat yourself physically?

❑   ❑ Do you ignore your mind-body connection?

❑   ❑ Do believe that your feelings and emotions are related to your physical health and well-being?

❑   ❑ Do you harshly judge yourself for feeling sad about a loss in your life?

❑   ❑ Do you have difficulty accepting your grieving process?

❑   ❑ Are you embarrassed that you still feel sad about your childhood?

The questions above highlight the six classic areas where shame hides in a person's life. Shame is never obvious or easily recognized because of how it silently operates in your life. The chronic malaise shame creates makes it feel like it is simply a normal part of your personality, your relationships, your family, your health, your finances, and your core sense of yourself. Shame has taken years to development, so it seems natural and acceptable. In what areas and circumstances of your life does shame play an active role today? Try to consider the different circumstances in which shame is taking a front-row seat in your life.

> *We delight in the beauty of the butterfly, but rarely admit the changes it has gone through to achieve that beauty.*
> —Maya Angelou, 2004

The courage to look at your life is no different from the despair and fear a caterpillar goes through to evolve into a place of emotional freedom when it becomes a butterfly. In chapter 6, we will going to explore the connections between trauma, shame, and addictive behaviors. The steel cord that binds shame with our hidden and unresolved trauma is the formula for all addictive behaviors.

CHAPTER 6

THE BIG COVER UP, SUPER GLUE: ADDICTIONS AND SHAME

Shame and addiction go hand-in-hand. But shame is not a good motivator; when people are shamed, they shut down and their personal growth stalls.
—Caroline McGraw, "The Toxic Mix of Shame and Addiction," The Clearing, blog, May 16, 2016

Shame is so painful to the psyche that most people will do anything to avoid it.
—Darlene Lancer, "Shame: The Core of Addiction and Codependency," *Psych Central*, October 8, 2018

These quotes demonstrate the powerful bond between addiction and a person's shame. Addictions serve a vital purpose in concealing one's unresolved trauma and keeping it buried deep within its victim. The psychological need to conceal unspeakable emotional trauma is the primary reason that addictive behaviors are so powerfully destructive and so difficult to understand. The process of uncovering the shame of addiction involves peeling away the concealed layers of embedded emotional pain and fear. One of the myths surrounding the treatment and healing of any type of addiction is the addict needs to be shamed in order to motivate change and amend self-damaging behaviors. Shaming someone for his gambling, drug use, sexual behavior, or any other self-defeating habits, however, is counterintuitive and non-curative. Shaming an alcoholic for her lapse of judgment only reinforces the negative behavior. This outdated belief unfortunately is widespread in the addiction industry.[1] Shame is independently funding a growing addiction treatment business. Additionally, like the analogy we used earlier, shaming someone caught in a cycle of addiction and self-abuse is similar to telling a drowning person to go get swim lessons while he is gasping for air.

Blaming, shaming, and devaluing someone for her addiction is the quickest way to reinforce her negative behavior. Addiction and shame blinds (i.e., causes amnesia) the victim to the short- and long-term personal consequences of her actions. The truth is that men and women who struggle with any type of addiction are already besieged by their own shame-fueled self-loathing. These pop-psychology, family approaches and industry practices are commonly performed without any long-term healing or resolution of the deeper core problem: shame.

Shame is the rocket fuel, emotional substance, and silent force behind all addictive behaviors. Addictions and shame have a magnetic relationship. One attracts the other and they bond seamlessly, each reinforcing the effect of the other. The power and function that an addictive behavior has in your life is only half of the story, though. The other half is how emotionally connected and psychologically defensive a person's shame is when it comes to his self-defeating behavior. Any repetitive behavior that serves as emotional "comfort" over time can and will become problematic. The psychological detour and the avoidance of uncomfortable feelings, situations, and traumas is a never-ending cycle of terror. This pattern of avoidance has its beginnings in a young child's life, and it evolves into early adulthood with ever-increasing challenges and consequences personally, socially, occupationally, physically, and romantically.

PSYCHOLOGY OF ADDICTION

Drug addiction is the only disease that kills you before you die!
—Drug Rehabilitation Advertisement

Historically, the research on the use and abuse of alcohol, prescription drugs, opium, heroin, and related substances has minimized the ironclad emotional bond between trauma and shame. Trauma and shame are two integral parts of the bigger addiction-shame cycle. Self-destructive addictions aren't limited to just drugs and alcohol; they can also involve sex, gambling, video gaming, eating, exercise, money, smoking, shopping, love relationships, work, or many other behaviors. The destructive nature of substances, the medical model of addiction (focusing only on the physical and not the emotional), DNA predisposition, and disease theory are important issues surrounding addiction, but the role shame plays in self-destructive choices is just as important. Neither addiction nor shame can survive in this relationship without the other's existence The real challenge when addressing addictive behaviors is a person's relationship with her shame. Her belief system and psychological defense structure has been under construction since her elementary school years and now serves to protect her wounded inner child. When she begins to explore the possible unseen reasons behind her addiction and psychological suffering, regardless of its nature, the effect is transformational. Insight breeds self-acceptance, which diminishes the power of unspoken shame. Self-destructive addictive behaviors can't function without the energy of a person's shame.

We aren't going to discuss the validity or importance of genetics or a preexisting family history of addiction as contributing factors for a person's self-defeating behaviors. Our primary focus here is on the powerful behavioral avoidance, psychological denial, and emotional amnesia of the shame-addiction model. Like the shame scale we talked about in chapters 1 and 3, addictive behaviors are also experienced in degrees of severity, with their own shades of white, grey, and jet black. We will discuss the addiction scale later in this chapter, but for now remember that addictive self-defeating behaviors are solely for the psychological purpose of avoidance. For example, addiction isn't taking prescribed pain medication after a spinal back fusion.

> *All addictions have one meaningful purpose:*
> *avoidance of emotional pain.*

Emotional Regression

The psychology of addiction is based in the mental and emotional experience of regression. What's regression? Regression is a term first used by the godfather of modern-day psychoanalysis psychology, Dr. Sigmund Freud. Freud identified regression as a psychological defense against feeling powerless or overwhelmed. When our emotional shame triggers are activated, either because someone is shaming us or we are shaming ourselves, our minds begin spinning and our emotions take over. Regression happens when our mature inner adult feels psychologically threatened, scared, or anxious. These terrifying emotions cause us to seek immediate relief, and in the blink of an eye the regression cycle takes us back to our early childhood defenses for protection.[2] In this way, the trauma and feelings of powerlessness are instantaneously dismissed and avoided. Years of repeating this psychological regression cycle whenever we feel any uncomfortable emotion, traumatic memory, or vulnerability is how we discover addictions. Getting rid of these paralyzing emotions is the function and purpose of addictive behaviors. When our thoughts and feelings begin to panic, we push the emotional eject button. That button is our core shame belief. Our unconscious avoidance creates self-soothing maladaptive solutions to calm our suffering and dis-ease.

In chapter 4, we discussed the seven emotional shame triggers and how they lead us into behaviors that minimize and calm our unspoken terrors. To review, these triggers are: fear of embarrassment, having a distorted view of yourself, imposter syndrome, isolation (i.e., feeling alone in your life), being suspicious of people and authority (i.e., lack of trust), fear of intimacy, and fear of criticism. These seven triggers can hide and disguise themselves in any area of your life (see chapter 5), where they automatically activate your shame cycle. By age fifteen, these shame behaviors and psychological defense mechanisms are in place to help the young person avoid mental re-experiencing their childhood trauma. The brick wall of security put up in adolescence holds the emotional development of the addict in place, so that the forty-five-year-old adult who smokes marijuana morning, noon, and night remains emotionally an adolescent.

The emotional age of addiction is approximately fifteen years old.

Teenagers tend to have a mindset of invincibility. They typically do not have a great deal of insight and perspective, leaving them with no concern about the future and a false sense of omnipotence (feeling themselves to be all powerful and bigger than life). Their normal lack of personal and relational responsibility is part of the way they often live in the moment with no regard for what the outcome will be tomorrow or in a few hours. While a sense of recklessness is common in adolescents, the same trait is abnormal in a twenty-eight-year-old man or woman. When these teenage traits persist into adulthood, they indicate the emotional wiring of a shame-based avoidant and addictive personality.

Addiction is much more varied than alcoholism, smoking, or using cocaine, and in a moment we will look at a number of addictions people face. According to the World Health Organization, over 185 million people throughout the world are addicted to illicit drugs alone. The problem with most of the addictions listed below, however, is the lack of data and research that would show how widespread these avoidant behaviors and actions currently are. Studies have estimated that one in eight people in the United States have some form of addiction.[3] I believe that number is far too low, as addictive behaviors are often ignored when they occur in socially approved outlets such as shopping, gaming, working, internet use, and smartphone social media obsession.

Self-reporting and personal insight into addictive behaviors is distorted by denial and psychological amnesia.

SOME COMMON ADDICTIONS

The addictions below aren't listed by any degree of severity or importance. Each of these behavioral actions, when repeated compulsively, will eventually lead to a shame-based addiction and emotional slavery. Each addictive behavior could have its own book, but the brief descriptions below are solely to illustrate the seamless bond of shame with addiction. This list is not complete, and it could easily be expanded to include another twenty-five or more addictive behaviors that all serve the same purpose—namely, avoidance of psychological, emotional, and physical discomfort and pain. The eleven addictive behaviors we discuss here all include brief vignettes of clients who struggle with these shame-driven addictions.

Later in the book, in section III, we will explore and discuss at length the different approaches to understanding and healing these shame-driven addictions. Addictions are emotionally fueled by an individual's avoidance of shame, and self-reporting makes addiction research very difficult to analyze and understand. People who engage in these self-soothing addiction cycles aren't a reliable source for the details of their private lives. Most of these behaviors tend to be kept secret or private, and people often conceal them so as to avoid feeling embarrassed or vulnerable. The psychological maze surrounding a person's shame and addiction cycle is complicated and very difficult to treat.

Tobacco

Tobacco was responsible for more than 480,000 deaths in the United States in 2016, and in 2017 an estimated 37.8 million American men and women smoked cigarettes (not including e-cigarettes, vape pens, or marijuana cigarettes, which would drive the numbers up).[4] Tobacco, as seen through these staggering statistics, is a major addictive behavior and a widespread health issue. Regardless of the vast amount of medical research on the hazards of smoking, tobacco continues to be a major addiction, which is largely due to its connection to shame. The new technology of vape pens and electronic cigarettes has made smoking even more assessable for self-soothing behavior and a quick emotional escape. Smoking is an oral fixation that can be very calming when a person is feeling anxious, scared, or shamed.

A young child will often suck his thumb when he feels fearful (e.g., after a nightmare, when there are loud noises, yelling, etc.). If the child doesn't learn to tolerate his feelings of dis-ease, frustration, and disappointment, a pattern of deprivation and shame begins to develop. When he becomes an adult, shame triggers his despair and his intolerance for frustration.

Oral fixations that remain into adulthood are connected to an incomplete emotional bonding process between a mother and baby. When a person feels the need for comfort, she unconsciously regresses to the emotions she felt when she lacked nurturing as an infant, and her need for soothing is met with a stick of tobacco. The frustration created in a young child when her emotional needs are not met, grows throughout childhood to become in adulthood a deep sense of inadequacy and emotional deprivation. Smoking temporarily alleviates the emotional shaming of emptiness and frustration that developed as a result of a mother's absence.

Sam Story, who is twenty-seven years old, has been a regular smoker since age sixteen. Sam has discovered that when his anxiety is high he will crave more and more cigarettes to relax. He has also noticed a pattern of feeling scared (due to imposter syndrome) and anxious about his job (shame) and then smoking a pack of cigarettes and wanting to drink or do drugs. Sam said, "When I am worried about my job or girlfriend, I immediately crave a quick smoke. What's now happening is, I want a stronger drug. I only use coke [cocaine] on the weekends. My girlfriend says I do coke far too frequently when I start smoking. I feel kind of trapped and know I should stop. I feel dirty after I stop and very shamed when I do coke. I am planning after my birthday in August to stop all drugs for a while."

Alcohol

Everyone is aware of the addictive nature of alcohol, but most people dismiss its seriousness. Because alcohol is widely available and inexpensive, it's a very popular choice for avoidant behavior. According the World Health Organization, alcohol is linked to at least sixty types of diseases or injuries, including those caused by accidents that can occur while intoxicated.[5] Social drinking, binge drinking, and daily drinking are all very common and require self-diagnosis for underlying addiction and shame. The standard of measurements for problematic drinking are the frequency, quantity, and motivation behind drinking alcohol. These three elements can be shame driven or not. Having a social drink isn't a problem, but it's a problem when someone has eight vodka tonics in ninety minutes, can't stand up, can't talk, and vomits on his partner.

Alcoholism is a fatal progressive habit with no positive outcome for the abuser. The link between unresolved childhood trauma and addictive drinking is very strong. When a person lifts a glass, takes a shot, or pounds a beer, these behaviors all seem very normal and acceptable. However, the emotional bond between trauma and feelings of shame are what create the horrors of alcohol addiction.[6] The unexplored traumatic reasons behind the excessive drinking are how shame will keep the drinker isolated from her pain and prevent her from healing. Addictive drinking is a major mood destabilizer and simultaneously breaks down the physical and emotional body. There are many different theories and ideas about alcoholism, but here we are focusing on the shame-induced self-destructive behavioral pattern of alcoholism.

Ron, a thirty-four-year-old medical doctor, grew up in the South where drinking was like eating fried food—everyone did it. However, Ron's drinking was becoming problematic in his work as a physician. He was recently confronted by his business partner about the smell of alcohol on his breath during the day. Ron told me, "I have my drinking under control. I need to relax after doing ten surgeries in the morning and seeing twenty patients in the afternoon. I enjoy having a few shots of vodka in the evening. Everyone is making a big deal about my drinking. I don't drink the nights before I do surgery. I drink afterward and on the weekends. I hate all the pressure my patients put on me and my office staff. I am not going to stop my only source of genuine relaxation!" Within a week of this therapy session, Ron was suspended by the California medical board for three years, pending alcohol rehabilitation and treatment. As of this writing, Ron is still drinking.

Drugs

Drugs, whether legal prescriptions (e.g., pain medication), street drugs (e.g., heroin, cocaine, etc.), or legal marijuana, have physical and psychological addictive effects and many have addictive chemical properties. Most of the commonly abused drugs are very effective in providing instant pain relief and mind-numbing qualities. The psychological and physical dependency is very difficult to manage with regular use. The physical tolerance and addictive nature of prescription drugs means that with regular use they will develop into a serious medical and emotional addiction. Over time, the user must increase the dosage and frequency to achieve the same desired effect of emotional and physical relief. Because of the inherent nature of denial and avoidance, the user can continue to raise the dosage amounts and frequency until they reach lethal levels; many times, the outcome of drug addiction is an overdose and/or death.

My twenty-seven-year old client Alan explained to me why he does cocaine: "The idea always starts off as fun early on Friday evening and then gets crazy around 4:00–5:00 a.m. Saturday morning. When I wake-up at 1:00 p.m. the next day, I never think or feel that doing a few bumps was a good choice. I never think it was a good idea to party all weekend on Monday morning. By Friday afternoon again, I have forgotten how awful I felt the weekend before. I need to stop doing this cycle because coke [cocaine] takes my life over. I forget everything and everybody in my past and present and how tough my job is. The biggest problem is how much shame I feel for doing cocaine behind my girlfriend's back. I feel so awful about myself."

Gambling

Gambling is a very seductive addiction. The lure of power, quick money, and fame makes gambling a type of avoidant behavior. The classic behavioral reinforcement of random winning keeps the addict betting more and more for the one-in-a-million payoff. Gambling is an all-consuming endeavor that allows a person to escape into their fantasy world of endless riches and power. The results of chronic gambling are desperation, potential bankruptcy, homelessness, and loss of family and friends. Shame is emotionally disempowering and anxiety inducing, but the core childhood sense of feeling inadequate is offset by the illusion of fame and fortune offered by gambling, sports betting, and "beating the odds." A person loses his self-control while gambling because he gains a false sense of emotional empowerment and a false feeling that he can control his money. The metaphor of "beating the odds" in life will never be accomplished through betting. The shame of feeling defective and not good enough can be eased for a few moments when a football game ends in your favor, gambling addiction, like all self-destructive excessive habits, is linked to poor health and chronic homelessness.[7]

Adam, age twenty-five, was a math major in college and was always intrigued by the lure of gambling and sports betting as a professional career. Adam is socially anxious, smokes marijuana daily, and gambles as a full-time profession. Adam came to see me for his social anxiety, insomnia, and family conflicts. I asked Adam what he was doing for a job. He said the following without a pause or hesitation:

> I am trying to support myself with sports betting. I have had some luck and bad moments. My parents refuse to give me my inheritance from my grandparents. They f—ing owe it to me. I gamble so I have money. I feel bad when I lose big on the weekends and wipe out my credit line from my bookie. When I win, I feel awesome and my life is positive. When I lose I can become very depressed and angry. I am currently out of money and my parents aren't going to bail me out this time. I do sell marijuana on the side for extra cash. I know I need to stop but it's my lifestyle. I don't know what I can do for a career or a job. I feel like a loser. My friends all work during the day while I sleep. I am not winning much this year. I really hate when my parents tell me to get a job. This whole gambling thing is mentally draining. I am always worrying about a point spread.

Food

Food addiction is very difficult to diagnosis. We all need to eat. People can live very well without ever doing cocaine, drinking, or smoking, but food is a challenging silent force. Emotional eating, comfort-food binging, stress-relief cooking, and eating when feeling anxious, depressed, or not good enough are very common food-related behaviors. The numerous health issues surrounding obesity are closely related to shame and trauma. Overeating can create an emotional cushion between the scared child and his world. The lure of food can trigger all types of eating disorders, body distortions, and endless self-loathing. The key to understanding any food addiction is the emotional intention of the consumer. People eat either to nurture themselves or else to escape feeling powerless, sad, or any other shameful emotion.

Another critical element of food addiction is whether a person eats out of the nurturing element of self-care or the destructive element of self-abuse and self-loathing. How we eat and what we eat are reflections of our intrinsic sense of shame. The ability to tolerate our emotional discomfort and not turn it inward is part of our ability to nurture and self-accept. Food and nurturing are two sides of the same coin. Shame is the intruding belief that tells us we aren't good enough, that we are defective and need to seek immediate comfort. Food behaviors, such as eating and cooking, are capable of providing emotional comfort for a moment. The emotional bond of feeling shame and then escaping through eating or cooking food is a very powerful behavioral addiction. The short- and long-term consequences of a volatile emotional relationship with food are endless and can lead to severe health problems. For example, another possible element of a self-destructive food addiction cycle is the craving for a specific food group, such as sugar, carbohydrates, or "junk food." Eating excessive amounts of foods from these groups to try and meet the unconscious need for emotional comfort and pleasure is what becomes physically and psychologically dangerous.

Cindy, age thirty-one, came to see me for her sudden onset of panic attacks and health-related weight problems. After meeting with Cindy for approximately six months, her panic attacks stopped, and her binge eating started. I asked Cindy to explain to me her emotional relationship with food. Cindy said, "When I am upset, I crave sweets, desserts, and fried food. Eating stops me from crying and thinking about my frustration and anger. My family upsets me all the time. I know I shouldn't use food to stop my feelings, but it works. I feel bloated after overeating when I am mad. I used to cut myself. Now I stuff my face and it works. Food stops all my bad feelings. Can you be addicted to food? If so, I am addicted to food. I am overweight and don't know how to stop overeating when I am upset."

Sex

Sex addiction is a much larger problem than most people would like to admit or acknowledge. Pornography, random sexual encounters, sexual escorts, sexual affairs, chronic masturbation, and the use of sexual encounter websites make the addictive behaviors very difficult to understand and treat. Shame can be a very powerful force in one's sexuality and its healthy or unhealthy expression. Sex is a private experience and its relationship to shame is therefore difficult to discuss and expose. Couples, single adults, young adults, and teenagers all have their own ideas about how to feel sexually comfortable. Shame skews a person's perception and experience of sexual intimacy at any age or developmental stage. Objectification (i.e., viewing your sex partner as a sexual outlet and not an equal participant.), sexual abuse, and sexual perversions are all shame-driven behaviors connected to unresolved childhood trauma of all types.[8]

Non-addictive sexual practices are formed around intimacy, equality, and emotional and physical safety. The psychology of sex includes emotional bonding, communication, and intimate expressions of love. The impulsive and addictive outlet of sex, on the other hand, becomes a physical exercise driven by the buildup of anxiety and shame. The psychological issues concerning power, anger, control, and force originate from the inner child who feels inadequate and now lives in an adult body. The uncomfortable feelings of unexpressed inadequacy can develop into a shame-driven sexual addiction. Sexual addiction is not intimate, emotionally inclusive, consensual, or relationship focused, it is, instead, object focused (i.e., based on the need for a physical release of emotional tension). The goal is a pleasurable physical outlet for internal "dis-ease" regardless of the consequences (e.g., personal risk from unprotected sex, etc.) surrounding the addictive behavior. There is an aggressor and a victim with any type of shame-driven sexual addiction (e.g., rape or sex trafficking victims).[9] The underlying psychological issue of shame-motivated sex is the attempt to regain control (i.e., by feeling good) and escape the tension of feeling powerless (i.e., of feeling awful). The shame of being sexually impulsive, reckless (e.g., having sex with strangers), and without regard for the consequences is a paralyzing emotion, overwhelming and secretive. The practice of secretive and shameful sexual practices (e.g., sexual abuse, date rape, rape, anonymous sex, affairs, incest, etc.) is a very strong behavioral habit.

The principle of seeking pleasure to avoid feeling "bad" is a dangerous psychological minefield to manage. The pleasurable release or desired sexual result (e.g., sadomasochism) by the aggressor is short lived and never truly satisfying. The underlying personal issues are never healed in the shame-sex addiction loop. The seeking of sexual pleasure to avoid shameful feelings and thoughts is a relentless cycle of blame, guilt, power, and excitement. The sexual cycle repeats itself when the individual is feeling their emotional shame triggers and has no insight or understanding of their self-destructive addictive behaviors.

Don, age forty-four, recently remarried a younger wife (thirty-two years old) after fifteen years of marriage to his first wife. Don has had a long history of having female sexual companions on a regular weekly basis. Don rationalized his behavior during his first marriage because he and his wife had different sexual needs. Don wanted to have sex five times a week and his ex-wife never wanted sex. Don met his new wife while traveling for work, and within in a year he was divorced and remarried. Don came to see me because his new wife found a hotel door card in his suit coat. When confronted, Don admitted to having a sexual encounter with a woman he met at a local bar. I asked Don what he was trying to find with so many different sexual partners over the years. Don said, "I love hot looking younger women. It's not wrong to want to sleep with younger women. It's a guy thing. Don't you want to?"

I asked Don about his family background growing up. Don looked at me with a frown and said, "As a child my mother was very cold and distant. Not until I started making big money in my thirties did she ever pay attention to me. My father is nice, but emotionally aloof.

I have been in therapy before and discussed these issues. What's your point?" I asked Don what triggered him to engage in finding escorts or female companions. Don replied, "When I am worried or scared that a client is leaving I will have afternoon encounter for two hours or so and then go back to the office. I find the sexual outlet very comforting with my high-pressure job and all its demands. I like to be desirable to young hot models. It feels really good. It's my mistake that my wife found the hotel key. I will be more careful in the future."

Video Games

Video games, and gaming in general, are very common among children, teens, and adults. The compulsive nature of video games, and the emotional rush from killing the enemy or building an empire, is emotionally intoxicating and exciting. The isolating nature of video games prevents critical social connections, relationship interactions, and peer-group friendships. With the touch of a keyboard, someone can escape into a fantasy world where their anger and fears can be acted out. The computer impairs the user's ability to feel competent and capable of direct, face-to-face encounters. The video screen is a shield against learning the necessary social, emotional, and psychological tools for fulfilling adult relationships. The balance of video usage isn't the topic at hand. Video games aren't problematic by themselves, rather, the way they are used by the user can be problematic. Escapism, avoidance, hiding, and withdrawing from life through gaming is the concern. The emotional and psychological need to numb out and impulsively avoid uncomfortable feelings, new activities, or interactions creates the addictive nature of gaming.

The surreal world of a video game is the perfect platform of escape from feeling socially rejected, emotionally damaged, or undesirable. The line between the imagery of the game and the real world can become very blurred. The ability to problem-solve peer group relationships is a critical developmental step that can't be achieved through online gaming. For example, my client Josh is twenty-seven years old and since about age ten he has preferred gaming to real-life relationships. In order to avoid making new friends, dating, or socializing with work colleagues, Josh will spend his entire weekend playing the newest video game. Josh doesn't like to feel vulnerable or meet new people. In the workplace, Josh has been criticized by his coworkers for not being a team player. The addictive part of gaming doesn't enhance the development of the necessary social skills for conflict resolution, interpersonal communication, and the ability to be empathetic with yourself and others.

The false sense of power and control by imaginary conflicts gives people, especially boys, a heightened sense of confidence and invincibility. The mind-numbing repetitive nature of gaming can be very hypnotic and isolating for all participants. Escaping into an imaginary world can appear wonderful when the real world is full of shame and despair.

Max, age thirteen, loves to play a very popular video game online all day, every day, year-round. Max recently had an emotional outburst while playing a game and smashed his keyboard with his fists. When asked about the many blowups he has had, Max seemed to have no recall or memory of prior incidents. Max is small for his age, unathletic, and doesn't like to socialize with anyone other than his gaming buddies from around the country. Max is smart and very comfortable with only having cyberfriends.

I asked Max what makes him so angry while playing online video games with other players. Max said, "I don't like getting bullied or pushed around on the game server. No one can pick on me while playing. I got scammed the other day for the first time ever and hit my desk. I didn't realize it, I broke my keyboard until it stopped working. I have a lot of friends online and they are cool." I asked Max if he feels comfortable playing video games in person with his school buddies. Max replied, "I don't have many friends at school, and I don't like them anyway. The guys online don't know what I look like. My user name is: The Beast! Everyone knows me as a tough guy, they all want me on their team. My parents don't understand that video games are my only interest and what I love to do. Please tell them I don't want to do a sport in the fall and spring. I am going to be a professional gamer like some of my buddies on YouTube who I follow."

The Internet and Handheld Devices

The internet and handheld devices—the immediate connection to the cyber world—are very powerful. The ability to automatically connect to any social media platform or website and endless social options makes the internet a very strong instant escape mechanism. The internet has become a primary emotional outlet for people of all ages. The need to be plugged into your phone, computer, or social cyber network can feed into an endless shame cycle. The false self a person can show to the world may be immediately visible to millions. The public image of having many friends, lots of attention, traveling, socializing, and partying can all be elaborate forms of self-deception. The self-perceived power of social status and cyber friends around the world can be very addictive and overwhelming. The need to feel important, valuable, and connected are all reactions to the nagging inner negative self-dialogue. People can be completely devastated, despairing, and even suicidal when they feel publicly embarrassed or exposed on the internet. Cyber bullying, stalking, and instant gratification are all self-defeating behaviors that lead to a person to seek that emotional outlet to an even greater extent. The emotional craving for self-acceptance is only momentarily met through social media, and it is lost in the next minute. Shame and social media are best friends.

Shame keeps covered up and stays secret, hiding the wounded child deep within the adult man or woman. The public self-image put forward on any social media platform can be an excellent cover up for the real person within, who is terrified to be revealed or exposed in a negative light. The constant need to be seen and acknowledged is relentless, and offers no lasting peace of mind or self-acceptance.

The wounded self and shame work together to keep the real self buried in the shadows of a person's online appearance. If someone's public image on a social media site appears wonderful and exciting, then his lurking feelings of being an imposter have been concealed under five thousand "likes" when he posts his new profile picture. The addictive nature of social media and internet surfing is widespread and is not slowing down. This is only a cursory psychological overview of the addictive nature and ever-expanding social, personal, and professional impact the internet can have.

Jade, age twenty-two, is a self-reported social media addict. Jade is currently a senior in college, and I have known her since she was in middle school. Jade talked to me when she came home for a quick weekend visit. She had had a major panic attack, thoughts of suicide, and drunk until she blacked out after she was blocked on all social media platforms by her best friend. The event had happened two days earlier, and Jade told me that she was thinking of leaving school and coming home. Jade believes that much of her popularity at school is based on her social media presence and her well-crafted exposure.

I asked Jade about her emotional attraction to her chronic social media obsession. Jade said, "Remember Dr. Poulter, when I was in high school I didn't date until I was a senior. Now that I lost weight and appear very popular, guys around school and at our college bars recognize me. I know if I wasn't so active on social media, I would be forgotten. My girlfriend is a bitch for blocking me and removing me from all the group text chats. I don't know why she did it, but it was after I posted a picture of her drunk at my apartment. I try not to look at how many likes and views I get every time I post something. I know I shouldn't care so much about the followers I get. It's hard not to do it. I know I am addicted to my phone. It feels great and then it feels awful."

Risky and Reckless Behavior Addiction

The popularity of extreme sports, high-speed endeavors, and designer hallucinogenic drugs such as ecstasy (which distorts reality) is due to people trying to feel alive and to release stress. The rush of excitement these behaviors bring is an emotional and psychological anesthesia to self-doubt, trauma, and feelings of inadequacy. The emotional rush and the sense of omnipotence they can cause become behaviorally addictive. Increasing the dangerousness of the activity adds to its psychological "high." The relentless pursuit of the adrenaline rush created by the risky behavior can cross the line from excitement to become a passive suicide attempt. The degree of danger a person seeks can be correlated to the degree of shame a person has experienced. Many times, the tragic result of these reckless behaviors is physical injury or, in worst cases, death. The resistance to psychologically accepting the possibility of an unspoken death wish with extreme behaviors is the blind spot of this addiction. What is considered courageous, fearlessness, and "gutsy" is actually the adolescent denial of danger and a false sense of invincibility.

Jeff, fifty-one years old, has had a very problematic relationship with his father since he was a young boy. Jeff has felt and still feels criticized, not approved of, and unloved by his father. The urge to push life to the limits is something Jeff thrives on and his father adamantly opposes. Jeff also likes to participate in extreme sporting activities. He grew up in Southern California beach cities and has been an avid surfer all his life. He has had several surfing accidents, including being hit in the head by his surfboard while surfing some of the world's biggest waves. Jeff feels empowered and alive when he is surfing the most challenging conditions. He feels that surfing allows him to be good at something that his father can't judge, compete in, or understand.

Jeff came to see me after suffering a severe head injury while surfing in Central America the previous winter. He was hit in the head twice by his surfboard and knocked unconscious. Jeff's longtime surfing partner saw the accident and was able to pull Jeff to shore and save his life. Jeff had to spend three months at a hospital in Central America to mend his fractured skull. He couldn't fly until the swelling in his head went down and the internal bleeding had completely stopped. Jeff, after explaining this story to me, said,

My wife wanted me to come see you in case I am suffering any brain damage. I can't surf anymore because of the possibility of suffering another skull fracture. Any severe head trauma could possibly kill me according to my neurologist. I am pissed off because I was warned by my dad and wife to stop chasing the endless wave. Now my dad looks at me when I see him with a look of pride that he was right, and I was wrong. My father has never accepted me because I didn't become a medical doctor [Jeff's dad is a very successful orthopedic surgeon], even though I have done very well as an investment banker. Regardless, I can't go snow or water skiing, cycling, surfing, or any other sport where I could smash my head again. I should have died but I was lucky my buddy saved me. I don't remember anything after catching the wave. My head hurts every day and I have problems with my vision. I am alive but what a loss of never surfing again. I have had a lot of near misses with death and now I will not do too much crazy stuff.

Shopping: Retail Therapy

Compulsive shopping and spending is an addiction that affects an ever-increasing number of people, who have easy access to millions of shopping options. High-end shopping malls and a Rodeo Drive mentality of being powerful and rich play into the need to keep consuming. As we discussed in chapter 5, hidden shame is embedded in compulsive spending, credit card debt, bankruptcy, and emotional deprivation. The unspoken need to offset the feelings of emptiness and inadequacy creates the incredible pull toward a shopping and spending addiction. The problem is that buying something new gives someone a false sense of control and a brief emotional rush that offers a momentary relief from her nagging uneasiness. Ultimately, the ongoing cycle of emotional hunger, inner emptiness, and despair is only satisfied until the next wave of shame hits. Another challenge is that shopping and spending behaviors are socially approved and therefore aren't considered a serious shame-based problem. The overspending and addictive shopping patterns are not only encouraged by marketing companies but are also presented as necessary for your happiness. The retail world endorses the chronic desire for buying "something new" regardless of whether it is practical or needed. The holiday seasons, birthdays, weddings, seasonal changes, and any other special occasions are perfect opportunities for over-spending and attempting to hide from the inner emotional terrorism of shame. Additionally, most retail therapy seekers are in serious debt and living beyond their means. Even if finances aren't an issue, though, the shame-driven addiction will lead a person further and further into despair and hopelessness.

Hugh, age forty, is a widower with two children who struggles with poor health and weight issues. Hugh's wife, the boys' mother, died two years earlier. His sons are teenagers and play year-round baseball. Hugh wants to keep his boys busy so they don't get depressed about their mother's death. Hugh feels that shopping with his smartphone is a great stress reliever for himself and a convenient way to find the best deals on baseball equipment, groceries, and anything else the boys need. The problem is that Hugh has a membership with Amazon for free shipping and immediate delivery of his purchases. Hugh is eighty to one hundred pounds overweight, needs a knee replacement, and has severe back problems. Shopping for anything online is a recre-ational activity for him, filling his time since his wife passed away.

Hugh came to see me to discuss his compulsive shopping, sudden weight gain, and grieving. I asked him if he blames himself for his wife's death. Hugh smiled at me and said the following:

> I feel guilty and ashamed that I am alive, and my wife isn't. She had health problems and developed ovarian cancer and died within three months of the diagnosis. I feel I could have helped her, but I just put my head down and looked at my phone all the time. I now can't stop looking at my phone every hour for the deals of the day. I feel like a horrible fat ugly dad to my boys. All the fathers at baseball look like GQ models and I am the fat one. Shopping does give me a great distraction and consumes me when I am not working or doing something. I have spent more than 200,000 dollars since my wife's death with online shopping. We still have plenty of money in the bank, and I feel momentarily good when I pur-chase something. Regardless of how many jokes I make about being a shopaholic, I ultimately feel like a failure every time I shop. I can't stop.

Now my boys are worried about me instead of me being worried about them. My whole life is messed up.

Work: Type A and B Personalities

Men and women struggle with not being completely defined, ruled, and governed by their job position, income, and social standing at work. Addictive work habits in the United States are often driven by the wounded inner child who needs approval, acknowledgment, and to feel competent. The unspoken need for approval from colleagues, superiors, clients, and friends creates a very strong pull. The addictive side of seeking to get rid of shame-based feelings is that a person never feels correct or good enough. The ruthless competition between coworkers can often be a disguise for feelings of insecurity and imposter syndrome. If someone outworks their peers or their competition, then they are seen as "good enough." The deep need to feel loved, understood, and supported is very difficult to achieve on an ongoing basis in a business setting.

The workplace can be a metaphorical replay of your childhood family trauma and abuse. The absent father/boss, the critical mother/clients, and the selfish siblings/coworkers are all early inducing events that can be replayed again in your career. Work is a business-driven element that can't heal or mend a shame-based man or woman. Many adults in their thirties, forties, fifties, sixties, and on into retirement age will give their heart and soul to their career in hopes of finally feeling loved and acceptable. The corporate world is a cold and shaming place, however, with an empty well of hope and acceptance. Employees will forsake their families and relationships to gain a bonus and the fleeting approval of their company. The relentless need for approval in the workplace becomes problematic and addictive when it is paired with the unsolvable shame of the wounded child within. Wealth, career achievement, and position are wonderful additions to life for an adult who doesn't struggle with shame. The chronic need for acceptance and feeling adequate and noticed are childhood needs being played out in the adult work world. Any degree of obsession or work-a-holic behavior has its roots in a person's early childhood wounding and despair.

Lisa Marie, age thirty-six, came to see me about addressing her biological clock crisis and desire to have children. Lisa Marie is a single, wealthy, ambitious business owner with a fashionable women's shoe store. She is the only child of teenage parents who were unable to fulfill their dreams of becoming successful professionals. Lisa Marie explained to me that when she was seven years old her mother would tell her that she had to go to an Ivy League business school, be financially independent, never marry, and maybe adopt children after her career was established. Lisa Marie has an MBA from the University of Pennsylvania's Wharton School of Business.

Lisa Marie described to me the way she is in business: "I am very tough, bitchy, and I know what I know. I know how to brand women's shoes, fashion accessories, and designer clothes. I always thought about having children someday. All my college girlfriends have settled down and have families. I have always felt this pressure to be successful and never be vulnerable to a man. My mom was brutal growing up about never putting anything in front of your career. Now I am regretting never considering having a family or marriage and always working seventy hours a week."

I asked Lisa Marie if she felt work was an addiction for her? She replied, "Yes. If I am not working six days a week I feel lazy and useless. Work has been my saving grace and refuge from feeling like a bad daughter. My mother is still very critical of me and what I should do with my business and clients. She is very controlling from three thousand miles away [Lisa Marie lives in Los Angeles and her mother lives in New York City], and I feel awful for always arguing with her. I work so I don't have to deal with my personal life. It's not good but it's better than a drug habit."

No one and no addiction is beyond the hand of change and personal transformation.

What's your emotional default behavior, action, or compulsion when you feel stress, fear, or shame? Everyone has a default behavior and emotional release they automatically seek to offset the terrible unconscious wave of shame and dread when it appears on their emotional horizon. The addictions we have discussed are laced and seasoned with shame and are complicated by all of shame's insidious feelings, distortions, and psychological blocks. Addictions are complicated behaviors to decode, understand, and resolve for the person enslaved to them. No amount of self-loathing, denial, avoidance, and amnesia will remove the power and pull of addictions as escapes from shame's terrible tyranny of terror and fear. All the addictions listed, plus countless others, revolve around the cycle of shame's relentless terror and emotional paralysis. The people we looked at all struggle with finding inner peace and contentment in their lives and face addiction on a day-to-day basis.

Consider what addiction, behavior, or impulsive action you engage in to rid yourself of shame's terrible control. How do you calm your inner storm when shame is threatening? And this question remains: Is your self-soothing behavior productive or destructive?

YOUR SELF-REPORTING SHAME-ADDICTION STRESS SCALE

The following scale is a self-reflective, self-disclosure tool to help you assess how you manage your shame triggers and behaviors. When you have a buildup of emotional energy, you are drawn toward your default outlet for coping with fear and stress. All addictions have a pattern to their expression, emotional response, and your automatic actions. It takes patience to sincerely look beyond your pre-existing psychological walls, old beliefs of dread, and self-soothing addictive behaviors. It's important to remember that addictions separate you from your true self with a wall of denial and fear. What is your response to feeling shame and engaging in self-defeating behaviors?

How do shame, denial, avoidance, and amnesia operate in your daily life? The scale below will help to clarify and possibly expose some of your emotional blind spots. We all have emotional blind spots, and the key is to be emotionally receptive to looking at yourself from some different angles and new perspectives.

What Do You Do When You Feel Anxiety, Shame, and Despair?

0. You don't engage in behaviors that are repetitive or self-defeating when feeling uneasy. Addiction of any type isn't your concern or outlet.

1. Allowing yourself to feel frustrated, depressed, joyful, happy, and any other emotion is a normal behavior. You don't avoid, deny, or have amnesia about conflicts in your past and present.

2. You don't avoid, deny, or ignore difficult situations, emotional confrontations, and relationship challenges. When you feel a sense of shame, you don't allow that feeling to control your day or decisions. You understand your occasional self-doubts and accept them as a normal psychological process.

3. You allow yourself to be emotionally vulnerable and open to others' feedback, be it negative or positive. You have developed a balanced sense of self-acceptance, self-forgiveness, and understanding of your strengths and challenges. You don't emotionally blend your past with your present-day frustrations; your childhood struggles aren't your present-day resentments or issues.

4. Your self-doubts don't trigger a negative emotional cycle of self-loathing and shame. You have appropriate empowering self-soothing thoughts, beliefs, and actions. You aren't avoidant of uncomfortable feelings or situations. You have emotional self-control with any type of recreational habits (e.g., drinking, spending, excessive eating, etc.) when engaging in them.

5. When experiencing old shame feelings of self-doubt or insecurity you automatically seek out your drinking buddy, video
game, or friend to forget a bad day, upsetting encounter, or
argument with your partner. You occasionally drink exces-
sively, overspend, and over indulge when feeling "bad"
about yourself. You are hypersensitive to being seen as "not
perfect" and react very angrily when experiencing these
shameful emotions.

6. You sometimes like to lose control and get drunk or stoned,
or overindulge in food, sex, spending, or reckless behavior.
You seek out extreme behaviors once or twice a month. This
pattern of letting loose has been long-standing and a regular
emotional and physical outlet. When feeling sad, unhappy,
or fearful you choose high-risk behaviors to distract your
mind. These behaviors can range from binge drinking,
binge eating and vomiting, unprotected sex, impulsive shopping, social media stalking, extra marital affairs, fighting, etc.

7. You have an impulse, desire, and urge to avoid shameful triggers with your drug of choice (e.g., spending, video games,
sex, etc.) regardless of the consequences personally, physically, or socially. Your friendships center around partying,
gambling, or any type of addictive behavior. You can't stop
your addictive behavior when you are agitated, emotionally
upset, or feeling inferior.

8. You find it difficult to abstain from your shame-driven
outlets, reactions, or self-loathing behaviors. You are unable
to manage, understand, or keep perspective when experiencing your emotional rush of despair, frustration, anger,
and hopelessness. You don't believe you have the ability or
psychological tools to stop or change your shame addiction
cycle.

9. You have been told by your close friends, family, or partner
that you have a problem with drinking, drugs, food, or
some other type of addictive behavior. You must engage in

this behavior or you become increasingly upset, angry, or enraged.

10. Your entire life is controlled, dominated, and impaired by your addiction. Every area of your life is controlled by the drug(s), alcohol, and/or reckless behavior. You have no emotional will power and no desire to stop this negative behavioral cycle of shame and destruction. Your ability to feel or understand your emotions is extremely impaired. Your life is on a downward spiral toward complete devastation and the possibility of death. You resist any type of assistance to stop your shame cycle addiction.

> *[Addiction] is a chronic illness that we must approach with the same skill and compassion with which we approach heart disease, diabetes, and cancer.*
> —Vivek H. Murthy, MD, *Facing Addiction in America: The Surgeon General's Report on Alcohol, Drugs, and Health,* 2016

CLOSING THOUGHTS

The seriousness of any type of addiction needs to be exposed with care and self-acceptance. The quote by Dr. Murthy is correct and very helpful in approaching our ultimate emotional wall of protection that represses our deepest wounds and fears. If we are unable to uncover the reason behind our self-defeating choices, shame will keep feeding our deepest fears of annihilation. Our dread of facing our deepest shame beliefs is the core reason that addictions are so powerful and destructive.

What is your typical shame response cycle?

What's your addictive behavior?

How often do you become consumed and terrified of being exposed?

How do you handle conflict and your behavioral outlets?

What is a typical situation that triggers your anger and sense of shame?

How do you recover from a shame-addiction cycle?

What are some of the consequences of your shame-driven behaviors?

How do the people closest to you feel about your shame-based actions?

How do you feel about your shame-driven addiction?

All addictions serve a psychological purpose in a person's life. Addictive behaviors are purposeful in helping keep the repressed emotional trauma, terror, and abuse buried. It's important for anyone seeking relief from their addictive behavior, regardless of the severity, to consider the classic question: Why do I choose to do something that is harmful to myself?

Nothing is ever lost or wasted by approaching our unexplored fears with the question why. We have covered lots of interesting material and a wide range of reactions that are common when people displacing their uncomfortable feelings and try to control them. The casual outside observer might ask, "Why do you do something that is self-destructive and harmful?" There is no straightforward and commonsense reason for any addictive shame-driven behavior, however. The only answer to this important question might be something like, "I will think about it." The shame-addiction scale is a reminder that your feelings, emotional pain, and trauma only worsen over time when neglected or ignored. The seriousness of addictive behaviors can't be emphasized enough.

Ultimately, any self-exploration will lead to the rational conclusion that addictive behaviors aren't a long-term solution to our emotional struggles or healing choices. The shame-addiction paradox is that we lose more and more control when our enslaved emotional response is to react automatically to feelings of shame with self-destructive behavior. We discussed eleven of the most common addictive outlets for shame among all ages, genders, economic groups, and races. Shame is a universal psychological disorder that is pervasive in its counterproductive effects and expressions. Addictions will increase in psychological magnitude until they are resolved from within. Each of the short vignettes above are a reminder that the shame-addiction cycle comes in many different shapes, sizes, and actions. The old boy's perspective of, "I am not alcoholic, I go to work every day and have a great job," is a myth and a complete misconception. No one is bigger than the power and deception of denial, avoidance, and amnesia caused by unresolved trauma and childhood terror. The road to healing—emotionally, psychologically, relationally, physically, and personally—is to expose your hidden shame beliefs. This is why you choose to heal your deepest fears and begin to live a shame-free life.

Please take a moment, put this book down, and sincerely consider what is driving your sense of shame and self-loathing. Confronting your shame-driven addiction(s) is the royal road to inner peace and lasting emotional contentment. Ultimately, you will open your emotional closet, turn the light on, and realize that the terrifying monster was just old yellow rubber raincoat.

Chapter 7 will explore how we can tolerate the horror, psychological resistance, and anxiety of opening our emotionally sealed inner closet and buried wounded child. Our shame cycle loves to create fear, anxiety, and dread when it is about to be revealed, exposed, and discovered.

Shame has as much power as we give it!

YOUR PERSONAL BRAND OF SHAME: FEAR, AVOIDANCE, AND EMOTIONAL TERRORISM

Growth demands a temporary surrender of security.
—Gail Sheehy, *Passages: Predictable Crises of Adult Life*, 1976

Failure is not falling down but refusing to get up.
—Chinese proverb

The soul always knows know what to do to heal itself. The challenge is to silence the mind.
—Caroline Myss, Twitter, February 5, 2014

These three quotes are the theme, message, and substance of this chapter. Shame, fear, and anxiety are not an accurate standard of measurement for your well-being and never will be. Your decision to address these three monsters will allow you to start living your life to its fullest capacity. How do shame, fear, anxiety, terror, and despair coexist? What's anticipatory anxiety, cognitive dissonance, cognitive disagreement, and emotional sobriety? These questions are going to be explored and answered in the pages to follow. First, though, we want to look at how the emotional stalker shame/anxiety is wrapped around these powerful emotions, thoughts, and feelings.

Shame is the invisible element that underlies the emotional experience of fear, anxiety, terror, and despair. Many people are misdiagnosed with a severe anxiety disorder when it is really a shame disorder. Shame manifests itself as anxiety, avoidance, and/or depression. The impending doom of the unknown, coupled with the various paralyzing feelings of shame, creates a chronic state of despair and fear. Many psychological mood disorders, emotional conditions, and personality problems are exacerbated by the complex functioning of shame. It's important to remember that shame is a slippery emotional villain with an incredible capacity to stay hidden. One of the best and most effective ways shame stays psychologically camouflaged is through fear. In the treatment of anxiety disorders, the ways shame keeps pushing your psychological, emotional, and personal buttons and fears is rarely considered. Anxiety and fear don't exist in a mental vacuum, though.

We all agree that fear is a basic and necessary human emotion. Fear's function is to keep us from driving off a mountain road, running into the freeway, or confronting a grizzle bear. Shame distorts, skews, and dramatically impairs the psychological functioning of fear. Shame hijacks our emotional wiring at a young age and uses fear to keep us from living a productive, peaceful, and purposeful life. *It's impossible to feel safe and secure when you are simultaneously feeling anxious, fearful, and defective.* Fear and shame are like white and red blood cells—it is very difficult to see the difference between them without careful examination. The two blood cell types and all the different parts of your blood look the same until you look at them under a microscope. Fear and shame require the same degree of examination and scrutiny.

Shame and fear appear psychologically inseparable until you carefully sort them out. Giving your full attention to your unconscious and conscious fear cycle is necessary so you can begin questioning and exposing shame's control in your life. When it has been separated from your fears, shame's power and influence in your life is dramatically reduced. Shame can't exist without your fear supporting its function. Your anxiety, despair, hopelessness, and feelings of impending doom all originated from your core sense of shame. Shame is the root cause of chronic anxiety, panic attacks, and fear of the future. Shame helps create the emotional terror of uncertainty.

Shame camouflages itself as dread, despair, and fear of the unknown.

Fear and avoidance serve one primary purpose: to protect you. When you add the emotional ingredient of terror to your shame core, the combination can be psychologically disabling. Anxiety is the active ingredient in your experience of fears: real, imaginary, or distorted. In chapter 2, we discussed how, by preschool age, a child will either feel competent or inadequate. This critical developmental fork in a child's life can either breed confidence and courage or fear, insecurity, and shame. We know that when a child feels psychologically competent, she isn't scared of the world or of trying new things. Learning about the world isn't embedded with a sense of fear but is, instead, approached with resiliency, courage, and a sense of adventure.

The child who feels intrinsically inadequate, defective, and not good enough is predisposed to avoid new tasks and be resistant to challenges. A shamed child's first response to any new activity or change is "No!"; their only control is resistance because their inner world is frightening and scary. By the age of ten, the sense of inadequacy has evolved into a fear that the world is not a safe place.

Fifth Grade Crisis

Not long ago, I received a frantic phone call from a desperate mother, whose fifth-grade son had threatened to commit suicide in front of his class if he was forced to go to the four-day science sleepaway camp with his school. I immediately met with young Robert. The trip was two weeks away, and the school administration was threatening to expel Robert because he was now considered a risk to the entire fifth grade. Everyone was in panic except Robert.

When we met on the same afternoon that he had made his suicide threat, I found Robert's calm demeanor inconsistent with a young boy who had been sent home from school and was facing expulsion. I asked Robert why he would want to die if he had to go camping. Robert, age eleven, said, "I am not going to kill myself. I just said that, so I wouldn't have to go to the camp and be away from my home. Both my parents travel every week and I only see them on the weekends. I don't like being away from home in case something happens to my parents. If I am home, nothing bad will happen." I asked Robert, if he felt that doing new things was fun or scary. Robert paused and said, looking up at the ceiling, "I feel scared a lot. I don't like to be away from home. My parents think I am lazy, and I don't try or do as well as I could in school. They also make me work-out five days a week with a trainer. I don't like the kids at my school and my parents think I am lying. I don't like being picked on for being fat. [Robert is about twenty pounds overweight for his height but looks very fit and healthy.] My mom and dad push me all the time to get A's and I don't care."

After meeting with Robert multiple times, he reluctantly agreed to go camping, stop threatening to kill himself, and tell his parents why he feels like a "loser." His parents never came to therapy because of their work schedules, although they called me after each session to discuss Robert.

Chronic anxiety is a symptom of shame and unresolved childhood trauma.

Robert is a classic example of an eleven-year-old who emotionally experiences any change as life-threatening. Robert has yet to develop a sense of competence, and instead feels afraid to try new things. Change or new activities must therefore be avoided at all cost. This illustrates the birth and development of shame, which breeds fear, which breeds anxiety, which breeds emotional terror. Even at a young age, Robert embodies this insidious shame and anxiety pattern. The psychological progression of shame shows briefly how shame, fear, and anxiety become so tightly bonded. The shamed young child becomes an adult who struggles with control issues surrounding other people, circumstances, emotional expression, and relationships. For a shamed adult, maintaining control equals safety. Without control there is no safe place for this man or woman. The problem is that the only real control a person has is self-control, and he cannot control the outer world.

The never-ending sense of feeling uncomfortable, inadequate, and unsafe in the world is exhausting mentally, physically, and psychologically. Feeling that you have to be hypervigilant for every single moment of every day, on the lookout for some impending doom, is symptomatic of unresolved shame and trauma. There is no emotional or psychological rest or peace of mind in keeping all the elements of the shame and fear cycle silent. In severe cases of feeling inadequate and defective or of chaotic childhood trauma, such as sexual abuse, people can develop psychological distortions of reality leading to the formation of a multiple personality disorder. Severe psychological disorders are often a young adult's reaction to terrifying and overwhelming circumstances. These coping mechanisms are the inner child's escape from their reality into a fantasy world of peace, harmony, and emotional safety.

Emotional safety is a lifelong pursuit despite feeling shame, fear, and anxiety.

The way you process your primal fear (the shame that makes you feel the world isn't a safe place) in different circumstances—social, professional, and romantic relationships, personal challenges, etc.—is often manifested as anxiety. Making it your psychological goal to disconnect your shame from your fear is powerful, courageous, and necessary. To gain a sense of emotional freedom—an important piece of your overall well-being—involves reevaluating your personal relationship with fear. One of the major benefits of emotional freedom and choice is that you can fully live in the present moment without the dread of the future or the fear of the past. Shame keeps you in a perpetual state of terror, worrying that something disastrous is going to happen. Shame can be seen as a terrorist or a hunter: it demands everything from you and if you don't comply with its outrageous demands you will be exposed, humiliated, and killed. Fear is the emotional bully that reinforces shame's ridiculous claims, demands, and internal threats.

> ***Shame stays hidden, as fear threatens your impending demise if you expose it.***

Fear is our inner safety monitor, but unresolved trauma changes the way fear works within us, so that it is not useful in our psychological, emotional, and relationship challenges. Instead, fear buries our unresolved trauma, covering it up with the mud of shame and anxiety. Shame operates by demanding to know the future and the outcomes of your actions before the processes have finished or even begun. Anticipatory anxiety is irrational and psychologically paralyzing. The demand of shame and anxiety to know the outcome of something before it happens is very common. Often, though, people will dismiss this symptom of shame as planning, being responsible, and acting prudently. The hole in that argument is the sense of dread, paralysis, terror, and excessive worrying that accompanies looking into the future. The worry and fear is disproportionate to the event. As you recall, Robert threatened suicide to offset his impending dread of the unknown (the fifth-grade science camp) as a means of regaining control. Good planning and being responsible breeds peace of mind and excitement, not fear and end-of-your-world scenarios.

> ***Anticipatory anxiety is a thinly veiled cover for shame's controlling nature.***

Regardless of where your fears take you emotionally, psychologically, and intellectually, it's never to a calm and peaceful place of mind. Living in shame, fear, and anxiety can be compared to projecting a horror movie into your future and wondering why you feel scared and terrified. Each of us has our own horror movie of shame, threatening us with losing control, exposure, humiliation, and ultimately death. Your defensive psychological walls that were built in childhood to protect you from this continual onslaught of terror and trauma must be updated and redesigned. What was useful between the ages of five and twelve is less productive for you in your adult life. This is why we discussed regression and addiction in the last chapter. Those behaviors can be triggered by your anticipatory anxiety, but the power of shame-based fear is a learned reaction that can be unlearned and rewired. There are many steps to your rewiring process; we will discuss a few of the basics in this chapter, and then we will talk about the steps more extensively in section III.

COGNITIVE DISSONANCE: THE FIRST STEP

The medical, psychiatric, and psychological bible of mental disorders is the *Diagnostic and Statistical Manual of Mental Disorders, Fifth Edition.* This mental health industry manual is commonly referred to as the *DSM-5.* It serves as the textbook for all diagnostic psychological issues and their related disorders. One of the challenges that the writers of the *DSM-5* describe when treating clients for anxiety, obsessive-compulsive, trauma- and stressor-related, dissociative, or somatic disorders is the lack of insight the client has regarding their psychological impairment. The other compounding issue is the undiagnosed impact of the individual's shame beliefs and various secondary symptoms and maladaptive behaviors. Shame and anxiety issues are complicated and closely interwoven, creating a very well-designed wall of defense against change.

Change and cognitive dissonance aren't friends for many

reasons. First, though, what are the emotional experiences of cognitive dissonance?

- The person's core belief is resistant to new information (i.e., shame-based). Any ideas or suggestions for changing the mental status quo are automatically rejected. The person fears things changing and fears losing control. Change equals terror, and change is therefore avoided whenever possible.
- There is limited psychological ability and insight allowing the person to accept new evidence that is contrary to her preexisting beliefs. Shame and fear feel familiar, comfortable, and safe. Contradicting, confronting, and exposing shame beliefs, defenses, and reactions is an unnatural, awkward experience. Shame is opposed to changing the status quo of despair.
- The emotional experience of separating your shame from your anxiety is extremely uncomfortable. The cognitive dissonance comes from separating out your old mental paradigm and making emotional room for the new and evolving paradigm. The emotional terror that comes with this process can be psychologically paralyzing, filling the emotional gap between the new and old information.
- The challenge in transitioning from old core beliefs it that you automatically rationalize and ignore the problems, even denying that anything isn't working. Blending new beliefs with the old is a conscious choice. The struggle between the new, shame-free response and the old way of responding out of shame, fear, and anxiety is what creates cognitive dissonance.
- A person typically avoids bridging the emotional gap between his old, shame-based beliefs and his healthy new beliefs until his suffering exceeds his old comfort level. Change is only possible when a person's psychological suffering exceeds his preexisting level of contentment and happiness.
- In order to build lasting cognitive changes and shift into healthier ways of thinking, you must develop emotional tolerance and

resiliency for the discomfort caused by bridging the gap between your old beliefs and actions and your new beliefs and actions.

Cognitive dissonance is the necessary first step in creating a psychological wedge between your shame-driven anxiety and all your related feelings of despair. The discomfort of unwrapping your shame from your fear and anxiety is possible to handle. Creating a "gap," space, and room for a new response in place of your old reactionary habit is the new beginning. The second step involves developing emotional stamina to tolerate the inner tension that comes with making room for new reactions, beliefs, and experiences. Changing your way of thinking is like cleaning out your favorite closet; it's difficult to get rid of sentimental items from your past to make room for new things (new beliefs and emotions).

> *Cognitive dissonance is a mental disagreement between your wounded self and your healthy self.*

Despite your desire to know and feel better, and despite all the wisdom and knowledge you have gathered during your life, shame can make you feel that you have no choice but to keep enduring tyrannical beliefs. Fear and anxiety are learned behaviors, and shame reinforces these negative feelings in your life. There is no safe place when shame is operating in your life. Everyone needs a safe, relaxing, and refreshing psychological place to recharge in order to keep a positive perspective on their life. Shame, though, is incompatible with any type of safety and rest. Shame feeds on fear, terror, and threats of annihilation and impending doom. This dynamic is the seedbed for all addictive behaviors, as we discussed in chapter 6.

> *Bridging the gap between your head and your heart reduces shame's power and control over your day-to-day life.*

Try to visualize cognitive dissonance as an inner argument between you and your mind, your head (intellect), and your heart (emotions). Cognitive dissonance is an ongoing disagreement between your healthy adult self and your scared and wounded childhood self. Beginning to recognize the psychological disagreement between these two parts of you is the start of the process of removing shame's hold on your scared inner child. Would you allow your child or a beloved pet (I love beagles and have two of them) to be emotionally abused by a stalker? This stalker also randomly grabs and shakes your four-year-old child and beats your dog. There is no way you would allow that to happen, and I suspect that the intruder would be quickly and aggressively subdued and apprehended. Shame isn't any different from such an intruder in how it terrorizes you, your life, your career, and your relationships. Shame, with its combination of fear and anxiety, ruthlessly beats and terrifies you emotionally, psychologically, and intellectually every day, and every time you think of your future. Although you may look cool, calm, and serene on the outside, inside you are terrified and your stomach is tied in knots about some possible impending doom or unforeseen danger.

THE ENDLESS CIVIL WAR: YOUR INTELLECT AND YOUR HEART

I want to further illustrate the huge emotional gap that can lie between your wisdom and your controlling shame beliefs. The scale below demonstrates the ways that gap can function in the patterns of your thinking, feeling, and healing. At the bottom of the scale is despair and at the top is emotional freedom—shame-free living. A person starts the list when they have a desperate desire to want to change, to stop feeling like a prisoner to her fears and shame. The different emotions, feelings, and thoughts on the list that lie between despair and emotional freedom are some of the typical emotions you will experience as you deal with your shame beliefs. People embark on this healing path when they have become tired of being scared. The psychological crisis created by wanting to change starts when a person is ready to stop feeling chronically anxious and scared: Your fears, worries, and habitual feelings of dread are "killing" you. The mounting pressure you feel is reaching a tipping point of complete despair, with thoughts of escaping the way you are currently living (i.e., suicide). You want lasting relief, resolution, and to not feel like a captive to your obsessive thoughts of hopelessness. This process is waging cognitive war in your head and heart.

How do you get out of your head and heal your heart? The first step is to begin intellectually addressing your free-floating fears and shame in order to reduce irrational panic, terror, and despair. The process of cognitive change will ultimately transform your self-loathing into a sense of well-being and self-acceptance. Consider the sequence of cognitive dissonance steps, feelings, insights, and psychological beliefs that we will discuss below, which will lead ultimately to cognitive acceptance and peace of mind. The gap between where you are and where you want to be is filled with threats, distortions, and terror—all of shame's colleagues. With lasting positive changes and insights, however, the cognitive gap can be closed, and peace of mind is achievable.

In the list below you will find your personal psychological process of moving from cognitive dissonance (self-loathing and shame) to cognitive acceptance (shame-free self-love) and lasting change. Please write in the book and mark your process as you move from despair upward to acceptance, healing, and change. The different emotions listed are all stepping stones to your healing and emotional freedom.

Your New Normal

Clients frequently ask me what a shame-free and anxiety-free life looks and feels like. My answer includes living peacefully in the present, healing your past trauma, being shame-free, experiencing constructive emotional responses in all areas of your life, and having a positive self-image, self-acceptance, self-forgiveness, the desire to expand your life experience, and an inner sense of purpose and hope. All of these qualities begin to evolve within you as you start to consider some different emotional options from your automatic shame-based worry, anxiety, and fear.

The list starts from where you want to live psychologically and descends down to despair and hopelessness. If you start from the bottom of the list, with feeling miserable, you will notice that the steps upward illustrate a lessening of the shame and dread that has plagued your sense of well-being all your life. The traumas of your past fade into the shame and fears of panic today.

- Emotional freedom—You have a new perspective on your life. You have arrived in a new place psychologically and emotionally; your wounded child has been healed, your shame has been exposed, and you are no longer controlled by your past. There is now a connection between your head and your heart. Your life feels empowered and you have new opportunities, hope, and no fear of the future.
- Openness—You are willing to build new relationships, try new things, and let go of your critical inner voice.
- Receptiveness—You have cognitive acceptance of your life (i.e., self-forgiveness and self-acceptance).
- Change—You are considering new options to your fears.
- Courage—You are willing to do something different (e.g., self-care).
- Insight—You are cognitively open to your emotional blind spots of shame.
- Less Terror—Your old fears of exposure and embarrassment aren't stopping your life.
- You are allowing your heart and your new insights about your life to take center stage in the present moment.
- You experience a big shift in your emotional reactions and you are developing a stronger sense of self-acceptance.

- Despair versus Hope—You are struggling with cognitive disagreement; your head and heart are arguing.
- Hopelessness—You have no idea of how to change but you want to anyway.
- "I am not going to die"—You are considering big changes.
- Anxiety and panic attack—You feel vulnerable and scared.
- Anxiety—You can't control everything anymore.
- Amnesia—You are trying to repress your past.
- Denial—You are trying to forget about why you are scared and shameful.
- Avoidance—You wish you didn't feel the way you do now.
- Anxiety—You worry about changing your life.
- Anger—You are experiencing cognitive dissonance. You are very defensive and focused on self-preservation.
- Chronic disease—You are uncomfortable but willing to consider changing.
- Miserable—You want to change your life. (This is your starting point for walking through the valley of indecision, outlasting the fears, terror, shame, and cognitive disagreements within you.)
- Your Bottom Line—You are controlled by shame, fearful and anxious about the future. You are resistant to any changes, big or small. You have a fear of death but an underlying anxiety about life. You have a negative self-image and are emotionally cut off from yourself and others. You avoid change and anything different from your shame beliefs.

This emotional chart is designed to show upward movement, starting with acknowledging your negative self-talk, fear-based emotions, and anxiousness about changing. Your current bottom line isn't your finish line! Your shame baseline is only a starting point. Every cognitive journey has a beginning and also a destination to reach. The journey out of cognitive dissonance and disagreement is no different, with the end goal being cognitive acceptance with emotional freedom, insight, and self-acceptance.

At the shame baseline, fear, anxiety about the future, fear of living, and terror of the unknown are all-encompassing. The steps in the above list illustrate the enormous intellectual and emotional gap between the syndrome of shame, fear, and anxiety and a place of self-acceptance and emotional freedom. Each step toward self-acceptance and healing exists in the gap of your life. Closing the gap between your head and your heart, by resolving old shame beliefs and finding psychological freedom, feels overwhelming. The chart shows how you can go beyond your ingrained self-doubts and dis-agreements—your personal fears and cognitive dissonance. At the top end of the scale is cognitive acceptance, positive changes, and emotional freedom within yourself. You are no longer controlled by the stalker, terrorist, and hunter of your heart and soul. What a huge relief to be rid of your emotional terrorist!

Shame's Insidious Resistance to Change at Any Age: Two Stories from the Valley of Despair

The two vignettes below illustrate the automatic, knee-jerk resistance to changing from a shame-based life to a self-accepting life, with living-in-the-present peace of mind. The two stories point out the intense conscious and unconscious psychological resistance to letting go of perceived control in exchange for something foreign. The final point in the journey is the experience of cognitively accepting the embedded trauma and allowing the defense walls to open to con-sider new ideas, solutions, and healing. As we have said, asking an anxious, fearful, and shame-driven adult to change is like telling a drowning person to just stop drowning. The process of exposing the embedded maze of shame, fear, anxiety, terror, and despair doesn't come through a one-hour course in self-awareness. It is, rather, a deliberate journey in self-discovery that holds many secrets and sur-prises that might seem overwhelming. Jon and Lynn, in the below stories, demonstrate the agony of being controlled by shame's relent-less tyranny of fears and demands for perfection.

Jon, Age Sixty-Two: "I Am Never Leaving My Patio"

Jon is an Ivy League graduate, a business owner, and the father of two adult children. He has recently remarried and loves his new wife. Jon's story begins about ten years earlier when his first wife demanded a divorce after twenty-six years of marriage. Jon told me,

> I pleaded and begged her to reconsider but to no avail. The divorce was a civil war centering around money and future business profit payouts. I was emotionally devastated, depressed, and shocked by her anger and resentment. My anxiety over having the security of my partner leave was beyond my mental or psychological comprehension. I now don't feel like doing much these days. I sit on my patio and look at the ocean. I am withdrawn and not very social over the last four years with my old friends, colleagues, family, and wife.

Jon came to see me to discuss his chronic dread of dying and a feeling of impending doom about the future. Jon explained,

> My wife suggested I come see you because my anxiety is increasing. I don't like being around people. My life was turned upside down when my first wife left me. According to her, I was too anxious and fearful. She complained for years that I would never do anything new or different. She didn't want to die sitting in the house waiting for me to do something. Unfortunately, she wasn't all wrong. I wasn't very flexible or open to doing new things. I regret being so rigid.

I asked Jon if his anxiety and shame had increased since getting remarried four years earlier. Jon seemed puzzled by the question, and said in a low tone of voice,

> I think I have always been anxious since I was a boy. My parents were very strict and demanding of me as a child. I have always worried about bad things happening. I don't feel very successful or courageous as a father, husband, and business owner. I just don't feel good about what I have done. I always have this nagging self-doubt that I am not doing enough. I have no idea what enough is or what it could be.

Jon paused, visibly upset, and his eyes welled up with tears. He continued, "I am very cerebral, and not much of a touchy-feely type of guy. I am struggling with this chronic dread of something awful happening again in my life. On the surface, my business is fine and my health is good. It doesn't make any logical sense to me. I should feel great, but I feel like I am one-step away from living on the streets, alone and worthless."

We will continue Jon's story in chapter 11 and talk more about what transpired for him.

Lynn, Age Twenty-Nine, Single Female: "I Am Moving Away"

Lynn is a retail store manager for a national clothing company. At the request of her girlfriends she came to see me about her on-again, off-again relationship with her boyfriend. I asked Lynn to tell me a little something about herself and what would be important for me to know about her. Lynn said,

> First off, I have never been in therapy with a man. I was raised by my dad. My mom died when I was eight years old. My dad died four years ago. I feel bad about both of my parents' deaths. I feel like I could or should have done something. My boyfriend is a lawyer and not emotionally expressive. We are together but not together. We go for weeks at a time without talking. We haven't made any formal commitments to each other. I have never had a close emotional romantic relationship in the past. I am usually the one that keeps my boyfriend at arm's length but Brad [her boyfriend] keeps me at a distance. I just wish he would open up to me.

I asked Lynn why she keeps people and intimate partners at a distance. Lynn said,

> I get too anxious if someone gets in my space. I don't want anyone controlling me or seeing all of me. I am a very private person. When I get disappointed or hurt, I move away. I have moved around the world since I was eighteen years old. After my dad died, I haven't lived anywhere for more than two years. I don't want to always run away when I get hurt or

scared. I know I have intimacy issues, but I love being in a relationship. It's very odd to me.

We will revisit Lynn's story in chapter 11.

EXPOSING YOUR HIDDEN FEARS, ANXIETY, AND TERROR

We have discussed some very powerful concepts in this chapter relating to shame's close relationship with fear and its operating system of anxiety, dread, and emotional terror. We now know that shame combines with fear to create a web of anxiety issues that limit, impede, and psychologically paralyze its victims. Shame is a major factor in the never-ending struggles of your attempts to change your thoughts and feelings about yourself. The cognitive dissonance of shame opposed to cognitive self-acceptance is deliberately avoided. My clients will frequently say to me, as a throw-away line, "My mind controls me." This statement is actually code for emotional avoidance, and is saying, "I don't want to think or feel any discomfort." A person's mind and heart are designed to work together, not in a conflicting internal struggle. Shame, though, is inherently at odds with all the positive parts of your being.

> *Shame, fear, and terror live inches below the surface of their victim's life.*

It's always important to ask how we can resolve and heal our insidious combination of shame and fear. The first step is to recognize their silent operation in your day-to-day relationships. The amount of energy that Jon and Lynn spend keeping their fears alive is beyond mentally and physically exhausting. Shame and fear beliefs will make you pass up the opportunity to take a big career or life step forward or move out of your childhood neighborhood. The next step can be as simple as allowing your children to experience their lives without you being the controlling helicopter parent. Unrestrained fear is a constant personal torture that can be activated by any routine daily event or life situation. The ingrained panic that is fueled by shame-fear beliefs is always just below the surface of a person's life.

> *We have to know the relationship patterns that drive us before we can break free from them.*
> —attributed to Dr. Nadine Macaluso,
> Hermosa Beach, California, 2018

The need to control the people, events, and relationships in your life is an exhausting task, with new worries lurking around every corner. Anxiety and chronic worrying are all symptoms of the deeper issue of shame and its best friend, fear. All the emotional, psychological, and intellectual beliefs protecting your unexposed shame and fear are something that you can uncover. The list of questions below are intended to shake up the emotional denial, avoidance, and amnesia that insulates you from understanding your fears. As the quote above reminds us, we can't change or heal what we refuse to see, acknowledge, or address. Answer the following questions with your first thought, idea, and/or impulsive response. You might be surprised at how defensive you are about your vulnerability, your disdain for anything uncertain, your cognitive resistance to change, or the irrational fears that seem rational to you. Answer the following questions briefly, writing your answers in the margins or next to the question.

Questions for Exposing Your Fears, Anxiety, Shame, and Despair:

- What drives your need to control people, events, and things that are not under your control?
- What is one of your unspoken fears?

- What is one of your shame fears?
- What makes you anxious?
- Do your loved ones know about your anxiety, fears, and shame?
- Do you consider yourself hypervigilant (always focusing on possible disasters or feelings of impending doom)?
- What emotions, situations, and circumstances do you actively avoid?
- How do you manage your fears and concerns about the future?
- Do you chronically worry about something or somebody, or dread the future?
- What do you actively avoid for fear of feeling your dis-ease?
- Do you avoid conversations or relationship issues that might require a confrontation?
- How were conflict and difficult situations handled in your childhood?
- How do you and your romantic partner resolve disagreements?
- Do you allow important people in your life to express their feelings to you?
- What is one thing, issue, behavior, or action that you are embarrassed about?
- Who in your life knows your private self (i.e., your unspoken fears, shame, and trauma)?
- Do you allow yourself to be completely honest, transparent, and vulnerable with anyone in your life?
- Do you fear death?
- Have you ever had a panic attack?
- Do people consider you an anxious and controlling person?
- Do you consider yourself an uptight, nervous, or "tightly wrapped" person?
- Can you relax and disengage from your life, technology, and work?
- Who or what scares you?
- What is one thing, issue, or concern about yourself that you avoid, deny, and have amnesia about?

This list is brief self-reporting inventory for exposing common emotional blind spots. We all have blind spots (i.e., issues in our life that we avoid). What is one of yours? In what ways are you burdened by your underlying anxiety concerns, buried fears, shameful feelings, and unresolved issues from your past? Do you know the difference between carrying an emotional burden (i.e., self-loathing) and resolving your past (i.e., self-forgiveness)? The above questions are designed to find an emotional opening in your psychological wall and hopefully crack it open. That opening is your growing new personal insight, which breaks the silence between the real you and your emotional terrorist, shame. Beginning to emotionally resist simply accepting your old shame commands is liberating and empowering. Shame can't withstand your disobedience that comes with your new-found psychological insight and clarity.

Do you notice a theme in your answers? Or something that stands out to you about them? The connections between shame, fear, and anxiety are difficult to understand in a logical way. Shame isn't logical, nor are its associates fear and anxiety. These questions are designed to help you to see yourself and your world from a larger perspective. The automatic defensive reactions—"That's all psycho-jargon," "I don't have any of those issues," or "I am in control and it's not a problem"—are all reflexive avoidant responses. These types of resistant, close-minded reactions are all automatically working to protecting your wounded and scared inner child. The psychologically ingrained defenses keep a person's unresolved trauma, childhood abuse, domestic violence, and current maladaptive shame behaviors concealed.

> **Shame perceives any personal change as dangerous and deadly—all change must be avoided!**

The emotional blocks and intellectual disconnections between the different parts and aspects of you are called *fragmentation*.[1] These fragmented aspects of you include your adult self, your adolescent self, your shame-wounded self, your core healthy self, your public self, your professional self, and your loving self. Mental health and long-term well-being are gauged by a person's integration and the cohesion of all these different aspects of his life. Shame, fear, and anxiety work together to keep all the different aspects from peacefully coexisting for your highest and best purpose. We will explore in section III how to integrate the painful, blocked off, shameful parts of you. Assimilation of all the different pieces and aspects of your life means freedom from shame, fear, and anxiety.

There are five common shame and fear areas that anxious adults hide, ignore, and avoid. As a psychologist, I can't emphasize enough the absolute cement wall of resistance brilliant men and women often have to the suggestions listed in the following pages. Many times, I act more as a psychological litigator, advocating for the value and purpose of change and emotional health. People who are consciously or unconsciously invested in keeping their status quo experience of living "fearfully" have the greatest degree of trauma when faced with change. Anxious adults, who are driven by shame and fear, unconsciously equate change with death. Death and change are the core terrors of a fear-driven worldview that began with feelings of inadequacy in childhood.

The following ideas are steps to guide you through the process of cognitive and emotional healing. Each of these areas are important to examine as you shift your shame-response cycle and its symptoms of fear and anxiety. These five truths, and their distortions caused by fear and anxiety, are necessary to consider to reduce shame's role in your life.

FIVE KEYS TO EXPOSING YOUR FEAR CONNECTION TO SHAME AND ANXIETY

1. Expanding Your Comfort Zone

The idea of emotional, psychological, and relationship expansion sounds easy until you push your inner walls of security outward. All fears are not the same. For example, it's important to understand that there's a difference between survival fear and emotionally learned fear. Survival fear, as we discussed earlier, makes us avoid a fist fight with an eight-hundred-pound grizzly bear, use the crosswalk during rush hour in downtown Los Angeles, and not stand on the very edge of the Grand Canyon. These are all appropriate responses and important for your personal safety.

What we are discussing here, however, is emotionally learned fear. Learned fears may include fear of intimacy, schedule changes, vacations, social gatherings, kids going away, having a pet, having a messy house, marriage, driving, public places, or taking a calculated risk. Expanding your comfort zone starts with differentiating between your survival fear and your learned shame fear. The goal is to no longer allow your learned emotional rationalizations to control your destiny, choices, relationships, and well-being.

2. Built-In Fear Limits

Your learned fear, caused by shame, will increasingly limit, restrict, and impair your ability to live by creating emotional walls to protect you. The threat of change and expanding your comfort zone is terrifying, and shame tells you it must always be avoided. Your false shame belief makes you think that avoiding your life challenges is a way to keep yourself safe. The irony is that fear breeds more fear, not comfort or safety. A fear-driven and shame-controlled life is literally a chronic anxious existence. Fear-based decisions lead a person psychologically into a progressively debilitating condition. In the long-term, lifestyle choices made out of fear and anxiety create a maze of chronic dis-ease. Some of the common psychological side effects of this way of living are social phobias (i.e., fear of interactions with strangers), ago-raphobia (i.e., fear of public places), and obsessive-compulsive per-sonality disorder (e.g., fear of germs and death). The victim tries to find safety by making the scope of her life smaller and smaller and attempting to keep some control of the dreadful unknown. Exposing the irrationality of your shame-fears is another important step in uncovering the underlying reasons for your unspoken terror.

3. Emotional Terrorism: Relentless Force

Terrorizing shame is like a chronically dripping emotional faucet. The impending threat of embarrassment and the dread of some-thing traumatic happening is always on your psychological radar screen. Shame's all-consuming threat of the unknown controls your need to question, worry, resist change, or take any kind of coura-geous personal action. Any change of daily routine or natural transi-tions of a family, a growing career, or an aging body are automatic triggers that cause panic, terror, and a sense of impending disaster. Shame, supported by your self-doubt, tells you that you can't manage or handle any changes. The force of the emotional terror washing over you feels like you have tried to drink out of a fire hydrant that's spraying out at full strength; you are washed down the street of despair and hopelessness. The natural psychological reflex to this is to create more self-imposed limits and to isolate you further from the world. Emotional terrorism whispers into your ear, saying, "If you don't listen to me, you will die." The emotional links developed over years of negotiating with your unreasonable self create a behav-ioral pattern that is very powerful controlling force in your life. Your life is organized around avoiding your terror, despair, and emotional dread. By repeatedly exposing the irrationality of your shame-based fears, you can begin to create new emotional connections of self-acceptance and well-being.

4. Loss of Control: Change Is in the Air

Many psychologists and mental health professionals believe that effective treatment of any type of depressive disorder must first consider an underlying untreated anxiety disorder.[2] My premise is, rather, that depression, anxiety, and fear all have many of their roots in shame's silent functioning. Shame flies under the radar of treatment because of its amorphous existence. Many researchers consider depression and anxiety to be different sides of the same coin in each person. Shame creates that coin and puts it into the person's heart and soul. People can and do spend their life's energy resisting what lies beneath their greatest anxiety and their deepest, darkest unexplored fears. The ultimate source and the major core cause of anxiety and shame disorders is the fear of death. The fundamental sense of having no control comes from fearing death and being afraid to live life.

These free-floating fears are connected to our lack of perspective about our life, relationships, and sense of well-being. When we begin to embrace our death, the need to control everything dramatically diminishes. Appreciating the natural cycles of life, with their ups and downs, reduces shame's control of your emotions and decisions. Our fear of losing control comes from our early traumatic experiences. The traumas we have gone through, including chaotic family situations, deaths, abuse, and psychological instability, breeds a terror of life within us, and a sense of impending doom and death. Because these fears developed when we were so young, we were unable to fully understand or psychologically process them. Our present-day emotional terror, amnesia about our traumatic past, and catastrophic thinking are connecting to the ultimate villain—shame. The fear of death is a misunderstanding of the natural developmental process that is connected to our unresolved childhood, adolescent, or adult trauma. Death, control, and shame are a powerful combination that can negatively impact anyone.

5. Your Full Acceptance

Death isn't going away because you avoid it or live in denial about your reckless lifestyle (e.g., your self-destructive addictions). Dealing with all the anxiety and depression issues in your life leads to the ultimate action that will end shame's control over you: acceptance of death. Once a person accepts that they will not live forever and thus stops avoiding the feelings of death, they then can start to live their life shame-free. Death isn't the big unknown that restricts your natural life flow: you are. We are always the problem and we are always the solution to any and all of our challenges, regardless of their magnitude or seriousness. At some point, everyone must walk down the pathway of embracing, accepting, and resolving their own thoughts about their death and their life choices.

Resisting this natural life path creates a chronic source of shame laced with fear, anxiety, depression, and terror. When you stop avoiding your personal and professional interests, desires, passions, and goals, though, your life immediately transforms. The possibilities, new horizons, and old dreams all start with your acceptance that your death is something to embrace not fear. Embracing your end game allows you to live in the present with hope, confidence, and passion. Eastern psychology believes that accepting your death is your starting point for living your life to its fullest capacity.[3] Shame has zero power and is rendered useless when you embrace the natural cycle of death and living.

CLOSING THOUGHTS

> *Nothing great was ever achieved without enthusiasm.*
> —Ralph Waldo Emerson, "Circles," 1841

> *And now that you don't have to be perfect, you can be good.*
> —John Steinbeck, *East of Eden*, 1952

We are slowly unraveling the intricate emotional bonds between shame, fear, and anxiety. These strong emotional and psychological reactions is a complicated maze, which keeps a person very controlled and limited. The above quotes by Emerson and Steinbeck illustrate the energy and fresh perspective that can diminish the role shame has in your life.

There is a wounded child inside all of us that must be rescued and protected from experiencing any degree of harm or abuse again. Developing emotional safety is an ongoing theme throughout this book. To feel safe and competent and live peacefully in your world requires a systematic removal of the old and outdated cognitive hardware and information. Reducing your anxiety, and stopping avoidant choices begins to pull shame's distorted beliefs, self-loathing actions, fear-based decisions, and abusive relationships out by the roots. The threat of your inner terrorist staging a complete and utter meltdown declines with your new insights, cognitive awareness, and the larger perspective of your personal power.

When you accept your life, you gain emotional power, essentially taking the keys away from your jailer (shame) and unlocking your psychological prison. Shame has no power, influence, or emotional leverage when you embrace your childhood beginnings, your present day circumstances, and the end of your life. This timeless truth allows you to start living shame-free.

In the next chapter, we will be discussing how shame controls your relationship world. Shame and loving relationships are inherently incompatible, but unraveling the role of shame in your relationships will allow you to resolve and change it in your life going forward. Chapter 8 is going to uncover shame's role in your emotional bonds, your attachments, and your disappointments.

SHAME AND RELATIONSHIPS: YOU, YOUR PARENTS, CHILDREN, AND LOVERS—HOW IT'S ALL RELATED

Stress, anxiety, and depression are caused when we are living to please others.

—Paulo Coelho, Twitter, May 24, 2016

Unresolved emotion from the past is often turned against the self.

—John Bradshaw, *Homecoming*, 1990

In any given moment we have two options: to step forward into growth and change or to step back into safety.

—Abraham Maslow, as quoted in
*How the Best Leaders Lead: Proven Secrets to
Getting the Most Out of Yourself and Others,*
by Brian Tracy, 2010

SHAME'S ROLE IN RELATIONSHIPS: THE BIG COVER-UP

Shame's greatest "fifteen minutes of fame" is in the arena of relationships. It's a commonly accepted fact in all areas of mental health that relationships are directly related to a person's sense of well-being. Our entire life, past, present, and future, is a composite of multitude of relationships. Everyone develops certain relationship styles, patterns, and attachments. Shame is the unseen element that deteriorates, erodes, and destroys the natural ability to develop stable and secure relationships. Healthy, supportive, functional, loving relationships can't coexist with shame's involvement; they are incompatible. Shame is a volatile emotion and belief, while self-acceptance and inner peace are calming feelings. Abusive, codependent, fearful, and addictive relationships all thrive in with shame. Why and how does shame work in relationships? This chapter is going to expose, explore, and demonstrate the insidious dysfunction and cause of shame within you and in your relationships. Removing the role of shame in your relationships is the single most courageous act you will carry out as adult. The pain, agony, embarrassment, abuse, suffering, disappointment, rage, and despair that shame causes in relationships are destructive and needless. Shame is like being infected by a flu virus: it contaminates you, your relationships, and your emotional health.

> **Shame and self-love are incompatible and can never peacefully coexist.**

Most people won't truly accepts that they have any shame issues or concerns until their relationship world blows up like a cheap firecracker: loudly, traumatically, and painfully. Shame comes with an ingrained psychological blind spot, denial, avoidance, and amnesia behavior, which is how it silently controls you and all of your relationship decisions, behaviors, and choices. Marriages, dating and romantic relationships, business contacts, family, social connections, and casual acquaintances are all measuring sticks that people use to gauge their emotional well-being and self-worth. That works until you run out of denial and you hit the brick wall of shame. Shame distorts the balance between you and your important emotional bonds, connections, and attachments. When your love life or job blows up, and you are emotionally flooded with shame and despair, it's at that point you are aware that something isn't working in your life. Shame never feels psychologically right or completely comfortable within you and your friendships.

> *Your relationship with your Self sets the tone for every other relationship you have.*
>
> —Robert Holden, *Happiness Now!*
> *Timeless Wisdom for Feeling Good Fast*, 2011

Shame has been forming your relationship template since your early childhood. The quote above illustrates how that template, formed by shame, self-doubt, and fear of abandonment, can affect all your relationships. Every relationship has a flow and rhythm; the tempos and rhythms of your relationships have been shaped and formed by your wounded sense of self. Your early relationship with your parents was the beginning of developing maladaptive shame behaviors, and these behaviors strengthened as you were unable to feel secure with your preschool friends. Who was your first friend? How did you feel about having friends? How did think that your friends viewed you?

How would you describe your relationship with each of your parents when you were in elementary school? Your early experiences of love, along with your feelings of emotional security or disappointment, formed the beginnings of your relationship style. We know from chapter 1 that children either feel competent or inadequate by preschool, depending on their parent-child relationship. The psychological crossroads of competence and inadequacy marks the beginning of your journey into the world of relationships. The early childhood feelings of inadequacy, self-doubt, and despair taught us that we weren't "good enough" to have loving, caring, supportive friends. Instead, we learned during our elementary, middle, and high school years that we had to hide, conceal, and keep secret our shameful and defective private self. Throughout our childhood and teen years, our self-esteem is affected more and more by our fear of feeling unlovable, unacceptable, and defective. The natural human need to feel loved, accepted, and understood is destroyed by our shame factor. Our ever-increasing sense of insecurity, despair, and worthlessness carries follows us into adulthood, marriage, career, parenting, and retirement. Shame cripples our ability to fully experience the power of love, acceptance, and understanding in our relationships. Shame is a glass wall between you, self-love, self-acceptance, and loving relationships.

> *The natural human need in relationships*
> *is for* **love, acceptance, and understanding,**
> **which is aborted, denied, and made impos-**
> **sible with shame and codependency.**

In order to survive as a child, teenager, and twenty-something, we create a false public self to keep everyone and everything from seeing our scared and wounded inner self. Many boys overcompensate for their wounded inner child with bragging, bullying, hyper-sexuality, and becoming either super-achievers or super-underachievers. Girls more frequently cover up their insecurities by forming exclusive mean-girl cliques, overemphasizing appearance and designer clothing, hyper-sexuality, and emotional withdrawal.

There is no relationship in your life that isn't impacted by shame, especially the one with yourself. Shame is at the core of our vulnerable sense of self and colors how we view our world, those we love, our self-worth, and our self-acceptance. The ways shame has played out in your life will come as a surprise when it's finally discovered and exposed. Shame negatively impacts all types of relationships, from your personal friendships to your romantic connections and your professional associations. Clients ask me frequently: what shame does in relationships. Untreated shame creates extreme self-imposed social pressure, demands a perfect professional appearance, builds chronic family stress and unending romantic struggles, and causes fear of rejection, self-loathing, and personal self-doubts. Shame—the hunter, terrorist, and the monster in the closet—is an active player in your relationships and your day-to-day life. In relationships where shame is simply accepted, endorsed, and allowed to live, it is the most destructive. Consider the following questions regarding shame and its negative impact on you, your relationships, and quality of life.

Questions about Shame in My Relationships

Answer these questions in the margins of the book. Write down your first thought, whatever it is. There are no right or wrong answers; they will, rather, offer a look into your relationship style.

- Do you frequently feel like a martyr in your marriage, romantic relationships, and close friendships?
- Do you feel that no one is ever concerned or considerate of your needs and wants?
- Do you feel good when people are pleased with you?
- Do you seek the approval of others?
- Do you avoid sharing unfavorable personal details of your life with your close circle of friends?
- How was your relationship with your mother while you were growing up?
- How was your relationship with your father while you were growing up?
- Did you feel cared for and loved by your parents prior to age twelve?
- Do you become anxious when someone is mad at you?
- Are you a very private person?
- Do you really like yourself?
- Are you always the responsible one in your relationships?
- Do you like "fixing" people?
- As a child, did you emotionally act like an adult to take care of your family?
- Do you have a lot of self-doubts and insecurities about your abilities and goals?

- Are you uncomfortable with accepting compliments?
- Do you feel more sympathy for others than for yourself?
- Do you allow yourself to be nurtured and cared for without feeling guilty?
- Do you seek people out for fear of being forgotten or ignored?
- Do you try to make everyone in your life feel good?
- Does anyone know your private self-doubts, fears, and concerns?
- Do you have difficulty setting boundaries with your friends, partners, and children?
- Do you placate people to "keep the peace" despite your opposing feelings?
- What person in your past or present would you like the approval of?
- What person currently holds the most emotional power and/ or influence in your life?
- Do you avoid conflicts in order to be liked and so that you are only viewed in a positive light?
- Do you resent your partner?
- Do you have a relationship history of being abused or being the abuser?
- Do you defer to others before you consider your own opinion and desires?
- Do you avoid being alone?

CODEPENDENCY EXPOSED AND DEFINED

These questions are intended to uncover and expose the multifaceted relationship tumor, trauma, and chaos commonly known as codependency. Codependency can't function or operate without your hidden shame driving it from behind the scenes. Shame manifests as the self-defeating, self-loathing personal belief system that guides and dominates your interactions. Shame taints, skews, and distorts your interactions with yourself, your partner, and your children, and twists the way you relate in your social interactions and your career. Navigating through shame is like pouring bleach into a glass of water and then wondering why it's poisonous. Everything appears fine in a relationship until you are required to grow and expand, and then the dysfunctional shame-based codependency appears.

Unfortunately, very smart, well-meaning, and accomplished adults from all walks of life spend years of their lives trying to make their codependent relationships work. The toxic mix of shame and codependency is fatal to all relationships. This may sound extreme, but it's a reality that few people accept until their relationships become a series of major disappointments, betrayals, and heart-breaks. These types of low-functioning relationships don't allow for mutual respect, emotional equality, or a balance of love and responsibility between two people.

Codependency means that one person is constantly seeking approval while the other person is withholding that love and acceptance. A codependent relationship is never a balanced relationship, with concern, care, and mutual interest for each other. Instead, the relationship is built around one person's needs, while the other person is always attempting to meet those needs. One person benefits from the effort and the other person ultimately feels exploited, used, and resentful. Codependent relationships are a one-way connection that doesn't include the best interest of both individuals. Shame is the emotional and psychological foundation of all codependent relationships.

Shame contaminates and destroys relationships!

The questions listed above illustrate a behavioral pattern of approval seeking, lacking self-acceptance, self-doubt, insecurity, avoidance of conflict, and personalizing everyone's behavior. I frequently get asked what codependency is. During my many years of personal and professional experience, I have developed the following description of codependency:

> Codependency means having an ongoing need for the approval of others; lacking of a feeling of self-worth in relationships; feeling unlovable; having a psychological need for people to accept and like one; and holding self-loathing and self-hatred as core beliefs. A codependent person uses relationships to find self-acceptance in spite of their sense of self-loathing. Codependency is a behavioral pattern of seeking approval regardless of the consequences to one's well-being; believing that someone else can heal one's wounded child if one serves that person. A codependent person feels worthless and underappreciated in their relationships; they feel like a martyr and that their relationships aren't based on mutual respect.

This ongoing working clinical definition shows how codependency and shame function together in chaos to create a relationship pattern of misery, emotional disequilibrium, resentment, and despair. Shame pushes a person into the emotional emptiness of chronically seeking approval in order to offset his private feelings of believing he is unlovable, replaceable, deeply flawed, damaged goods, valueless, and not good enough. The adjectives and descriptions coming from shame are a constant indictment and a never-ending flow of emotional terror. Codependency becomes a person's behavioral model to compensate for feeling inadequate (due to shame) in all his different relationships and in both formal and informal settings. While I am most frequently asked what codependency is, the second-most frequent question I receive is: "How did I get that kind of relationship disease?"

How and Where Did It Start?

Codependency begins when a young child's basic and natural emotional and psychological needs of feeling loved, accepted, and understood aren't met or properly appreciated; the child's interests, ideas, and personality aren't fostered or encouraged. These early emotional disappointments are devastating to the young child's sensitive heart and soul. As the child grows up, the repeated pattern of psychological negligence by her parents is detrimental to her evolving self-image. The end result is that the child feels a sense of emotional deprivation, self-doubt, and insecurity in her relationships. The painful sense of feeling emotionally empty, defective, not good enough, and unlovable all started in the parent-child relationship from birth to approximately the age of ten. The early experience of trauma, dysfunctional parenting, and lack of nurturing happens in degrees of severity and within a range of psychological damage. Some children are able to get their parents' attention periodically and develop a fragmented sense of competence. Other children are unable to get their parents' attention, interest, or time at all and then personalized that neglect as being their own fault or failure (i.e., they believed they were not good enough for their parents). The early parent-child relationship is where the shame-codependent relationship model begins.

Children believe they are at fault for their parents' emotional neglect.

The complexity of shame's operation in your adult relationships can result in a series of repeated failed attempts to feel loved, accepted, and understood. These unmet childhood psychological needs become the endless source and cause of feeling angry, disappointed, and afraid of intimacy. In chapter 2, we discussed the emotional magnitude of whether a young child feels either loved or inadequate. The unloved child becomes a neglected teen, who then becomes an anxious adult, having grown up with a nagging sense of feeling emotionally empty. The early trauma, parental neglect, and emotional hunger (brought on by deprivation) evolves into a shame-driven personality. The effect of shame in relationships comes in the form of codependency and self-defeating relationships. We know from our discussion throughout the book to this point that shame isn't helpful or interested in being healed, exposed, or understood. The unconscious psychological defense against feeling defective, not good enough, and like damaged goods is how shame operates in your relationship world; the shaming of your needs, natural desires, and hopes develops into the codependent cycle of disappointment and feeling inferior, damaged, and unlovable.

> *Shame and codependency are a serious rela-*
> *tionship illness that is ignored and/or mis-*
> *understood by its victims and participants.*

Codependent tendencies, such as placating behaviors, start to form early in a young child. If a child's mother or father was narcissistic, emotionally absent, or abusive, the child learns instinctively how to attract his parents' attention, interest and love. When raised by these types of self-absorbed and emotionally absent parents, children instinctively learn how to psychologically survive. All children crave and need their parents' love and approval, and kids of narcissistic parents learn how to make their parents "feel good" so they can receive positive emotional attention from them. For instance, my client Eric would make his mother and father's nightly martini starting around age seven. He received more praise for learning to make this nightly cocktail than he did for getting straight A's in school. Eric told me, "My parents were more concerned about their martini than my life. I knew it and that was how I was noticed."

Children of abusive, narcissistic, absent, or delinquent parents always find ingenious ways to get bits and pieces of emotional "bread crumbs." These children grow up to be approval seeking, placating, and codependent adults, hoping to find love, acceptance, and understanding in the world. The codependent adult never considers that the ability to fulfill her need for love, acceptance, and understanding lies within herself. The emotional void of an undeveloped core self leaves a person feeling empty, insecure, and seeking to find a relationship that will fix their inner wounds. The psychological wound of shame can only be healed from within, however, not by having the "perfect" relationship or a "hot" partner. Codependency is the unspoken agreement between two adults to fix each other's inner child. This agreement doesn't work, though, and usually leads to divorce, heartbreak, and emotional despair. Healthy relationships require the participation of two independent adults to create a safe, secure, and thriving bond. Codependent relationships are inherently flawed because of the lack of mutual respect and the lack of understanding about the roles each partner will have.

Codependency prohibits a person from discovering his genuine passions, goals, and hopes. The codependent adult is always seeking to be "good enough" and he ignores his true desires and wishes. The children of codependent parents become adult who personalize their parents' poor parenting, believing it to be their fault. This double negative creates a very emotionally insecure, frightened adult who secretly believes the world doesn't like, love, or care about them.

> **What's codependence? "I am not codependent, I don't need anyone."**

> Finding your passion isn't just about careers and money. It's about finding your authentic self. The one you've buried beneath other people's needs.
> —Kristin Hannah, *Distant Shores*, 2002

HOW CODEPENDENCY LOOKS AND WORKS AT ANY AGE: FOUR SCENARIOS

Scenario 1: Silent "Abusive" Neglect

Debbie, twenty-nine, was engaged to a man she met on a popular social media dating website. She came to see me about wanting to improve her relationship with her estranged mother before she got married in nine months. Approximately two months before the wedding, Debbie started missing or rescheduling our weekly therapy appointments. The behavior patterns of shame and codependency between Debbie and her fiancé, Mike, were starting to become noticeable and were increasingly problematic. Debbie believed that she couldn't get married because of her mother's negativity about relationships and men, and because of her own self-doubt. Debbie's mother had divorced her father, and the end of the marriage had been very contentious and had created a great deal of disillusionment. Debbie was emotionally paralyzed when she has to confront Mike's rage, anger, and mean-spirited behavior whenever he got frustrated with her. Mike verbally demeaned Debbie for wanting to plan the wedding immediately after they were engaged. Debbie didn't believe Mike truly wanted to marry her because of his emotional resistance to finalizing the wedding. The following discussion was a painful example of Debbie's fear of abandonment and fear of rejection and the way she placated Mike when she disagreed with his actions.

> Debbie: "I am getting blamed and yelled at because I found the wedding venue. Mike feels pressured and yelled at me for three hours last night. He accused me of being selfish, self-centered, and insensitive for wanting to plan the wedding. I didn't argue or defend myself because I was afraid he would blow up and break up with me."
>
> Dr. P: "Does Mike yell and verbally devaluate you?"
>
> Debbie: "Yes."
>
> Dr. P: "Do you feel scared when Mike yells and calls you names?"
>
> Debbie: "Yes, the verbal rage has gotten worse lately with the wedding planning. Mike gets mean-spirited and calls me insulting names. He makes fun of me and my parents. My dad is a cardiologist and has a very big medical practice and lives in Malibu [a very exclusive beach community in West Los Angeles, California]. Mike grew up in northern Florida, and his parents were divorced. Mike and his family struggled financially after the divorce. I try not to personalize his negative comments. It's hard to listen to the barrage of negativity. He says, for instance, that I am spoiled, self-entitled, and I want to be a kept wife. None of it's true, I work my ass off, and I am making 80 percent more than he is currently."
>
> Dr. P: "Why are you marrying someone who resents you and your life?"
>
> Debbie: "I am hoping things would get better. If I keep the peace and not upset Mike, maybe his mood will change."

One month prior to the wedding Debbie received an email at work. It was a twenty-five-page prenuptial agreement from Mike, with whom Debbie had just spent a tense weekend. Mike had mentioned several months earlier that he wasn't going to support Debbie if she ever stopped working. Mike repeatedly told Debbie that he didn't want a lazy, self-centered wife. The prenuptial agreement outlined how Mike wanted no legal responsibility for Debbie during or after the marriage—no community property and no shared bank accounts—and included a clause about infidelity and payment for emotional damages. Mike also requested repayment for everything he would spend on the family during the marriage. Debbie called me and requested an emergency two-hour therapy session that afternoon. It's important to mention that Mike had *no* assets coming into the marriage. Debbie, on the other hand, owned her own home, ran her own business, and had no debt.

> Debbie: "I sent the prenuptial agreement to my company's attorney. The lawyer called me on the way to your office and said he can't legally or ethically advise me to sign the prenuptial agreement. The lawyer said he will not represent me because the prenuptial is so disturbing and irrational. He also said I shouldn't enter a marriage when the groom wants nothing to do with me, our future children, and/or build a life together. Lastly, the lawyer told me not to marry someone who appears to be very abusive and disrespectful of me. I am in shock because Mike said he isn't negotiating the prenuptial at all. It's his final word on our future. What do you think of all this, Dr. P?"
>
> Dr. P: "I think you need to do several things. First, get a second opinion from a family law attorney. Second, ask yourself why you want to marry someone who clearly resents and doesn't trust you. Third, think about what kind of marriage you want for yourself, Mike, and your future kids. Most importantly, do you believe that no one will marry you, and that Mike is your only option?"

Four days later, and approximately four weeks from the wedding day, Debbie canceled the wedding. She explained the following to me:

I have never truly understood my codependency and people-pleasing tendencies until now. Your question about why I was marrying Mike rang in my heart and head all week. There is a part of me that believes that Mike is my only hope of getting married. I don't want to be that woman who was never married and never had children. I do feel very unlovable. I know it's messed up, but I think Mike wasn't wrong for yelling and making me feel bad. Yet I really know I am a great person and not a selfish bitch. I don't feel secure, confident, or clear-headed in relationships. In the past, I believed whatever a guy said about me must be true. I know that kind of thinking isn't right or emotionally healthy. This is the third guy with whom I have broken an engagement. Mike is by far the most abusive and mean-spirited to me of all my boyfriends. Two years ago, I would have signed that document and not told anyone, hoping things would work out. I am going to resolve my codependency and approval seeking with men. My denial is scary because I would have married Mike despite all his devaluing, abusive moods, and rages. I promise myself, before I start ever dating again, I am not going to ignore these warning signs of abuse.

Codependency requires the victim to be solely responsible for both individuals in the relationship.

Scenario 2: I Am Embarrassed

Jack was forty years old, married, and the father of three children (ages three, five, and eight). Jack came to see me regarding his avoidant behavior with his wife, Carol, to whom he had been married for twelve years. Jack described himself as a people pleaser, and he avoided any type of conflict or emotional tension. Jack and Carol had never had a very active or fulfilling sexual relationship. They had sex about twice a year, when Carol was amenable to the idea. Jack felt rejected and emasculated because Carol frequently told him he wasn't masculine enough for her. Jack described himself as having been very sexual before he met Carol. He married Carol because she was emotionally stable, predictable, and very mild mannered. The dialogue below is a sample of how Jack viewed himself, women, intimacy, his fear of conflict, and his mother.

Dr. P: "How do you manage your frustration with Carol when she rejects your sexual advances?"

Jack: "I have ignored the cumulative rejections over the years until last summer. I realized then that I am scared to confront Carol about her demeaning comments about me, my career, and our sexual relationship."

Dr. P: "What happened to shift you from being passive to being more direct with your wife?"

Jack: "I told Carol that her comments about me and our sex life were very hurtful and unwarranted. She told me that I should get over it and not be so sensitive and soft. She also said that if I can't let go of her comments, maybe we should get a divorce. I was speechless about her coldness and lack of insight and empathy. I realized at that moment I had married a newer version of my mother."

Over the next four months, Jack and I met to explore his mother-son relationship. Jack began to realize the physical and verbal abuse he had received from his mother during his childhood was still affecting his relationships, especially his marriage. Jack realized that he was scared of upsetting or disappointing his wife. Emotional terror and panic would flood Jack whenever Carol was unhappy with him. Another shame-codependency issue Jack uncovered was his difficulty in setting and keeping psychological boundaries with his children, coworkers, and with Carol. He felt responsible for everything and everyone, and he felt that he must keep the peace. Jack saw how his shame beliefs that he was bad, not good enough, and at fault for everything controlled his life. He was also humiliated that he had allowed himself to be terrorized by Carol's anger. Jack began to resolve his childhood trauma of being physically abused and emotionally blackmailed by his mother. These hidden shame issues allowed Jack to challenge his wife to start couple's therapy for their communication issues.

Jack told me the following after their first couple's therapy session:

Carol started the session by telling our therapist [a woman] that I have anxiety and shame issues that have ruined our marriage. The therapist asked Carol what her role was in the marriage discord. Carol told the therapist that she doesn't have any issues and that's why he sees Dr. Poulter. Our therapist told both of us that unless we are both going to take responsibility for our role in the marriage, couple's counseling was a waste of time. Carol immediately got up and walked out of the session. I feel torn about not upsetting Carol and continuing to pursue therapy. It's our only chance for staying married if we work on developing some emotional balance between us. I can't always be the cause and the blame for everything.

> **Shame and codependency control the victim with self-blame, self-loathing, and fear of abandonment.**

Scenario 3: Never Leave Me

We met Dave in chapters 1 and 3. Dave was a self-described recovering "rage-a-holic." He openly admitted to having outbursts of toxic shame. The most recent verbal outburst had been when his siblings got together for a family reunion weekend. The theme of the blowup had to do with his mother's resentment about Dave's lack of love and support for her and the family. Dave came in to see me to resolve his ongoing despair about his mother, sister, ex-wife, and daughter. Dave had been married for twenty years and divorced for the last five years. He had two adult children who lived out of state (a daughter, twenty-five, and a son, twenty-two).

> Dave: "I feel this weird emotional bond with my mother [Dana]. You know she moved from New York City to Los Angeles ten years ago. She lives a mile from my home in Santa Monica [California]. My mother gets very jealous of my ex-wife and daughter when we are all together. It's like I am my mom's boyfriend or something like that. It's very uncomfortable. I feel emotionally suffocated when I am around my mom. She is relentless in badgering me to take care of her."
>
> Dr. P: "Dave, don't get upset, but would you consider the idea that you might create emotional distance from your mother and friends with your rage and unpredictable outbursts?"

Dave: "Hmmm, that's interesting. I yell at my mother all the time and feel horrible afterwards. She gets everyone in the family to be on her side whenever we argue. I have always felt that if I don't do what she wants, something awful would happen. It makes no sense, but I feel it with her. I have a hard time saying no to women in my life. I haven't dated since my divorce. I don't want to be controlled by another woman."

Dr. P: "Dave, do you seek your mother's approval?"

Dave: "Yes and it's sick."

Dr. P: "What happens if you don't get it?"

Dave: "I never get it."

Dr. P: "How would your life be different if you sought your own self-acceptance?"

Dave: "I have no f—ing idea! I cater to that woman and all she wants is more money and a new house. My parents divorced when I was fifteen years old and I was left to take care of my mother. I still resent her dependency and mean-spiritedness. It feels like my mother has some funky incest thing with me. I don't think I was ever molested by her. It just feels creepy how she talks to me like a husband. I get why my dad left her. She is so needy and manipulative."

Dr. P: "Dave, you didn't answer the question. How do you react emotionally when you feel ignored and dismissed by your mother?"

Dave: "I blow up and scream at her. I hate myself afterwards. I did this in my marriage and with my daughter. I get so mad when women dismiss me or ignore me."

In therapy, Dave continued to address his issues of emotional enmeshment with his mother. Recognizing the psychological connection between seeking his mother's approval and feeling defective allowed Dave to approach women and view relationships without needing to be "good enough." Dave, for fear of becoming emotional fused and codependent with women, had chosen to stay away from romantic relationships. He increasingly became aware of how his self-doubt would cause him to help "save" his wife, girlfriends, and mother. Trying to "save" and emotionally "fix" his mother was the primary source of Dave's childhood, and then adult, rage and anger. The conversation below is a sample of the new insight Dave found about his shame, codependency, and anger.

Dr. P: "How are you doing with tolerating your feelings of shame when you don't engage your mother's requests for help?"

Dave: "It's hard not to run in and fix her. I feel a lot of tension, dread, and doom that something bad is going to happen. Then nothing happens other than me feeling relieved and more relaxed. I never saw the connection between my shame and being a rescuer as a big source of my anger. I just started dating a few weeks ago. I have gotten so much of my self-esteem and self-worth from rescuing people."

Codependent relationships leave the victim feeling devalued, emotionally starved, and with very little self-worth.

Scenario 4: I Am a Good Person

Emily, whom we met in chapter five, was hospitalized for suicidal ideations. She was placed in a psychiatric eating disorders clinic for sixty days. During this therapeutic time, Emily began to understand her self-loathing issues, her insecure emotional connections, and the shame-based patterns in all her relationships. Emily came to see me as part of her outpatient treatment and her continuing personal growth.

Emily told me,

You know Dr. P, I was never suicidal or ever going to kill myself. I just didn't know how to get rid of this ball of anger, bad feelings, and fear in my stomach. I have carried around this fear that no one really liked me or was really my friend. When my girlfriend became a "mean girl" [emotional bully] to me, my whole world crashed. I didn't realize how much I was emotionally dependent on my social media popularity. I then would starve myself to look cute and attractive to guys. My drinking was out of control, with weekly blackouts and random sexual hookups. In the hospital, the staff took away my phone, laptop, and iPad. We had no internet or connection to the outside world. It was the first time in way too many years that I wasn't on my phone or checking my social media posts.

Dr. P: "What did you began to notice about yourself with no distractions?"

Emily: "Wow, at first I felt like a heroin addict looking for my emotional fix. It took me ten full days to stop obsessing about my life on the internet. Around day eleven, I started to calm down and feel more grounded and stable. I noticed how much time I spent running away from myself and my emotions and was hiding with food and drugs. I never really believed the shame idea until I had to be with myself every day for the next fifty days!"

Dr. P: "What did you notice about your cycle of shame?"

Emily: "I remembered after about three weeks that I buried my sexual abuse history. We were in group therapy and another girl was talking about her sexual abuse at age ten and how she ate her feelings. I had a flashback about my incident and how my family dismissed it as a nonevent. I remember feeling incredibly enraged at my mother for not believing me and ignoring the truth. After that day, I have never trusted myself or what I thought or felt. I was also very ashamed of being sexually abused [the perpetrator died seven years earlier]. I know it's odd, but I have felt guilty and embarrassed about it."

Dr. P: "Do you see the connection between your addictive need to be noticed and your abuse history?"

Emily: "Yes. I have been trying to get everyone's approval and never giving it to myself. I struggle with liking myself and not feeling like the ugly one in my friend group. [Emily has distorted perception of herself.] I am trying to stop my need to be needed with my friends. I am more focused on connecting emotionally and talking about real issues, not how many followers I get on my social media site. This might be the first time I haven't been worried about my popularity, looks, or what people are thinking of me. It's very odd but very refreshing not to be worried about everyone's opinion of me."

What did we see from these relationship scenarios? Codependency is always seeking to fix all the gaps in one's life by first fixing the other person. The problem is that all the needs, desires, and hopes of the codependent adult are ignored and dismissed in service of helping the other partner first. The relationship isn't equitable, balanced, or functional. One person is the adult, and the other person is an approval-seeking child.

Debbie, Eric, Dave, and Emily couldn't be the people pleasers, the blamed ones, and the only cause for their relationship dysfunctions. It's impossible for one person to be the sole cause of all the issues in their relationship. The codependent relationship style of always seeking approval and pleasing others to their own detriment is a formula for pain and suffering in any relationship. The four scenarios above painfully point out the great intentions of the shame-filled, codependent partner who is trying to play both sides of the tennis court. Every high-functioning relationship requires both individuals to meet and develop their own balance.

The Game of Tennis: Player 1—Shame/Codependent Relationship Control, Player 2—You

The game of tennis is a wonderful metaphorical illustration of how shame and codependency directs your relationship style. Tennis is a game that requires two players (at minimum) to hit the ball back and forth to each other. In order to play the relationship game of tennis, you must be on one side of the court, and the other player must be on the other side of the court. The psychological premise behind this metaphor is that in any type of relationship you can't handle both sides of the relationship. You are 100 percent responsible for your side of the court (i.e., relationship), while your partner must be 100 percent responsible for their own side of the court. Anything less than 100 percent participation on either side of the relationship will, over time, create an emotionally imbalanced, selfish, and exhausting dynamic.

> *Codependent behaviors require that one partner do all of the relationship work.*

Shame whispers to you that unless you play both sides of the relationship you will not be loved, accepted, or appreciated. The primary reason for a person trying to carry more than their share in relationships is their core self-belief of not being good enough, of being flawed and unworthy. A common shame myth is that if you don't take all the responsibility for your partner then you aren't a loving,

caring, and sensitive person. This deceptive myth and the dysfunctional pattern of shaming relationships is the primary reason these
relationships ultimately all become nonfunctional. Loving, caring,
mutually supportive relationships can't survive with imbalance, self-
centeredness, and blame or shame. Shame-based codependency is
a solo game of tennis you try to play in your relationships, hoping
that your partner will eventually participate to the same degree that
you do. The problem is that one person (you) over-functions and
the other (your partner) under-functions. When shame is involved,
the relationship scales of love, support, concern, and care are never
balanced. The unconscious unbalanced dynamic is something that
both participants unspokenly agree upon. All four scenarios above
are examples of someone trying to play both sides of the relationship
court and ultimately resenting their partner for it.

> *Tennis is never played as a solo experi-*
> *ence, and neither are relationships. It takes*
> *two people to fully participate in a healthy*
> *relationship.*

There are many important relationship strategies to metaphori-
cally hitting the ball over the net while staying within the lines of love
and respect. The basic idea is to hit the ball to your partner and then
let them hit it back to you, not run to the other side of the court and
hit the ball back for them—right? This sounds ridiculous but it's how
shame and codependency fundamentally operate in your relationship
world. The lack of emotional, psychological, and physical boundaries
allows you to play both sides of the court to your own peril. No one
really wants to play both sides of the court with their partner, family,
colleagues, or children. The amount of worry, loss of control, fear, and
self-loathing that is required to be two-players at once is exhausting.
Common sense would dictate that playing for everyone else isn't a
good relationship style or productive long-term strategy. Ultimately,
codependent relationships are impossible to maintain.

No one can play both sides of a tennis "rela-
tionship" game without eventually feeling
resentment, anger, and betrayal.

It makes sense that figuratively running back and forth to keep all your relationships working is impossible to maintain long-term. The four scenarios above all point to, in this analogy, an imbalanced tennis game, filled with shame and no genuine psychological safety within relationships. The psychological energy required to take care of all the people in your life with no regard for your own thoughts, feelings, and emotions creates a never-ending cycle of despair. The codependent behavior has many unconscious motivations, such as a longing for self-acceptance, feeling loved, and finally being "good enough." Codependency is an endless cycle of placating the other person and hoping they will fully accept and love you. The problem is that unless a person has developed his own individual sense of self-love, self-acceptance, and self-forgiveness *it's impossible for someone else to develop it for them.* It's our own responsibility to grow and to create our own sense of self that will resist and dismiss all the varieties of shame-based beliefs and behaviors. Before we discuss some common relationship styles, we need to revisit the idea of how emotional boundaries are the first line of defense in stopping your cycle of codependency. No relationship can function properly without clear-cut boundaries.

Emotional Boundaries

The importance of boundaries in all facets of life is irrefutable. Without boundaries we can't endure physically, psychologically, or relationally. Our physical body has boundaries that allow us to survive in the world. Countries go to war over land rights and boundary disputes. There is no sport, business, or relationship in which boundaries and limit setting aren't needed. Knowing, under-standing, and establishing your boundaries in your relationships is paramount to healing and creating the life you desire. Having physical boundaries for yourself and others is a critical piece of your life and well-being. Setting emotional and psychological boundaries means applying your values, desires, and sense of self-worth to your relationships. The things you are willing to tolerate, and the ways you involve yourself emotionally in life, are all facets of your personal limits and related to your sense of self-worth. Developing your core values and sense of self automatically helps you understand the purpose of boundaries and put them into use. One of the major measurements of mental health is having clear and strong personal boundaries. In chapter 4, we discussed seven common emotional triggers and ways that shame functions in your life when there are no boundaries and limits. Developing emotional boundaries with yourself and others, and understanding their purpose, is the pathway to healing and to resolving your shame factor. Shame has no boundaries and no respect for your desires, wants, and needs. You are the only one, not your partner or friends, who can develop your own set of emotional, psychological, and physical boundaries.

Emotional boundaries can be defined as follows:

> Emotional boundaries (EB) are the psychological, emotional, and intellectual ability to see, experience, and have your own ideas, opinions, and actions separate and apart from others. You can feel empathy for another without becoming the other person. You can tolerate disapproval without reconfiguring your life to placate the situation or relationship.

Understanding and implementing emotional boundaries stops the cycle of codependency and exposes your shame factor relationship style. A prime example of not having EBs is seen when your partner, colleagues, family, and children demand, verbally or nonverbally, that you play both sides of the court in the relationship. Without EBs, you would automatically assume that it was your responsibility to be more concerned about others' lives than your own. Unclear EBs result in not being able to express your opinion, voice your concerns, or take action on your own behalf. Emotional enmeshment, when your emotions are fused with those of another person, is a symptom of undeveloped EBs with yourself and others. We will discuss these self-acceptance issues in section III and talk about how to develop a core sense of self with clear emotional boundaries. When a partner, friend, parent, or colleague lacks EBs between them and their partner it allows shame-based codependent relationships to grow and develop. We are now going to see how the shame-driven codependent style works in five different types of relationships.

FIVE COMMON RELATIONSHIP STYLES AND THE SHAME FACTOR

> *Conflict cannot survive without your participation.*
> —Dr. Wayne Dyer, *Everyday Wisdom*, 1993

- Addictive Relationships
- Noncommittal Distant Relationships
- Placating Relationships
- On-Again, Off-Again Relationships
- Secure Relationships

This above list includes some of the most common relationship styles. Our purpose here is to uncover, expose, and observe the insidious nature that shame-codependency has in each type of relationship, regardless of the circumstances. Each style typifies a pattern of relating that can be changed and improved over time. No relationship style is either "good" or "bad." Our purpose is rather to discover some of the strengths (security) and weakness (shame) inherent in your own style of relating. Someone can operate in all five styles in five different settings. For instance, Eric, from our scenario above, is very secure in his relationships at work. He is overly codependent and placating with his wife and children at home. Eric has an on-again, off-again ambivalent relationship with his mother (his father died seven years ago) and a noncommittal distant relationship with his two older brothers. Eric has an addictive relationship with his use of the internet, where he is always searching for some emotional security and comfort for stressful circumstances in his life. He is keenly aware of the emotional undercurrents of shame and codependency in all his relationships. Below is a brief description of how shame and codependency can silently operate in each of these different relationship styles.

Addictive Relationships

Addictive relationships occur, for example, when two teenagers, or adults, cannot handle being apart or separated emotionally, physically, or psychologically. The two individuals cling to each other as though they were actually a single person, afraid of being alone again in the world. At the beginning, the relationship takes off like a rocket, feelings of love are like a drug. The two people in the relationship fuse into one being that can't tolerate separation or any type of emotional space. The two people act as one person, living, working, eating, and sleeping together. The couple's first date lasts six months, with no emotional space to individually process the relationship—or the new job, new friend, or other new change. The inner emptiness that had been present is no longer felt or active. The shame and codependency is all mixed together in an emotional blender of fun, empowerment, sex, and recklessness. The problem is that this type of relationship is not sustainable in the long term; any type of addictive relationship is impossible to maintain and it will eventually crash into the brick wall of shame and codependency. Often, these types of addictive relationships are called "camp crushes" because they start quickly and intensely and end with the same force in a short period of time, after a week or a month, and with tremendous disappointment.

The relationship feels like a natural high, allowing the couple to transcend their prior self-doubts, shame, and emotional emptiness. This intense style of attachment can be described as "fused" or "enmeshed." The high energy created by the fusing together of the people in the relationship is legitimate and real. This incredible feeling of finally having found your "soulmate," your other half, is a psychological fulfillment of the secret wish to heal your childhood abandonment and shame issues. Addictive relationships are attempts to avoid and skip over the uncomfortable, fearful feelings of being ignored, dismissed, or neglected again. These painful feelings of shame and fear are all wiped away by the couple's intense emotional connection and fusing. The two individuals can meet in any situation or circumstance. Addictive relationships occur in all types of settings, although they are most usually found in romantic or marriage connections. The euphoria of connecting with someone who accepts you, understands you, and loves you is wonderful. The lack of personal or emotional boundaries are ignored for the sake of this new love and its importance in your life.

> *Like a strong drug, love in an addictive relationship can temporarily mask the effects of shame, which needs time and patience to truly heal.*

After the initial rush of emotion, addictive relationships have difficulty allowing either of the two individuals to grow and evolve. The magnetic charge in an addictive relationship is the fun new sex partner or new adventure, and in time this becomes routine and stale. It's impossible to develop a mutual loving relationship when there is only one emotional heart and one cognitive theme being shared between two people. It takes two complete people to build any type of relationship. Addictive relationships are time-limited, short-term fixes to long-term challenges. The unspoken wish to heal all the flawed, broken and wounded parts below the surface of a persons' life can't be achieved. The relationship ends as quickly as it started. Personal transformation takes time and patience; addictive relationships aren't conducive to the process of growth, which needs stability and persistence. The chronic need to be emotionally stimulated and fused does not work with the need for separation and mutual understanding.

> *The breaking-up process in addictive relationships reactivates unresolved childhood feelings of inadequacy and damage.*

The collateral psychological damage when an addictive relationship ends—with a sudden breakup, job loss, or loss of a new friendship—is devastating and heartbreaking. All the old issues of the person's shame and codependency rush back in and are overwhelming and very depressing. The emotional withdrawal from this intense psychological connection is fueled by all the unresolved shame issues and fears of abandonment. The breakup, however, can serve as an opportunity to finally address your shame issues, heal your wounded inner child, and develop emotional stability within. The challenge comes because addictive relationships are fun and feel good for a while, acting as a quick emotional fix to avoid the deeper issues of shame and codependency.

Noncommittal Distant Relationships

This style of relating is at the opposite end of the relationship spectrum from the addictive style. Instead of the impulsive supercharged kind of fusing and enmeshment involved in addictive relationships, this style is methodical, perfunctory, and very thought-out. The relationship is more cognitive, cerebral, and intellectual. The impulsive and rush of love is replaced with an intellectual experience over any emotional or feeling-based experience. The noncommittal type of relationship functions in many professional, work, social, personal, family, and marriage connections. The important element of this style is the avoidance of vulnerability and any type of strong emotional expression. The adrenaline rush of love is replaced with an emotionally cool and level-headed approach to intimacy and bonding. The personal communication is infrequent and without any pattern or obvious interest on the part of either person in the relationship. The distant style could be called the "survivor" style because of its protective emotionally uninvolved pattern. Men and women in these relationships are typically very polite and very guarded against revealing or exposing any emotional interest, wound, or shame issues.

Emotional distance doesn't breed safety in relationships, it only breeds an avoidance of close emotional connections.

The distant style in a romantic and marriage relationship can be functional but has no passion or empathy between the partners. The relationship is emotionally and psychologically distant, and those in such a relationship guard against any mentally heated exchanges for fear of one party being engulfed, suffocated, or annihilated. The ingrained habit of thinking through emotional experiences gives the illusion of control and safety. The built-in walls of avoidance, prohibiting any type of close emotional heartfelt bonds, are the result of severe unresolved trauma. A person in such a relationship has an unconscious terror of being engulfed and powerless again in any relationship.

The shame involved in hiding the childhood or adult trauma in any relationship compounds the lack of intimacy for the emotionally resistant and "cut-off" man or woman. For a person like this, shame and codependency can mean finding a partner, friend, or family member who will unconsciously express all of his emotions and vulnerability for him. His need to have people around him who are emotionally expressive is both scary and, simultaneously, something he deeply desires. The internal conflict between emotional expression and psychological suppression is ongoing. Distant noncommittal relationships are cool, aloof, and unfulfilling for both parties. The lack of nurturing, lack of emotional connection, and lack of passion over time becomes a major cause of the relationship ending. Shame, codependency, and a fear of losing control are major factors in why a person may embrace a distant style of relationships.

Placating Relationships

Placating relationships, by nature, mean that there is a unilateral focus by one person on the other person. The reciprocity of giving and receiving isn't part of this style. The focus, emotional energy, needs, and desires of one person control the other person's decisions, self-esteem, and well-being. There is no disguise or illusion that this relationship is out of balance and very one-sided. Both parties have an unspoken agreement about the dynamic of the relationship in order to potentially have their own needs met. This arrangement can exist in the workplace, within a family (between adult children and their parents), in marriage, and in friendships. The person who is in the placating position in the relationship finds fulfillment through constantly giving to the other party in hopes of feeling good enough. The problem, however, is that neither party has any concern for the well-being of the giver, whose actions work to their own detriment. This relationship style is the classic example of the self-defeating nature of shame. The placating style is problematic due to its under-lying sense of emotional deprivation in both parties.

> *Shame can't be hidden in a relationship;*
> *eventually all the irrational beliefs and fears*
> *are exposed, despite efforts to the contrary.*

The placating relationship style is based on the inequality of the partners, with one person always being in the giving position and the other always being in the taking position. The giving partner's anxiety about not being good enough and her fears of upsetting the other partner controls the relationship. Neither partner wants to know or understand the awful shame feelings that the other person carries and hides. The chronic imbalance helps to keep the relationship superficial and in denial about any problems and challenges. The partners unconsciously share the burden of concealing each other's shame and codependency. Their unspoken fear is that one person's shame will be discovered, which would then reveal the other person's flaws as well. The sooner the emotional bond is formed, the sooner the fear of being discovered as a fraud is assuaged—though it's a temporary fix. The recurring problem with this style of relating is that the core sense of shame and insecurity in both individuals doesn't go away with new activities, crisis, or by blaming the other. The tension and anxiety of shame's irrational beliefs begin to appear over time, regardless of the denial, avoidance, and amnesia of the people involved. Both parties are constantly fearful that their "secret" will come out and that they will be exposed and humiliated as other than who they had originally presented themselves. The amount of emotional energy that is expended to keep one's shame hidden ends up being greater than the amount of energy that would have been spent in developing a safe secure connection. The sense of desperation a person feels when trying to hide his shame is only matched by the need to be perfect so that no one sees anything negative about him.

On-Again, Off-Again Relationships

On-again, off-again relationships are when one partner makes a very strong verbal, physical, mental, and emotional connection with the other, while, the next morning, that same person might do exactly the opposite, being distant, cool, and aloof. The other person in the relationship—partner, friend, colleague, or child—has no idea why the relationship has changed. Whatever explanation is given by the on-again, off-again partner has nothing to do with the real underlying reason for her sudden psychological distance or closeness. The partner creating the distance, drama, and chaos has a shame codependency pattern of merging and then withdrawing whenever her strong feelings or emotions are triggered. This relationship is very different from the other styles we have discussed because it can develop a genuine connection full of hope and promise. The inability to tolerate the emotional closeness, required trust, and fear of intimacy and exposure drives this erratic style. The inability to trust another person is one of the primary problems with this relationship pattern. The instability in this relationship prevents intimate, stable, consistent, and secure bonds from being established.

> *Emotional distance is a form of shame that alienates partners from each other. Intimacy and shame are incompatible.*

Over time, the relationships of the on-again, off-again person become merely a series of intermittent random connections. The possibility of developing safe, secure, and consistent relationships is lost whenever his shame and childhood trauma fear are triggered. This person deeply wants a significant connection but he can't tolerate his unconscious need for safety and distance. His reflex to retreat to a distance combined with his craving for a loving, stable relationship is the burden this relationship creates for those within it. The people in this type of shame cycle feel like there is a glass wall between them. They can see each other but can't touch or feel the other person. The glass wall is shame covered up the fear of intimacy.

> *Emotional intimacy can trigger unresolved childhood trauma and fears of feeling emotionally trapped.*

The ongoing behavior by the on-again, off-again partner is fueled by her unspoken fear of being emotionally engulfed, swallowed up, and completely submerged by the other person. Her fears of emotional intimacy are rooted in her unresolved individuation separation process in her childhood relationship with her parents. As a young child, such a person was overwhelmed by her parent, emotionally, psychologically, and many times physically. As an adult, her sense of self is very fragile and she can only tolerate so much closeness before she must pull away as a defensive measure against being engulfed emotionally.

Secure Relationships

The four previous relationship styles all have some elements of a secure, safe, stable, and loving connection. One of the main differences between a secure relationship and the other styles is the absence of emotional upheaval, self-created drama, and issues surrounding unresolved old trauma. The men and women with a secure and stable style of relating all have a sense of their own individuality, and psychologically they have sufficiently separated from their families of origin. Security is a result of two individuals coming together to form a friendship, not to heal their own hidden childhood terrors. The emotional and psychological development of each person allows for the natural progression of a positive relationship. Shame has no role or active place among partners with this style of bonding, attachment, and intimacy. It's possible to be shame-free and not have terrible fears lurking inside of you. Shame can't coexist with intimacy and vulnerability to any degree or in any circumstance. Just as light dispels darkness, vulnerability exposes the secret world of shame.

> *Secure relationships embrace conflict as a vehicle for deeper intimacy and understanding.*

Individuals who form secure attachments with themselves and others allow their friends, colleagues, partners, and children to have their own opinions, needs, desires, and goals. Conflict, misunderstandings, and mood swings aren't viewed as personal attacks or some type of emotional abandonment. The emotional boundaries of this style offer safety and security. The natural differences between those in a relationship are encouraged, not viewed as a threat or an act of betrayal. These relationships are based on mutual respect, empathy, and love. People in such a relationship understand that their connection won't be only rainbows and unicorns dancing in the backyard as the couple holds hand sipping tea. Each partner knows from previous experiences the emotional pitfalls of the other four styles and chooses to embrace this secure relationship style. The importance of being an individual in this type of relationship style is encouraged, fostered, and understood. The natural emotional flow of acceptance, love, and understanding for one another breeds security and safety. The lack of terror, emotional instability, anger, fear, and arguing between the parties allows for the growth of empathy, loving gestures, and positive psychological support. This style has room for positive actions and fun experiences granted by having a good friend, a lover, and relationships that can be trusted.

The secure style of attachment is what the movie industry has historically depicted as magical. The partners in these relationships know that the love, support, and "magic" is the result of emotional growth, joint resolution of painful shame issues, and a cornerstone to heal and grow—something we can all strive for and attain.

CLOSING THOUGHTS

Shame and codependency are a serious impairment to relationship happiness, personal fulfillment, and the development of secure loving connections. I know we have covered a lot of material about the silent terrorist—shame—and its role in relationships. The purpose of our discussion has been to reveal blind spots that you might have had about your shame and codependency behaviors. Understanding all the different ways shame negatively impacts you, your relationships, and your entire life is a major step toward emotional and psychological happiness and peace of mind. No one I know personally or professionally (myself included) is exempt from shame's insidious influence in their relationships. I have met many who claim they have no placating issues, for example, until a closer examination of their relationships reveals an astonishing pattern of codependency mixed with shame.

> *To rid yourself of old patterns, focus all your energy not on struggling with the old, but on building the new.*
> —Dan Millman, *Way of the Peaceful Warrior: A Book That Changes Lives*, 1980

The three quotes at the beginning of this chapter are reminders of the importance of you, your relationships, and shame's self-defeating role in your life. Each of those statements point to the importance of focusing on the new and letting go of the past. Shame is the most powerful, and the most common, type of dysfunction in relationships. The shame operating system of codependency keeps its victim locked into a continuous cycle of fear, self-doubt, and dread. For instance, earlier we saw in the four vignettes the different ways that shame and codependency exist together to create a steel bond of relationship despair.

The four different dysfunctional styles of relationships are all symptoms and signs of a codependent template. These styles of relating are all attempts to conceal and keep everyone away from a person's greatest fears and self-doubts. Even among those who, on the surface, appear unaffected, shame can be a very active force and presence in people's relationships. The codependent element of shame is a psychologically debilitating pattern that must be exposed and healed. The comfort, hope, and belief of having peaceful, fulfilling relationships starts with you. I can't emphasize enough the developmental roadblock that shame is when it comes to individually developing your highest and best self. Shame clouds, distorts, and redirects personal growth into personal misery and despair. As we end this chapter, consider the following eleven questions as a personal report card of how your shame factor is operating today in your relationship world. Focus on today, not on your past relationships or prior disappointments.

Eleven Common Shame and Codependency Questions for Relationships

1. Am I always worried about my partner's mood?
2. Do I spend large amounts of emotional energy worrying about my partner's reactions?
3. Am I uncomfortable with emotional intimacy?
4. Do I resent doing everything in the relationship yet I like the control?
5. Do I have a sense of dread and worry about something bad happening in my relationship?
6. Do I allow myself to be verbally devalued, blamed, and/or insulted?
7. Do I have boundary issues in my relationships?
8. Does my partner rage at me and accuse me of being unsupportive of him or her?
9. Do I feel that everything is my fault?
10. Do I base my happiness on my partner's mood?
11. Am I afraid to be away from or separated from my partner?

These eleven questions are the heart and soul of the shame and codependency relationship dynamic. Accepting that you might have some shame-codependency relationship patterns isn't a problem. The problem is the denial, avoidance, and amnesia that often surrounds these dysfunctional behaviors. Shame corrodes and impairs loving men and women from experiencing the breadth and depth of secure, stable, mutually supportive relationships. In the next section, we are going to resolve your shame dilemma with insightful psychological tools, wisdom, and the power of practical change. This chapter gave an overview of just some of the insidious roles shame plays—and will always play until you expose it. The two quotes below are reminders to be present and outspoken in your relationships today.

I've had a lot of worries in my life, most of which never happened.

—attributed to Mark Twain

The most courageous act is still to think for yourself. Aloud.
—Coco Chanel, as quoted in *Believing in Ourselves*, by Armand Eisen, 1992

HEALING THE BIG SPLIT IN YOU AND YOUR OTHER SELF

The man who never alters his opinion is like standing water, and breeds reptiles of the mind.
—William Blake,
The Marriage of Heaven and Hell, 1790

Water is fluid, soft, and yielding but water will wear away rock, which is rigid and cannot yield. As a rule, whatever is fluid, soft and yielding will overcome whatever is rigid and hard. This is another paradox: What is soft is strong.
—Lao Tzu, *Tao Te Ching*, 600 BCE

When children know uniqueness is respected, they are more likely to put theirs to use.
—Dr. Dorothy Corkille Briggs, as quoted in
Awakening Your Child's Natural Genius,
by Thomas Armstrong, 1991

CHAPTER 9

NO MORE SECRETS: YOUR OWN HEALING EXPOSURE PROCESS— VIEWING ALL THE PARTS OF YOUR LIFE FROM 10,000 FEET

Progress is not achieved by luck or accident, but by working on yourself daily.

—Epictetus, *Discourses*, Book 3, 108 CE

Instead of saying, "I am damaged, I am broken, I have trust issues," say, "I am healing, I am rediscovering myself, I am starting over," positive self-talk.

—Horacio Jones

Your vision will become clear only when you look into your heart. Who looks outside, dreams; who looks inside, awakens.

—attributed to Carl Jung

There is an ongoing idea and theme throughout this book, and it echoes in the three quotes at the beginning of this section and the three at the beginning of this chapter. That theme, of course, is shame and how you deal with it. Regardless of how overwhelmed or powerless you feel or you think you are, you have the ability within to change, to stop and resolve your old emotional and behavioral cycles of shame, self-doubt, and self-loathing. Exposing and healing the core of your shame belief and shame identity is the goal of this section and the following chapters. You are going to discover who you truly are, reunite and reconnect to your healthy core self. One of the fundamental operating principles of all the many types of psychological approaches and theories is to assist an individual in reclaiming the parts of his personality he has abandoned, rejected, or dismissed. The process of integrating, developing, and establishing your own identity is referred to as the separation-individuation process, also known as developing self-acceptance, self-forgiveness, and a core sense of self.[1]

When you form your own identity primarily during childhood and adolescence, you learn how to establish relationships with other individuals. Without a formed identity, however, and with a lack of self-acceptance, a person will try to create their identity within another person. We know from chapter 8 what an emotionally painful and seemingly impossible task a selfless relationship can be. Attempting to create your own individuality in another person is a self-defeating process filled with despair, disappointment, and shaming codependent relationships.

WHAT ARE INDIVIDUATION, SELF-ACCEPTANCE, AND A CORE SENSE OF SELF?

In my practice over the last thirty years, I have been asked one type of question more often than any other. These questions are about identity and who and what a person is. These aren't esoteric questions or some vague intellectual exercise. People probe for answers with a sincere hope that they can find practical solutions leading to personal growth and lasting change. These types of questions point to the psychological development process called separation-individuation. I don't mean to sound dry or too academic; the answers to such questions are the pillars of our daily lives, our emotional connections, and ways we truly think and feel about ourselves. Shame, hopelessness, and despair block the natural developmental process of self-discovery, and this internal resistance to self-acceptance is a major problem.

The psychological base of a child's personal identity has been established by fourteen to eighteen years of age. If the base hasn't been built with more positive and competence beliefs than negative and shame beliefs, the child becomes adult who feels insecure and full of self-doubt. During adolescence, you form your core sense of who you are, what your place is in your family, your school, and the world, and how you act in and fit into various situations and circumstances. Many of your long-term life decisions, such as college, career, goals, and whether you want to marry and have children developing at this time. Shame aborts this important process with a barrage of self-doubt, self-loathing, and self-hatred beliefs. These negative emotions are in direct opposition and conflict with self-acceptance. All the various descriptions for self-acceptance, such as self-worth, self-esteem, and self-forgiveness, all refer to the same concept—having positive feelings about yourself. None of these constructive "self" terms work without a core sense of "self" within you.

> *Self-love, self-respect, self-worth. There is a reason they all start with, "self." You cannot find them in anyone else.*
> —Unknown

The negative voice, beliefs, and self-loathing feelings all hamper the natural development of your individuality into your thirties, forties, fifties, sixties, seventies, and beyond. As we discussed earlier in the book, your core beliefs about yourself were first planted within you from birth to around age five. The second major development stage for your individuality and core self was from about ten to seventeen years old. Let's break down the idea of what it means to have a positive self-image, self-acceptance, and positive internal picture of yourself (core self)? Below are some questions that are all connected to your personal identity, core self, and self-acceptance.

- What's individuality?
- What does self-acceptance feel like?
- How do I accept myself?
- What's the cure for feeling shame and being codependent?
- How can I individuate from my parents and partner?
- Can shame and codependency be healed in a marriage or other relationship?
- How can I accept myself when I don't like myself?
- Why do I have low self-esteem?
- Why do I feel insecure around certain people?
- Can I become a self-reliant adult later in life?

These questions and others like them beg to be answered from a practical point of view, with hands-on applications and tools for implementation. We all want a healthy self-esteem, a strong core self, and unconditional self-acceptance, but how do you find that? Let's first define some critical terms necessary for rebuilding you: self-acceptance, separation-individuation, and core self.

Definition of Self-Acceptance

Self-Acceptance means having an understanding of your life goals, and having the ability to feel compassion and empathy for yourself and others. It means having the ability to see yourself as separate and apart from others, having placed psychological boundaries between yourself and other people. You have your own opinions, ideas, and feelings, and you understand that your life experiences are unique and personal. You accept your personal differences, understanding that your life journey is yours to decide and implement. You know that you are imperfect, lovable, and capable of giving and receiving love as well as loving yourself. You're always changing, and life is a fluid process of learning, experiencing, and healing. You are comfortable with conflict and differences of opinion.[2]

What this definition means to you at twenty-two years old is very different than what it means to you at thirty-six or at sixty-four years old. Each stage of your life is important and necessary to embrace as you live in it. Your self-acceptance process isn't finished when you're eighteen years old, but, rather, this is the beginning of a process that continues until you leave this life. Self-acceptance is never finished and it is constantly expanding as you gain new insights. The idea that you are always processing new personal information and embracing change allows for continual new experiences of compassion, empathy, and well-being. Your life is never finished experiencing your choices and relationships, with all their different elements. The section-opening quote by William Blake about how becoming closed-minded creates "reptiles of the mind," serves as a warning against stubbornly restricting your concept of "self," rather than allowing it to evolve or keep changing. The quote that follows Blake's, by Lao Tzu, is on the importance of remaining fluid, flexible, and soft rather than rigid, and the benefit provided by personal openness.

> *A lasting benefit of self-acceptance is that it naturally creates emotional clarity, purpose, and the courage and ability to take risks.*

Definition of Separation-Individuation

During adolescence and the later school years (ten to seventeen years old), young people start to create emotional, psychological, and physical distance from their parents, important role models, teachers, and relatives. The teenager's increased personal space allows them to become a separate entity from their parents; the boy or girl separates from and rejects their parents as a means to create psychological space to create and experience their own emotions, opinions, likes, dislikes, values, and goals. The teen is then able to experience themselves as an individual apart from their caretakers, and, ideally, their new identity is acknowledged by their family.

The teenager will find productive ways (e.g., new friends, new interests, and new activities) or counterproductive ways (e.g., reckless behavior, legal problems, escapism) to create emotional distance and psychological room to become their own person. The degree to which a teenager or young adult successfully develops their individuality is the same degree to which they build their core self and gain psychological material for self-acceptance. This stage is very difficult for parents and teens, as it can be loaded with conflict, arguing, and, sometimes, dangerous reactions to all the changes taking place. Change is inevitable, however, and all families, regardless of their relationships, struggle with this phase of life.

> *Creating emotional space is not a form of rejection; it allows the young adult to develop their core self.*

A teenager who is in the process of becoming a separate person, with his own thoughts, feelings, opinions, desires, and dreams, has a critical need for empathy, approval, and understanding from his parents. If a teenager or young adult—or forty-year-old son or daughter—has to keep arguing with their family for their own emotional space and opinions, the individuation process becomes a psychological tug of war for control between all the parties involved. A teenager may use countless unconscious strategies to create emotional and physical distance from his family, such as running away, reckless drug use, pregnancy, chronic arguing, threats of emotional abandonment, and physical violence. This phase is normal and age appropriate, but the ways teens may seek to create emotional and psychological leverage can seem endless for everyone involved.

When a person gains psychological space from her primary emotional connections, her core self is able to develop. There is a saying in development psychology: *No space, no self!* For teens, the urgent issue of separating from their parents typically becomes the flash point of family crisis and drama. Parents who can't emotionally tolerate their son or daughter becoming a separate person, begin a dysfunctional civil war. No one wins such an on-going war, and shame spreads like a flu virus, infecting both the parents and child. In my personal and professional experience, the relationship damage that frequently occurs between a young adult and her parents during this process can last for many years, or, in the worst cases, the relationship may be irreparably fractured.[3]

The incredible conflict involved in the individuation process is the reason that so many teens and parents try to skip over and avoid this natural process. However, neither dwelling in the conflict nor avoiding the situation entirely is a solution to the teenager's necessary process of personal identity formation. I can't overstate the fact that in my clinical practice I see adults in their forties, fifties, and sixties who are still trying to negotiate their individuation process. A compounding problem comes when these adults' own adolescents are reaching the point of their own individuation and self-discovery process and seeking their own core identity. It's never too early to individuate and create your own life, opinions, decisions, choices, and core values.

Giving teenagers the psychological support and space they need to understand the different roles and identities they might try on is important for their self-psychological formation. The negative and positive messages from parents are projected onto the teenager, showing them what their parents will embrace or reject. Being allowed to make different choices from the rest of the family builds a young adult's inner strength and motivation, giving them the confidence to pursue their own life goals. This natural process between parents and children (including adult children) is shame-free is when neither party views it as rejection or unloving behavior.

Definition of Your Core Self

Your core self is the psychological integration of all the different aspects, ideas, and desires you have. It's the center of your moral, behavioral, and emotional beliefs, and the hub of the opinions that direct your choices. Your self-acceptance is the extension of your core self's values, dreams, goals, and relationships, and your psychological base comes from your core self. It is your intuitive "gut" feeling that guides you in creating your life and all its choices, your inner voice of reason. All the different parts of your life are connected to your internal feelings, emotions, and beliefs; they are your internal map for living your life, your sense of integrity and internal life compass. All aspects of your self-acceptance, self-worth, and self-esteem are externalized parts of your core self; everyone has a core self, and whether you feel fulfillment or emptiness is a reflection of your core.[4]

Your core self is comprised of all the different aspects, behaviors, moods, desires, beliefs, thoughts, and emotions that you experience every day of your life. My clients tell me all the time that they don't feel or know their core self. I reassure them that they do have a core self, but that they just don't recognize the invaluable role it plays in their life. Recognizing and connecting to your core self is a powerful experience of self-acceptance. Knowing you have this untapped resource of strength and acceptance covered up with the mud of shame is the first step in your healing process. No amount of denial, avoidance, or amnesia can cause you to disconnect from the unlimited resource within you. In the next three chapters, we will discuss how changing your conscious connection to your core resolves your previous failed attempts at individuation. If a person has not successfully individuated and gotten in touch with their core self, their twenties and later years continued their ongoing internal development of shame, self-loathing, and self-doubt. Self-acceptance is the psychological medicine and cure for these insidious beliefs and personal fears. If the individuation cycle is hindered or resisted, it results in a ripple effect, with the developing self-shame belief system growing and reaching all areas of a person's life. All the decisions concerning your relationships, career, and physical health stem from your core self.

The experience of connecting to all of your lost parts is both a relief and very empowering. Feeling emotionally connected and psychologically unified is an ongoing process that reaps huge personal rewards. Let's now discuss how these three parts can work together for you today while removing your cycle of shame from within.

> *When there is no enemy within, the enemies outside cannot hurt you.*
>
> —African Proverb

GOING FROM THE OUTSIDE TO THE INSIDE OF YOU: YOUR JOURNEY WITHIN

A question that is usually asked in therapy eventually is, "Why don't I have a stronger sense of self, better self-acceptance, and self-love?" The short answer is that we aren't taught that liking and accepting ourselves and developing self-awareness should be a primary goal that leads to success rather a byproduct of success. Western culture views the primary key to success in life as achievement, accomplishments, and fulfilling your dreams. This formula is backward, though. We are taught that outward accomplishments and high achievements will result in your inward growth and success. However, great achievers throughout the ages all had a strong core self, a clear vision, and a positive self-image before they accomplished their goal. Both inward and outward growth are invaluable in life, but the secret of success is in the order of their importance.

> **All inward journeys start with fear and end with you feeling empowered.**

Recently, I was at dinner party and a professional man in his early forties (Alex) started talking to me. He asked me what life meant after a person had made money. I debated on how to answer the question, since it was a Saturday night and I didn't want to get too deep psychologically. The conversation went as follows:

Alex: "I feel empty a lot. I work hard but I am now questioning my goals."
Me: "You know, you have all the answers to your questions within you."
Alex: "How do you know that?"
Me: "I don't mean to sound rude, but how do you not know that? Your
    life is directed by your core self and sense of self-acceptance. All your
    choices and feelings are related to your internal self."
Alex: "I don't know about that. I don't spend much time thinking about
    myself or emotions."

The discussion stopped at that point, as Alex didn't say a word and walked outside. I felt empowered that I answered the question with the truth and not with some polite non-answer to a soul-searching query.

My discussion with Alex shows how outward achievement is usually considered superior to inward awareness. Achievement and self-awareness do not need to be opposed to each, though, but, rather the order of their importance needs to be switched. Without the inner tools of your ever-expanding self-accepting process, life becomes very empty, and achievement doesn't deliver the lasting inward satisfaction that you had dreamed of. Your core sense of self feeds your self-acceptance, which gives you courage and a sense of purpose to pursue your ambitions. The gasoline that will fuel your dreams comes from your core self and takes you out into the world.

YOUR FIVE-STEP ACCEPTANCE PROCESS

> *A ship is always safe at shore, but that is not what it's built for.*
> —John A. Shedd, *Salt from My Attic*, 1928

How do I accept myself? The answer to that question is in five parts. After exploring this timeless question, we will then discuss how to keep uncovering your self-imposed limitations, fears, and trauma. You are now ready to leave your harbor of familiarity of shame and self-doubt. You are now going to new places within yourself, gaining new realizations, uncovering your life map and purpose, and finding healing.

Step #1: Roadblocks within You

We now know and accept that shame inhibits and distorts our natural emotional development, core self, individuation process, and present-day self-acceptance. It's important to step back from all the layers of denial, avoidance, and fear that have kept your core sense of self covered in the mud of shame. When treasures are covered in mud, it's very difficult to believe or imagine that they are worthwhile things, that they represent new potential, being gifts and desires that you have never fully understood or accepted.

The first step in uncovering your lost self and wounded inner child and connecting to your best self starts with some honest soul-searching. Shame creates dense psychological roadblocks that we unconsciously support and keep in place for fear of something bad happening. It's now time to remove these outdated beliefs, uncover your core self, and allow your emotional terrorist to be expelled from your life. Your answers to the following questions aren't meant for public discussion but for you to consider as your paradigm shifts from shame to self-acceptance. That shift began long before you read this book or you would have never been drawn to it for your continued growth and healing. Think about the questions below and write your answers in the book. Your first thought is usually your most truthful and repressed one.

What is your earliest memory of being embarrassed or humiliated?

What is something that happened to you in the past or that you did that made you feel bad about yourself?

When was the first time you felt feelings of shame about yourself?

The answers to these questions are a thread of information showing how, why, and where you first started experiencing the awful feeling of shame.

What is a self-statement that you have made to yourself about yourself?

This sounds counterintuitive, but it's very important to know. Based on the first three questions, the answer to this question shows the result of feeling inferior and embarrassed, which has become part of the mud covering your core self. We start to write a shame-based self-narrative that fills in for our fear of individuation, negative self-acceptance, and fear of looking into our trauma.

What is one thing that you were ashamed of, embarrassed about, and/or felt inadequate about while growing up?

This question covers the early school years of your life. The sense of not feeling "normal" or like the rest of the kids is a common shame legacy. The discomfort of not "fitting in" can, as an adult, become a major source of isolation, loneliness, and anxiety. It's important to recall the way shame imprinted on you through your early attempts to blend into your peer group. The rage that is triggered in early peer-group rejections can block the natural development of accepting yourself as valuable and lovable. The fear of intimacy has its roots in early friendship disappointments.

What is one secret about yourself that you can't accept, avoid, or deny for fear of being abandoned, ashamed, or harshly judged?

We are as psychologically healthy as our secrets. The shame surrounding sexual, physical, and emotional abuse requires us not to look inward for fear of uncovering and re-experiencing our trauma and sense of powerlessness. Remember that courage comes through small steps and small tasks. Answering these questions is very courageous and will lead to new insights and emotional relief from your self-inflicted terror. Facing your shame is something everyone (myself included) avoids until they can't tolerate the emotional suffering any longer. Now is a good opportunity.

> What is something about yourself or your family that you keep hidden and concealed?

Talking candidly about your family, childhood, or siblings might feel like a betrayal or some form of disloyalty, but your self-exposure is a very powerful action that will start to wipe the mud of shame off your core self.

> What is there about your past, your trauma, or your abuse that feels beyond your comfort zone to discuss?

Nothing in your past is beyond the reach and grasp of healing, relief, and resolution. Take a hammer and break the glass wall that is keeping you from connecting to your core self. We discussed in chapter 5 the six life circumstances we all face and manage. One of these six areas is a current trigger of your shame, embarrassment, and terror. Your life is bigger than any one shame-based belief, action, or thought. These circumstances are the challenges through which your self-acceptance becomes an action and not just a theory. Later in this chapter we will discuss how to rewrite your personal narrative regarding your challenges.

> *It's rigged—everything in your favor.*
> —Rumi, *Love Poems from God*,
> translated by Daniel Ladinski, 2002

Step #2: No Perfectionism—Life Is Messy

Perfectionist behavior is a form of self-loathing and personal disdain. My obsessive-compulsive clients hate when I remind them that their healing and relief means living life without perfection. Clearing away the mud and personal debris from your core self through the self-acceptance process means learning how to be comfortable with being perfectly imperfect. Perfectionism is a severe form of self-loathing based on the feeling that you will be unlovable unless you are perfect. The internal tension of accepting, acknowledging, and allowing yourself to see your mistakes, wrong turns, and miscues is life changing. Shame can't function or survive in a non-perfectionist personal belief system. Your inner judge, critic, and hunter is suddenly unemployed and has lost control of you.

> *Shame, however, corrodes the very part of us that believes we are capable of change.*
> —Brené Brown, *Dare to Lead*, 2018

Exposing the irrational belief of perfectionism is liberating and empowering. The shame factor drives the chronic fear of being discovered as not being good enough but rather being a fraud and an imposter. The quote above by Brené Brown underlines the deceptive distortion shame creates in our heart and souls by telling us we can never change or feel better. Such fears started very early in your life and have, since then, restricted all aspects of your life. It's literally impossible to try something new, have an adventure, or make changes when you feel you must be perfect. Perfection equals paralysis of your core-self.

Perfectionism is a form of self-loathing.
No one is perfect and accepting that fact is
self-acceptance.

The questions below will help you to explore the beginnings of your conscious and unconscious terror of imperfection and loss of control, and how it affects you today.

What is your first memory of trying to be perfectly well-behaved, perfectly dressed, get perfect grades, etc.?

Did you get extra attention from your parents when you were perfect?

Did feeling loved and accepted hinge on your good behavior?

What happened when you couldn't be perfect?

How do you feel today if your situations aren't perfect or under your control?

Do you feel unlovable and not good enough if your partner sees your imperfections?

How much energy do you think you spend keeping a perfect public image and hiding your true self?

These questions point out the endless black emotional hole that you have no prospect of ever filling; there is no date of completion you can point to as the time when you will have finally met the demands of perfection. How did it feel to allow yourself some emotional space to consider the concept of being perfectly imperfect in your career, family, marriage, finances, health, and personal desires? Accepting the theory of imperfection is challenging because it means cracking the hard casing around yourself, the one you have put up to protect yourself against shame. The terror, secrets, fears, and emotional blackmail that shame uses to play on your fear of exposure is the old childhood need to be perfect. For brief moments of time you can feel "perfectly" safe, and then that feeling is gone in a flash. The endless pursuit of perfection is tiresome and psychologically debilitating.

Step #3: Accepting Change in Your Life—It's Not Personal

The resistance, stubbornness, and refusal to change is, in the mental health profession, considered major stumbling block to self-acceptance. The ingrained anxiety and terror of trying to control or avoid issues, or blame them on others, is rooted in self-doubt and self-loathing and shame.

Men and women who are terrified to face themselves and what's inside of them usually end up having to do so. Why?

The only time when your resistance is open to change is during emotional heartbreak, loss, psychological pain, and physical suffering.

When a person's comfort level falls below their level of suffering, that is the exact moment when change is in the air. The discussion later in this chapter regarding the six common shame areas of life demonstrates the practical process of change.

> *The gap between suffering and comfort*
> *creates emotional pain, which is the crisis*
> *that drives change.*

Comfort-Shame Level of the Status Quo

The term "hitting your bottom" describes exactly the time a person is most willing to change and make emotional room for new information. This change involves moving from self-loathing to self-acceptance. The emotional bridge across the Grand Canyon of despair and death is only crossed when a person's life is no longer working, and their pain exceeds their old ways of shame. Self-acceptance is on the other side of the gulf of all the self-limiting beliefs and behaviors. Facing your shame is a personal crisis because you are evicting its suffocating and painful hold on you. The six life challenges are all examples of when your pain can be transformed into positive change, leading to a new perspective of yourself and your entire world.

> *Hitting bottom: where desperation screams*
> *louder than your shame!*

The following questions are about going beyond your fear of change and your resistance to new personal insights about yourself. Emotional resistance occurs when you fear the loss of control. Being vulnerable and open-minded feels very unsafe and dangerous. However, by reading this book you are looking at your life and its present challenges, which means that your shame is something you are willing to address. All change leads to self-improvement, which is another form of self-acceptance and love.

What is holding you back from accepting yourself?

When did you first start to dislike yourself?

What do you do to keep love and self-acceptance away from your feelings?

Who told you that you are unlovable?

Who do you wish would love and accept you in your past or in the present?

It's now your time to let go and allow your life to unfold—let's move any and all self-loathing debris off your core self. If there is only one concept or idea you get from this book, let it be this one: What is within you that prevents you from living a calm, peaceful, emotionally stable life? You know the answer and the solution, and we will discuss this further in the chapters that follow.

Step #4: Taking Personal Responsibility for Your Life

You live the experience of self-acceptance when you take full responsibility for your actions, choices, and decisions—whether positive or negative. The personal power that comes with "owning" your side of the tennis court is liberating and emotionally freeing. Personal responsibility stops the cycle of shame, blaming others, and resentment. This step creates emotional space between you and your family or any source of conflict in your life. The flip side of the self-acceptance coin is self-responsibility. These two elements help create the fabric and core of who you are. No one has ever made a mistake by taking responsible for their life and all the paths they have chosen. When you view your life from the perspective of a participant rather than an observer the effect is transformational. Responsibility breeds emotional safety for your wounded inner child. The healthy, strong, and loving adult core self is making decisions and acting on your behalf.

Shame can't survive or exist any longer when a person takes responsibility for his actions. The deception of shame tells you that you're either a victim, a suspect, or prey for your invisible terrorist. Shame can never function with a participant who isn't willing to give his personal power away or skip out on his responsibilities. Taking responsibility for your career, children, finances, and love-life choices creates new insights about your needs and desires. Accepting the limits of your control—the fact that you can only control yourself—and not attempting to control others, changes your entire relationship world. Internally accepting what you can and can't do and can and can't control removes the power of shame in your life. Personal responsibility allows for trial and error with any new task you try.

> ### *Personal responsibility breeds self-confidence, self-esteem, and self-control.*

Being able to accept your actions, decisions, and choices gives you emotional and psychological freedom and a sense of fulfillment. The sense of inner peace that comes with being honest with yourself and others is the practical application of self-acceptance. Shame has no traction or grip when personal responsibility is part of an individual's daily life, choices, and ethics. The ability to create emotional boundaries, secure relationships, psychological stability, and self-love all come from looking inward and taking control. The anxiety of the unknown and fear about the future or past are dramatically reduced with being emotionally present and responsible for your actions and choices today.

The following questions explore how and why your personal view of yourself might change by taking personal responsibility. There are no right or wrong answers but, rather, consider the psychological paradigm shift from powerlessness and shame to feeling empowered with emotional freedom.

What is something that you can take responsibility for but haven't yet?

How would your marriage or romantic relationship change if you took personal responsibility for your part?

What situation or relationship feels beyond something you can be responsible for?

What would change in your life if you were to take responsibility for it?

Who do you give your personal power away to, and why?

Step #5: The Power of Empathy and Self-Forgiveness

Accepting the challenges in your life regardless of the outcomes requires both empathy and self-forgiveness. Forgiving yourself is a large part of all the self-acceptance steps we've already talk about. This step requires you to find compassion, empathy, and understanding for you and your past. Shame is toothless and rendered powerless when you embrace personal forgiveness, empathy, and self-understanding. The critical demeaning voice of shame can't coexist with empathy and compassion. Personal understanding is an important piece of the self-acceptance matrix that keeps shame and emotional terror outside and powerless.

> *Everything that irritates us about others can lead us to an understanding of ourselves.*
> —Carl Jung, *Memories, Dreams, Reflections*, 1961

All the world religions, psychological theories, and mental health methods know that having empathy for oneself is invaluable to the development of a stable core and positive self-acceptance. Empathy, forgiveness for yourself, develops emotional clarity and self-awareness. Carl Jung knew that what we don't like in others is what we don't like in ourselves. The degree to which we forgive ourselves and accept our life circumstances will be the same degree to which we do so with others.

The old fears of being abandoned, rejected, or dismissed have no leverage with self-forgiveness. When you have the ability to see yourself as separate from others, you have the ability not to personalize someone's actions as your fault. Empathy allows you to know what you are thinking and feeling within yourself first and secondly for someone else. The shame codependence dynamic can't function with self-forgiveness because of you have emotionally separated from the other person. Shame doesn't contribute to the development of an independent individual; its function is to create codependency wrapped into emotional terror and fear.

Empathy and self-forgiveness keeps you from losing yourself inside of your romantic relationships, family, and career.

When you accept your relationship roles, your limits of control, and your decisions, you are no longer under the power and control of placating and people pleasing. Your self-awareness keeps you from losing yourself inside of your partner or any relationship. The old relationship styles of fusing with your lover, emotional enmeshment, abusive relationships, and personal neglect are incompatible with empathy, accepting, and understanding your role in relationships. Forgiveness requires you to interact with and embrace all the different parts of yourself. Fragmentation of your disowned and wounded parts are now reconnected with personal empathy and forgiveness.

The shaming power of rejection and self-loathing can't thrive within an empathetic and understanding environment of self-awareness and forgiveness. Your life is now a full circle of inclusion— you, your core self, and self-acceptance and love. Excluding aspects of yourself isn't part of your self-forgiving personality any longer.

> *What lies behind us and what lies before us are tiny matters compared to what lies within us.*
>
> —Henry Stanley Haskins,
> *Meditations in Wall Street*, 1940

No one can control you, and you can't give your personal control away any longer. Self-forgiveness requires you to separate and individuate from the relationships in your life, past and present. This last step in the self-acceptance paradigm is critical because it completely neutralizes shame's old voice of gloom and impending doom. The fear of the past and trepidation about the future is replaced by accepting of your life and relationships today. Mr. Haskins knew that the true antidote to the power of shame was the power of self-acceptance. Self-acceptance allows you to function in the present moment in every aspect, area, and relationship in your life. Here are a few questions to consider about embracing self-forgiveness and personal empathy.

When I feel empathy for myself, what happens within me?

What do I forgive myself for?

What area or relationship in my life do I choose not to be judgmental or critical of today?

What does self-forgiveness mean in my marriage, family, and health?

Who in my life presently understands me?

Who do I understand and forgive in my life?

The power of self-acceptance renders shame completely powerless!

WRITING YOUR NEW SELF-ACCEPTING NARRATIVE: SIX OPPORTUNITIES

The psychological technique of Dialectical Behavior Therapy (DBT) is an exploration of the existence of opposites. In DBT people are taught that two seemingly opposite strategies can exist in any personal issue or challenge. The acceptance of the possibility of positive change is taught. The ingrained addictive behavior, shame, and repressed trauma can be exposed with a new option: self-acceptance. We are going to apply this cognitive behavioral theory to the six areas of your life, which we discussed in chapter 5 in regards to how they can be the current areas of shame and suffering. I am going to contrast the typical shaming voice in each area with the positive and unlimited resource of your core self-acceptance. Then you will write down your amended self-empowered core values concerning each, absent of shame's haunting presence and emotional threats. Write down what you want to see happen, your goals, desires, and the direction you see your life going regarding each aspect of your life. The absence of shame is a new feeling and experience, and it is still unfamiliar to you. Give yourself permission to step into the next chapter of your life.

1. Money, Finances, Wealth, and Career

Shaming Money Beliefs

You experience emotional deprivation; there is never enough and you aren't enough. You withhold your life from others; you can't have a successful career.

Self-Acceptance Beliefs

You experience generosity, abundance, emotional support, personal fulfillment, sharing, and helping others. You feel that you are enough, have sufficient abilities, and are capable of creating your career.

Your Self-Acceptance Money Script

What does your script look like without shame, emotional deprivation, and self-doubt controlling the outcome?

2. Love, Romance, Marriage, and Emotional Intimacy

Shaming Love and Intimacy Beliefs

You don't believe you deserve a good relationship. You see yourself as damaged goods. You believe you are inferior, not appealing to others, unworthy, and that there are no good men or women left to marry. You think that you are too old for a new relationship.

Self-Acceptance Love and Intimacy Beliefs

You enjoy intimate relationships. You are in mutual supportive relationships. You are capable of love. You understand that you are a work in progress. You like yourself; you have empathetic abilities, and you take care of your inner child. You choose who you want to love and be with. You are a complete individual who can share that person's life.

Your Love-Relationship Self-Accepting Script

What does your relationship look like without approval-seeking, placating, or codependence?

3. Childhood Family Issues

Shaming Family Issues Beliefs

You experience emotional enmeshment and no separate identity. You are emotionally fused with your mother or father. You have unresolved denial about sexual or physical trauma or a chaotic family background. You are embarrassed about your background. You feel like you can't have your own life because of your family. You believe that you will be a bad person if you leave them, and that your family can't exist without you.

Self-Accepting Family Beliefs

You are able to individuate. You accept and value your own opinions. You have emotional boundaries. You approve of yourself as an independent man or woman. You have a passion for your own goals, career, and adult life. You respect differences. You see your family as a starting point in your life, not the finish line. You make and value your own decisions. You accept your background as part of your growth into a loving, caring, and empathetic adult.

Your Self-Accepting Family Script

Are you a separate, loving person individuated from your family?

4. Present-Day Family

Shaming Current Family Beliefs

You tend to be people pleasing. You can't have a family because of your wounded inner child. You believe you are unlovable and too damaged to have children; you think your past trauma would destroy your kids if they ever found out about it. You try to keep everything concealed. You limit your emotional exposure. Your kids hate you. Your kids and your partner know your secrets.

Self-Accepting Current Family Beliefs

You are capable and competent of having a marriage, children, and a stable life. You either are or can be a great parent. You don't have to have children to be acceptable. Your sexual orientation is yours to disclose. You can have a safe and secure family unit. You can empower your kids to separate and individuate in their life.

Your Personal Self-Accepting Family Script

What do you want your family to be and/or become?

5. Your Health and Your Body Issues

Shaming Health and Body Beliefs

You hate your body. You believe you are ugly. You wish you had better health. You are being punished. You think that no one likes your appearance. You feel resentment and self-loathing. You believe you are better looking than everyone else; you feel entitlement. You hate to eat. You cut yourself. You cover yourself up with tattoos. You think about killing yourself. You think no one cares about you. You feel bad when you hurt your body, but you do it regardless.

Self-Accepting Health and Body Beliefs

You like your body and appearance. Your life matters to you. You make good choices; you don't abuse yourself. You fully accept your physical traits and gifts. You are healthy, whole, and complete. Your body is a gift to you. You enjoy sex. You allow yourself to take proper care of your day-to-day life. You accept your physical challenges.

Your Self-Accepting Health and Body Script

I chose to nurture and care for myself and my body; I fully accept myself and my body.

6. Loss and Death: The Unspeakable and the Unexposed:

Shaming Loss and Death Beliefs

You feel that your life is hopeless. You don't know what the purpose of your life is. You believe that no one would miss you or notice if you were gone. You hate living. You feel like nothing ever changes. You feel that you can't take another loss in your life. Your pain never stops. You believe you have no future. Everyone you love leaves you. You are always sad. You that if you were to disappear no one would care.

Self-Accepting Life Beliefs

You have goals, plans, and desires for your life. You accept that change is part of life. You can overcome your losses with new connections. You are grateful to be alive. You have gratitude for your life today. You accept, love, and care about your life and everyone in it. You can help others overcome their losses, fears, and sadness. You embrace all the facets of your life.

Your Self-Acceptance Life Script

What do you want your life to be and become? You are the author and editor of your life path.

CLOSING THOUGHTS: HAPPINESS AND YOU

> *When I was five years old, my mother always told me that happiness was the key to life. When I went to school, they asked me what I wanted to be when I grew up. I wrote down "happy." They told me I didn't understand the assignment, and I told them they didn't understand life.*
>
> —attributed to John Lennon

I love this quote for many reasons. The theme of achievement over substance is captured in John Lennon's childhood story. It's interesting that at the critical age of five John knew that happiness was important. The insight to know the difference at age five between happiness and achievement is amazing and a fabulous inspiration. This message isn't dated or only for the older generation; it's for everyone age five and above.

Outward achievement is only fulfilling when a person's core self is formed and connected to her self-acceptance and healthy self-image. The goal of this chapter has been to demonstrate that you can create and develop a positive core self. The five steps to creating your functional self-acceptance are challenging, scary, and also invaluable to your life. The struggle to individuate and form your own identity is your personal pathway to emotional freedom and happiness. The application of your self-acceptance allows you to write a new and updated narrative about who and what you are and where you are going. All internal résumés and life scripts can be revised, corrected, and amended for your personal healing and transformation. The step-by-step self-acceptance process is ongoing and is never fully completed. There is no time limit or expiration date on change, creating your identity, or pursuing your deepest desires. You have the innate ability to heal yourself, your family, and your relationships with positive self-accepting actions. Your personal style of hope and happiness, and your feelings of competence, create a deep, sustaining core belief that the world is an adventure and something to embrace. We know how the opposite belief works, with its limitations of shame, fear, and emotional terrorism.

Your self-acceptance is a picture you carry in your psychological wallet throughout your life. It's possible, and necessary, to update this internal picture just as you update your passport picture or driver's license picture.

Self-acceptance looks and sounds like this:

> *It's a journey, no one is ahead of you or behind you.*
> *You are not more advanced or less enlightened.*
> *You are exactly where you need to be. It's not a contest,*
>   *it's LIFE.*
> *We are all teachers and we are all students.*
>   —Unknown

CHAPTER 10

REWRITING AND REWIRING
YOUR EMOTIONAL TRIGGERS

I will not let anyone walk through my mind with their dirty feet.
—attributed to Mahatma Gandhi

If beating yourself up worked, you'd already be rich, skinny and happy. Why not try loving yourself for a month and see what happens.
—attributed to Cheryl Richardson

We are what we repeatedly do. Excellence, then is not an act, but a habit.
—Will Durant on Aristotle,
The Story of Philosophy, 1926

We have discussed some very important issues thus far in our journey together, such as developing your self-acceptance, building your own identity, and individuating from your family. Now we are going to do some reprogramming. All three of the above quotes speak to the power and necessity of pulling the weeds of shame out of your emotional and mental garden. Simple cutting the weeds will only allow them to grow back stronger and fuller. Plowing your emotional, psychological, and intellectual garden sounds wonderful, like a nice commercial to watch during your favorite show. My male clients, regardless of age, hear the idea of plucking out the shaming weeds in their life and they roll their eyes at me. My female clients, again regardless of age, hear this suggestion and ask me, "How do you do that? That sounds impossible."

> *Shame creates silence, secrets, and a scared*
> *and wounded inner self.*

People of both genders have the same fear that there is no way for them to stop their automatic reflexive shame trigger cycle. The fear surrounding the idea of exposing their wounded inner child is beyond their psychological grasp. The ability to articulate and describe their personal repressed trauma, however, is possible and doable. The next question I am asked, without hesitation, is, "Do all my problems stem from my family?"

> *Your family is your starting line in life not*
> *your finish line!*

My answer is, "Absolutely not." I go on to explain that their family is a baseline, a starting line for their life and development. Our childhood isn't our finish line or a death sentence that we suffer under for our entire life. The option of healing and changing our emotional wiring is a real possibility. The problem is that we carry our childhood and family trauma with us into the present day, dragging it like a hundred-pound backpack full of bricks. Our avoidance, denial, and emotional amnesia about our trauma is what makes it feel overwhelming. The fear of exposing, resolving, and healing the trauma becomes our residual emotional suffering. Our emotional pain, trauma, and the fear that we will be annihilated if we ever confront our demons creates our elaborate shame triggers.

Another question I get asked is about the origin of shame and the creation of emotional triggers: "What role did my parents play in my emotional wiring getting mixed up?" I explain that it's a two-part process.

Part One: What were your mother- and father-factor messages regarding personal empowerment, separation-individuation, and your adulthood?

Part Two: How and when did you individuate from your parents?

At this point in our discussion, my clients are looking at me like I have three heads and they have no idea what I am talking about. Let's now describe these three elements in how to organically rewire your shame triggers into self-empowered actions, beliefs and emotional freedom.

YOUR MOTHER FACTOR, FATHER FACTOR, AND SHAME

The two questions above about your parents are threads to understanding and developing your core self, individuating, and developing your self-acceptance. Your parents were intimately involved in your early years and your relationships with them formed the first relationship templates through which you experienced the world. The first woman you loved was your mother. The first man you loved was your father. It's commonly understood and accepted that your parents, regardless of their relationship with each other, had a profound impact on your early messages to your core self. How we processed those messages leads to a myriad of psychological pathways that we all walk down.

The verbal and nonverbal messages you received from your mother and father (or did not receive), along with the guidance and beliefs they passed on to you, can be an untapped source of personal insights and information. Many of my clients say they never knew or lived with one of their parents. However, an absent, deceased, or uninvolved parent has a huge impact on a person's childhood, just as much as a super-involved, passive, depressed, anxious, or loving parent. Let's look at the obvious, the hidden, and the subtle influences your mother and father had or still have on your view of the world, your career functioning, relationship styles, finances, emotional intelligence, and your core self.

I refer to the incredible influence your mother and father had in shaping your life as the Mother Factor and the Father Factor. We can have many different mother and father role models, all of whom contribute your internalized ideas about men and women. The definitions guide who you understand yourself to be and how you function in and relate to the world around you.

The Mother Factor

Describes how your emotional functioning is shaped by your mother, consciously and unconsciously, including your emotional development, functioning, and ability to form meaningful relationships in your family life, social life, and with your intimate partners. An emotional template is created by your mother-child bond that influences your feelings of frustration, love, fear, hope, competency, and inadequacy. Your mother's style of relating is a template for your emotional disposition and your core sense of self, of who and what you are in the world.

The Father Factor

Describes how you develop your perception of your ability to problem solve, handle conflict resolution, and master your world—emotionally, psychologically, and in the areas of career, finances, and love. It involves your ability to be self-supporting, industrious, goal driven, competent, and individuated, and develops your innate ability to psychologically survive, form relationships with peers and colleagues. It is your foundation for your career choice and affects your conscious and unconscious ability to excel, your courage, your fear of failure. Your sense of competency vs. inadequacy in your career reflects your father-child relationship.

These definitions and concepts are brief summaries of two complete books that I have written. Your Mother Factor and your Father Factor—the influence of parents in your life—are ongoing in their importance and their ability to create a sense of competency or inadequacy and inferiority in you. For adult children, the Mother

Factor and Father Factor are always expanding in importance and residual impact. In chapter 2, we discussed styles of families and parenting, and now we are looking at the individual verbal and nonverbal messages you received from each of your parents. Regardless of marital status or physical proximity to your parents growing up, they contributed to the formation of your individuality and all of your different aspects.

Your Shame Factor Is a Blend of Your Mother/Father Factor.

What are five messages you received from your mother about emotions, relationships, and yourself? These messages can be verbal or nonverbal, implicit or explicit. Take a minute to consider what your thinking is now and what actions, reactions, and shame first began with your mother-child relationship. This isn't a blaming exercise, though, or finger pointing for what your mother either did or didn't do.

What are some themes, messages, and feelings you got from your mother about life, who you were, and growing up? These messages are pieces of your identity today and parts of your shame triggers. Typically, the most powerful messages from our parents are nonverbal, unwritten rules for emotional expression, communication, sex, finances, resolving conflicts, and how to build relationships.

Client Examples of Their Mother Factor Messages

Ann

"My mother told me that marriage was prison. Don't ever lose your freedom. My feelings about myself were always gauged by my mom's moods. I still find that I gauge my feelings by how someone else is feeling. She told me to never be dependent and always be self-supporting and free."

Dave

"My mother never wanted me to be independent or get married. She said family is first, but it really meant that she is always first in my life. Men don't leave. If I was independent, I was abandoning her. I always feel shame if I don't take care of her. I hate her and love her."

Jean, age, fifty-two

"My mom wanted me to go to college and have a big-time career. She didn't want me to stay home and take care of my kids. My mom always wanted to become a professional because it was her dream. She also told me to only tell my husband what he needed to know. My mom ingrained in me to be a career woman. She didn't like being a full-time mom. Me and my brother always felt like a burden. I think her unhappiness was why she became alcoholic."

Write in the space below five messages, both verbal and nonverbal, that you received from your mother about life.

Mother Factor Messages to You:

1.

2.

3.

4.

5.

Client Examples of Their Father Factor Messages:

Barry, age thirty-six

"My entire self-worth is wrapped up in my job, career, and how I am professionally progressing. My dad is very successful in finance and has always told me that I needed to try harder. I feel like I have never gotten his approval or love. I know he loves me, but it's hard to see that when his only concern is my career not me. I feel like I am always chasing his approval. I wish we were closer."

Cindy, age forty-two

"My dad always wanted me to be a boy. I work very hard and never feel like I have done enough. I try not to eat my emotions. I get super stressed at work, worrying about not being a good manager or employee. My dad was loving, and he always wanted me to be successful. I feel like I have to be a hard-ass in order to do well at work. My self-doubts are chronic, and I question myself all the time. I have my dad's work ethic and courage."

John, age fifty-six

"My dad was a public-school teacher for forty-five years. He found a way to get me and my two older sisters through college on a teacher's salary. He worked in a low-income neighborhood and loved it. I modeled my career and approach to life, marriage, family, friends, and traveling around my dad. I never thought much about the influence of my dad. It was never a question. My dad was a solid man and our family knew it. I wouldn't have been so successful at work, working with superiors without my dad's role model."

Write in the space below five messages, both verbal and nonverbal, that you received from your father about life.

Father Factor Messages to You:

1.

2.

3.

4.

5.

Mother Factor and Father Factor Impact and Insights

Your ability to emotionally, professionally, and relationally function at home and outside the home encompasses your Mother Factor and Father Factor integration. Your innate ability to resolve emotional issues, handle relational conflicts, and understand and feel good about yourself tends to be the Mother Factor influence. Your desire and ability to go out into the world, work, function, survive, and be independent tends to be the Father Factor dynamic. Historically, women have been defined by what they did inside the house and men have been defined by what they did outside the house. I know this sounds like a 1950s social studies class, but it's still a very powerful male/female relationship template today.

The ingrained male and female roles have been in place for centuries and have a residual psychological and cultural impact on all walks of life. The challenging part is that both men and women are now feeling torn between being both an excellent father or mother, a professional, and a jack-of-all trades for their families and partners. This impossible personal script telling each person they need to try to be "enough" become shaming triggers of not being the "perfect" mother or father, wife or husband, woman or man; this feeds right into one's feelings of self-loathing, isolation, and fear of failure.

A man's Mother Factor shapes his view of love, intimacy, and self-worth. A woman's Mother Factor shapes her identity, emotional expression, and self-worth.

Another important piece of everyone's Mother Factor and Father Factor is the intrinsic dynamic of approval and acceptance. Men who feel they have their mothers' support and approval will develop a sense of competence and security in relationships. Women who feel they have their mothers' support and approval feel very capable in their role as a mother, wife, and friend, and have strong secure personal relationships with women. Both men and women with a secure and positive Father Factor and Mother Factor can fully individuate and develop their core sense of self with acceptance, forgiveness, and a sense of responsibility and personal control.

Men who feel insecure, unloved, resentful, and neglected by their mothers have tremendous difficulty individuating and separating. The lack of maternal support, child-focused attention, and empathetic female-love disrupts a son's ability to form emotionally secure, functional and mutual supportive relationships with women. These sons often view women as objects to heal their sense of maternal deprivation and rejection. Men who experience maternal deprivation can develop a deep narcissistic psychological wound, chronic emotional deprivation, and a sense of never being good enough. All these feelings, wounds, and beliefs contribute to the formation of a man's shame factor. Women who feel unloved or criticized by their mothers have a difficult time forming trusting relationships with other women regardless of the setting. Maternal deprivation for a daughter creates a chronic emotional state of self-doubt and fear within her. The lack of internal courage in a daughter starts with feeling she isn't "good enough" to gain her mother's love and attention. Self-doubt evolves into a sense of shame within the daughter and causes her to avoid risks (e.g., career opportunity), challenges (e.g., relationships), and her own personal development. Women who feel emotionally neglected by their mothers develop a strong self-doubt and shame-driven personality covered up with anxiety and depression.

Adult codependent relationship patterns began with the child's sense of emotional neglect in their relationships with their mother and father.

Men who feel loved, supported, and understood by their mothers develop a secure male-female relationship template, consistent emotional stability, and competence in all their different relationships. These sons become men who are familiar and comfortable with expressing a wide range of emotions. Women who feel secure in their relationship with their mothers have the innate courage and wisdom to pursue their dreams, wishes, and goals. These women have an internal support system and core self that guides them in their life, relationships, parenting, career, and health.

Healing your mother and father wounds allows you to develop your internal life compass for your dreams, goals, and desires.

Women who have secure, accepting, and supportive relationships with their fathers have clear emotional, physical, and psychological boundaries with themselves and the world. The sense of internal acceptance passed from a father to his daughter is unseen confidence that allows her to individuate and develop her own identity. Women with a positive Father Factor can manage the male dominated work world with finesse and courage. The ability to productively work, live, and function at one's best in the world is a direct benefit of a positive Father Factor for both daughters and sons. Sons who feel accepted, loved, and understood by their fathers have innate ability to be empathetic and understanding of others in the workplace and in any relationship. These sons are "civilized men" who appreciate and respect the emotional and physical boundaries of others. The sense of integrity, honesty, and clarity in the workplace started at home with a secure relationship. Fathers shape their sons' ability to be a mentor, leader, and father by the degree of love and acceptance they give them.

Below, list five strengths of your Mother Factor and your Father Factor. You may feel that neither your Mother Factor nor your Father Factor has any noteworthy qualities or strengths. However, consider the idea that deep within you are many untapped talents, gifts, and abilities. Many of these same talents are within your parents. Focus on the positive parts within each of your parents.

1.

2.

3.

4.

5.

These insights and expanded understanding about your parents and their conscious and unconscious impact on you today are related to healing and rewiring your emotional shame triggers. The experience of individuating allows you to apply and keep the pieces of both your Mother Factor and your Father Factor that are positive and empowering. The parts, pieces, and messages that aren't useful or beneficial to your life today can be put aside so that they are no longer active ingredients in your relationships today. The idea of individuating from both your parents regardless of the trauma, loving support, or chaos is imperative. Creating your own identity, separate from your internalized parents, is a transformational life experience, whatever your age or situation in life. The exposure process of your hidden shame elements is ongoing and directly connected to your sense of peace and security in life. Self-discovery is the result of individuating, which is a lifelong process and always valuable in removing the mud of shame from your core self. Shame triggers develop when the parent-child bond doesn't naturally progress and evolve. These triggers, as we have discussed throughout the book, are insidious and tend to be resistant to exposure and change. Now is the time in your life to continue weeding your garden and pulling out all the roots of shame.

FOUR CORNERSTONES TO UPDATING AND COMPLETING YOUR SEPARATING-INDIVIDUATING PROCESS

> *When a child learns to walk and falls down fifty times, he or she never thinks to himself or herself, "Maybe this isn't for me."*
> —Unknown

The following four psychological elements, emotional variables, and internal paradigm shifts will help heal your wounded inner child and strengthen your core self. There are many stops and starts along the journey of self-transformation, healing, and growth that might seem overwhelming. When a baby is learning how to walk, she is determined to master her balance and stand up. The same holds true for you and your newly discovered self: keep trying and you will master the art of emotionally standing on your own. When considering your Mother Factor and Father Factor and rewiring your shame responses, you need these four individuating tools to withstand your own self-doubts. Each of these four factors are foundational to the functioning of your core self.

1. Emotional Boundaries: Staying on Your Side of the Court

Becoming increasingly responsible for your own feelings, emotional reactions, thoughts, and choices creates personal boundaries. The concept of not having to be inside of your partner's life to be loved or cared for is a liberating experience. Beginning to consider your own role, choices, and responsibility in all the important areas of your life is establishing internal and external boundaries. One of the greatest challenges is keeping yourself on your side of the metaphorical relationship tennis court. The learned behavior and emotional rewards of trying to save and fix your relationships has been the formula for misery and despair. Shame-driven and codependent relationships have no psychological boundaries between partners. Empathy, compassion, and consideration for others are all within the limits of allowing the other person to take responsibility for their choices. Start to recognize and know where you stop and start without placating for fear of annihilation. Self-acceptance, self-approval, and self-love are new pieces of your identity's emerging cornerstones. Boundaries breed confidence, strength, and competence.

Emotional boundaries require you to be conscious of your own needs, desires, and wants in any relationship. Trauma, shame, and fear impair a person from seeing his appropriate role in relationships. The fear of saying no is a classic symptom of a lack of personal boundaries. The despair in approval seeking and saying yes against your better judgment is valuable information to consider. Developing the courage to speak up to the opposition, voice your own opinion, and make your own decisions are all features of having personal boundaries. The empowerment of having psychological boundaries implies that you take full responsibility for your choices, actions, and outcomes.

What's your greatest difficulty in keeping clear emotional boundaries?

What situation causes you to lose your perspective and boundaries?

In what relationship do you need to establish clearer boundaries?

What is your unspoken fear if you say no?

2. Emotional Enmeshment: You Aren't Responsible for Your Parent's or Anyone Else's Life (Everyone Has Personal Responsibility)

The dynamic of two adults having one head and one emotional thought is relational enmeshment. The term enmeshment refers to the complete blending of two people into one entity—psychologically, mentally, and physically. This process begins at birth and is natural for the mother-infant bond. The problem comes when the young child matures and attempts to create their own emotional space apart from their mother, father, and/or other family member. Psychological enmeshment is the loss of your individuality within a relationship. The umbilical cord between a newborn baby and mother is cut at birth; the emotional umbilical cord must be cut starting at age five, which allows for secure and consistent development progress within the child. Unless emotional separation occurs, this umbilical cord will create developing paralyzing enmeshment and shame codependence based on living another person's life. Mental health experts never consider enmeshment as a positive trait or a relationship strength.[1]

Many negative behavioral traits are passed down from one generation to the next via the enmeshment process. The physical umbilical cord during pregnancy transmits life-sustaining nutrients to the developing fetus. Each child receives all physical DNA from both the father and mother at the time of the child's conception, with each providing half of the necessary chromosomes. The psychological and emotional transmission process occurs later, during childhood and into adulthood. The ability to separate and form your own identity is part of your life cycle, and it's imperative to create personal space between you and your parents in order for any degree of self-acceptance to develop. No identity or sense of self can form without emotional and psychological space and support.

When a child, teen, or adult individuates and is no longer emotionally enmeshed with their family, this can stop, breaking negative emotional family patterns. Many times, the cycle of sexual abuse, physical abuse, addictive behaviors, and emotional immaturity stops with the individuated son or daughter. The psychological need for individuation created the field of family therapy.

When a child is psychologically enmeshed with a parent to an extreme degree, it becomes emotional incest. Emotional incest is when a parent uses the son or daughter as a romantic surrogate, replacement, and/or substitute partner. The parent's unmet romantic feelings are downloaded and projected onto the child, causing the child to feel "bad" for not being able to reciprocate or fulfil the parent's unspoken desire. When emotional enmeshment mixed with unmet romantic feelings become the child's burden and role to fulfill, shame becomes the glue between the parent and child. The unspoken secret of emotional incest, due to poor boundaries between a child and parent, is traumatic and embarrassing. This is a very taboo topic because of its inherent problematic nature. It's important to address any type of emotional enmeshment relationship style in your past and present. All the steps in this section of the book are excellent starting points for creating shame-free relationships in all the areas of your life.

No child, regardless of age, wants the responsibility of being their mother's or father's intimate emotional support system. The need to create emotional and psychological space without a parent's permission, approval, or support is challenging but possible. The child's conditioned emotional response of feeling bad, feeling betrayed by the parent, and feeling fearful of rejection by the parent is terrorizing. Your need is to step back from the emotional functioning of others in order to allow the enmeshment process to change. Emotional boundaries allow you to think and fulfil your own needs, not the needs of your parents.

Questions about You and Your Enmeshment

What family trait would you like to change as it relates to you?

What does it feel like when you can't be enmeshed in a relationship?

How much of your identity do you seek in being enmeshed in others?

Who in your life are you connected to with an emotional umbilical cord, emotionally fused and enmeshed with?

3. Emotional Sobriety: Responding Rather Than Reacting

The cognitive ability to pause and reflect on emotionally "heated" issues allows for the opportunity to have a productive, non-shaming discussion. Stable communication breeds a stable and secure relationship bond. When you are feeling shame, fear, or powerlessness, the automatic reflexive reactions cloud and distort the issue at hand. Volatile emotional reactions are symptoms of an underdeveloped core self. Assimilating the separation-individuation steps above for emotional boundaries and disengaging from enmeshed relationships allow you the opportunity to remain cognitively clear and aware. In chapter 1, we discussed how emotional sobriety widens your ability to process new information, new ideas, and new perspectives and develop them within yourself and grow your calm inner emotional state absent your shame triggers, fear of the future, and feelings of impending doom. Shameless conflict can be experienced simply as disagreement, not the "end of your world." Staying cognitively sober allows you to change your internal view that conflict equals, "I am bad." Your growing self-acceptance foundation no longer experiences everything as a "do or die" proposition because of your higher intellectual clarity, instead of the fight or flight adrenaline response you previously lived with.

People can get physically sober from drugs and alcohol within a short period of time. The psychology of individuation, however, is a lifelong process of healing and freedom. The ability to pick and choose your reactions, opinions, and concerns is a level of personal mastery that is attainable for all. The absence of the old familiar emotional patterns of terror and neurological fight or flight and adrenaline surge allows you to be the person you choose in any situation. Your core self doesn't need or want the mud of shame, psychological drama, and emotional confusion as elements of your relationships. Responding to a disagreement, misunderstanding, or perceived betrayal keeps your personal power and control on your side of the relationship tennis court.

Questions about Understanding Your Emotional Sobriety

What is a common circumstance in which you feel shame, fear, or the imposter syndrome?

Who in your life, past or present, triggers your anger and rage?

How do you process feedback from your partner, colleagues, family, or friends?

What did you learn from your mother and father about how to handle disappointment?

What is one action you can take to not lose your emotionally cool composure?

4. Frustration Tolerance: Understanding, Accepting, and Developing Emotional Maturity

One of the strongest behavioral tools to healing and changing your entire life is understanding how your emotional triggers operate. If your psychological triggers are buttons on your mental keyboard, then you can learn to disconnect those keys, right? It's a commonly accepted fact in the drug and alcohol rehabilitation industry that a lack of emotional tolerance for uncomfortable feelings is the pathway to all addictions, codependent relationships, anxiety, despair, and rage.[2] The rehabilitation business knows that unless a person learns to accept and process their shameful feelings, the relapse is inevitable. The cognitive treatment for strengthening your emotional response cycle, commonly referred to as frustration tolerance, is to develop the ability and insight to tolerate the frustrations of your life. Unresolved trauma, repressed terror of childhood abuse, neglect, and sexual abuse create the emotional reflex of denial, avoidance, and amnesia.

Developing your core sense of self allows you not to personalize negative events as detrimental or a strike against you. Shame breeds impatience, avoidance, and the need to always have control. Maladaptive ways to control and avoid our uncomfortable feelings are the psychological foundation of addiction. Creating a new personal shame-free narrative about your life begins with approaching and sitting with uncomfortable thoughts, emotions, and feelings. We will discuss in chapter 12 when it's necessary to enlist a psychologist or other form of professional assistance to expedite your healing, this would be appropriate example of getting professional support.

> *Developing emotional tolerance for your life, relationships, and partner are all acts of self-acceptance and self-love.*

A positive cognitive response to day-to-day events can be established and become your new normal. Mental frustration tolerance is being mindful, self-aware, and living in the present moment to access a different outcome. Running develops physical endurance tolerance over time with practice, training, and commitment to getting in marathon shape. Similarly, cognitive awareness and increasing tolerance to your shame triggers requires a skillset of commitment, practice, and emotional retraining. With patience and with a foundation of self-acceptance, you can rewrite your reaction cycle to become your response cycle. Responding to your life, your relationships, and your emotions helps to form and define your core self and your personal identity and individuation.

The theory of impermanence is an ever-present element of healing: everything changes; events, situations, and challenges come and go. By accepting your life situation, circumstances, and facts, knowing that everything changes, and keeping cognitive flexibility you develop frustration tolerance. The quote at the beginning of this section by Lau Tzu, is an analogy of being fluid like water versus rigid like a rock and how this breeds tolerance and acceptance. Your emotional need to feel accepted, loved, and safe can't be met outside of yourself.

The insight that your life starts within you and then goes to the outside world breeds peace of mind, tolerance, and cognitive flexibility. Impatience, perfectionism, and frustration are created through the belief that if your outside world is perfect then your inside world will become perfect. This is one of the greatest myths in life. All of the changes, desires, goals, and dreams are inside of you waiting to come out into your life. The key is to keep pulling the weeds of shame from your emotional life, removing your self-imposed road-blocks and self-doubt.

Questions about Your Patience, Emotional Flexibility, Empathy, and Tolerance for Yourself and Others

What situation or relationship are you currently feeling impatient and irritable about?

Where is an area in your close relationships in which you could be more accepting and tolerant?

What is something you could do to be more flexible and understanding with your partner, close friends, or colleagues?

What do you feel when you become angry?

What is a quality in yourself that you would like to change?

How can you express yourself more lovingly to the important people in your life?

HEALING AND REMOVING TERROR FROM YOUR LIFE: CONTRASTING SHAME TRIGGERS WITH YOUR SELF-ACCEPTANCE RESPONSES

We discussed in chapter 4 the seven big triggers of shame. Each of these triggers hides behind the defensive wall of avoidance, denial, and emotional amnesia. These three ingrained safety mechanisms are no longer needed (and never were needed) or beneficial in your life and relationships today. In fact, these emotional psychological blocks only reinforce your chronic paralyzing shame. We will tackle these three psychological roadblocks to your personal well-being and freedom in the next chapter.

> *Being scared to ask for what you need is a*
> *trauma and shame response.*

Shame has seven common felons that keep women and men of all ages silent and scared of being exposed as something awful. The ability to recognize the insidious damage these shame-based emotions do as they control and terrorize you is invaluable to your healing. It's possible to challenge each of these seven cycles of automatic responses when you feel vulnerable, scared, and flooded with the words of your old internal shaming tapes playing over in your mind.

A psychological technique called "I AM" is a tool to expose your irrational ideas, shame-based beliefs, and chronic fear of being discovered as a "bad person." The technique allows you to pause, question, and expose the automatic psychological reflex of denial, avoidance, and emotional amnesia. It is possible to literally stop your internal panic when you feel waves of disdain, self-loathing, and imposter thinking. Refuting, rewriting, and rewiring your emotional brain starts with you. The I AM technique creates a cognitive space for you to question your automatic thoughts and reactions. This psychological tool can be applied in any setting or circumstance where you might be unclear about your role, your boundaries, or your personal responsibility.

I AM is a psychological tool that can be implemented for exposing your shame in a concrete productive manner. Seeing your own outdated reactions will allow your new self-acceptance responses to replace your existing emotional terrorism and self-disdain.

- I = Is this **Important** to me?
- A= Do I need to **Act** according to these beliefs and shaming emotions? What are the facts surrounding these shame-triggering beliefs?
- M = Can I **Modify** this belief, emotion, or thought? Can I change this situation with new action?

This simple and powerful three-step process for uncovering your unconscious denial, emotional avoidance, and selective amnesia requires you to take new action. The control of personal choices, taking responsibility for those choices, and exploring new possibilities, solutions, and alternative options to your old shame triggers is powerful. Your shame and all its collateral terror can't exist when exposed and questioned. The purpose of shame in your life is never for your psychological health, well-being, or your highest and best good. No longer can your undeveloped scared and wounded inner child try to create emotional safety while using dangerous shaming weapons of personal destruction.

THE SEVEN SHAME TRIGGERS AND SEVEN SELF-ACCEPTANCE OPTIONS

The following seven common emotional shame triggers, fear-based reactions, and haunting beliefs are the mud and debris covering up your core self. These reactions are the fabric and substance of your shame factor. Eliminating these cycles of psychological terror, paralyzing thoughts, and old addictive self-loathing reactions is your journey toward personal mastery. The application of your developing self-acceptance, self-love, self-forgiveness, and self-worth can now be expressed in an atmosphere of personal safety. The following rebuttals to these triggers are a starting point for you to refute every shaming emotion you experience. The genius of the "I AM" technique is that it gives you a tool to guide your own recovery and healing process. You are in control of your own healing, which is a very powerful concept.

Let's explore the seven triggers from chapter 4 and their deceptive beliefs and actions. Let's then offset these old reactions with a new narrative and a new perspective on you, thus creating lasting change.

1. Fear of Embarrassment (Emotional Paralysis)

Embarrassment Shaming Inner Belief Dialogue

I will be humiliated. I am inadequate, and everyone will finally see that. If anyone knew my sexual thoughts, they would see that I am a horrible person. I can't think when I am around my rich friends; I don't want them to know I am getting support from my parents. I have a loser job and no one can know. I have a secret addiction to pornography and I would die if someone found out. I hide all my awful feelings so no one will know about them. No one can know about my affair. My mother committed suicide. I can't be weak or vulnerable with my friends, colleagues, or family. My father went to prison. I was sexual molested by my neighbor. I was hospitalized for cutting myself.

The list is endless, with shame threatening to embarrass and humiliate you if anyone sees who you really are, knows your past, or realizes that you have problems today.

Self-Acceptance, Exposure, and Honesty Inner Dialogue

I am capable. People know and love me for not trying to be perfect. I can take action to be direct, honest, and transparent in all my relationships. I am no longer a small, powerless child; I have options and choices that can change my circumstances. I am not an emotional prisoner of self-doubt or my past. I am not ashamed of my past. I don't have to hide my needs and desires. My parents had their own problems and did their best with what they were capable of. I am in therapy for my addiction to spending. I accept my shortcomings, and I am working to change and grow. I choose to have meaningful, supportive relationships. I welcome new challenges in my career, family, and marriage. I have the courage to pursue my desire to be self-employed. I am loved and supported by close friends, regardless of my successes or failures.

Your I AM Rebuttal to Fear of Embarrassment

I = Is this important to me?

A = I will act according to what is in my best interest. Are my thoughts and feelings about being vulnerable rational? Making mistakes is better than hiding and avoiding a new opportunity. No one cares if I do something or not as long as I follow through on my responsibilities. I don't seek people's approval. I choose not to placate my partner tonight. I can say no to my family.

M = I can change this situation. Nothing in my life is terminal or hopeless. I have many options and choices. I have the courage, desire, and drive to achieve my goals. I accept my past and present actions as learning tools for my personal transformation and healing. I don't have to live in fear or trauma anymore. I control my life and any situation I am in.

Your Self-Accepting Dialogue about Becoming Empowered Rather Than Embarrassed

2. Feeling Angry, Invisible, or Worthless: Distorted View of Yourself

Anger and Self-Loathing Shaming Inner Belief Dialogue

Men don't cry or show weakness. Women can't be angry. I will not let anyone f— with me. I hate when I am disrespected. No one controls me. I didn't mean to punch the bartender, but he was rude to me. I yell and I am a bitch. No one listens to me until I get angry and aggressive. I feel so much shame after I rage. When I get angry, I can't stop myself from being verbally aggressive and demeaning. Anger keeps me safe and in control. No one messes with me when I am bitchy, mean, and irritable. People who can't argue and fight are weak. After I rage, I feel very sad and lonely. I feel like I am sitting on a time bomb inside of me. I only express my anger; no one cares about my feelings. It's not safe to be weak and emotionally vulnerable. People only respect and listen to me because I am tough. Men only respect a woman who is aggressive. My friends need a hard-ass person in their life.

Self-Acceptance of Anger and Emotions Inner Dialogue

I can express all my fears, hopes, and desires. I am no longer an abuse victim. I don't need to keep fighting. I am capable of expressing my frustration calmly. I forgive myself for being an a—hole. No one controls me but me. I am not a victim but a participant in my life. I have strong clear emotional boundaries. I can say no. I choose how to respond to aggressive people. I embrace my vulnerability and am open to differences. Conflicts can be settled peacefully. I am a likable person. I choose not to date a dangerous person. I pick my friends. I am no longer neglecting myself. I have my own opinions, interests, and hobbies. I don't need to fight or be hostile to make my point. I don't need to win every disagreement. My life isn't controlled by my past abuse, anger. and fear of vulnerability. Winning in life is understanding others. Genuine masculinity means expressing my thoughts and feelings. Genuine femininity means being able to express my anger and frustrations. Disagreements can be resolved peacefully and productively. Physical violence is never necessary or warranted.

Your I AM Rebuttal to Anger, Rage, and Feeling Powerless

I = Is this argument, disagreement, or conflict important to me? Do I need to be involved?

A = I will choose how to calmly respond and act appropriately when I get emotionally upset. I chose not to be controlled by my fear of being a victim. Physical violence is never a solution to any issue.

M = I have the self-control and emotional clarity to peacefully resolve this situation. I would rather be in a relationship than be right. I am able to walk away from any threatening or aggressive situation. I can create open communication in my life with a gentle, loving approach to others.

Your Self-Accepting Dialogue about Anger and Abusive Behavior

3. Imposter Syndrome: Feeling like a Fraud (Fear of Being Revealed or Exposed)

Imposter Syndrome Shaming Inner Belief Dialogue

I have relentless terrorizing emotions and fears of being discovered as am imposter and phony. I am not really very good at what I do. I fool everyone. No one truly knows my lack of ability. I am terrified of being exposed as a loser. No one truly likes me; it's all a cover-up. I have serious personal deficits that no one sees. My entire life is a lie. I make myself physically sick worrying about what others think of me. My colleagues like me to my face and dislike me privately. I will never succeed in my career. I am unable to function at my capacity at work, home, and with my partner. No one knows my secret self-doubts. I dream about moving away to a new country where no one knows me. Relationships scare me. I don't want anyone to see me. I have felt inadequate since birth. My partner resents me for not being more successful. I am afraid to take a new job because I won't succeed at it. My parents were right; I am not very smart. I have attention-deficit issues that I hide at school and work.

Self-Acceptance Empowering Inner Dialogue

Everyone has strengths and weakness. I don't have to be perfect. I acknowledge my personal and professional strengths. I enjoy the support of my coworkers. I like new challenges to keep me developing and changing. Risks are necessary. I approach my challenges. No matter the outcome of a situation, my life will keep going forward. There are no mistakes, only lessons. I can go beyond my professional and personal comfort zone. I choose to embrace feedback. Everyone has their own fears and doubts. I am not alone. I am not controlled by self-doubt or fears of being exposed. I have nothing to hide or avoid about myself. I accept disappointments as naturally occurring events. I can ask for help, support, and guidance. No one knows everything about everything. It's good to ask questions. Learning expands my insights and potential. No one controls my future but me. I choose to live in the present moment.

Your I AM Rebuttal to Imposter Syndrome and Emotional Terrorism

I = I choose to embrace and approach new challenges and opportunities. I choose not to hide or be controlled by old fears.

A = I will take action to be inclusive of others in my career growth. I will allow colleagues and other people to see my vulnerabilities and strengths. I am a perfectly imperfect coworker, manager, employee, supervisor, consultant, romantic partner, parent, and adult.

M = I have the ability, talent, opportunity, and experience to master and resolve any challenge in my career, relationships, and personal life. I don't have to hide my life from others.

Your Self-Accepting Dialogue about
Your Imposter Syndrome Fears and Fear of Exposure

4. Isolation: Feelings of Rejection, Defectiveness, and Inadequacy

Fear of Vulnerability, Feeling Defective, and
Not Being Good Enough Shaming Inner Belief Dialogue

I am damaged goods. I am messed up, and no one wants to know me. I can't handle dating and being rejected. I only feel safe being alone. No one likes me. People make me anxious. I hate to be bullied as an adult. I don't need friends. My colleagues know I am odd. I am overweight and no one wants a fat person. I have issues and problems that scare people. I don't want anyone to know me or my past. I don't like myself. I am ugly. Men only want sex, not me. Women only want money; I am not rich. I have always been a loner. I am terrified of being dismissed or ignored by women. Men never notice me. I don't like people. I don't know how to have close friends. I have never felt good enough to be close to people.

Self-Acceptance Feeling Competent Inner Dialogue

I am capable of loving another person. I accept myself and others as imperfect. Everyone wants to feel love, acceptance, and understanding. No one can reject me; it's not personal if a relationship doesn't work. I enjoy the company and companionship of others. I like my appearance. I am capable of intimate relationships. I desire secure emotional connections. I am sensitive and open to a loving relationship. I support my colleagues' success. I care about myself and others. Friendships are important to me. I enjoy feeling emotionally connected to my friends. I don't judge myself or others by appearance. Everyone has strengths and weaknesses. I am a loyal friend. Relationships are important. I have the ability to develop relationships. I choose to emotionally engage people in my life.

Your I AM Rebuttal to Isolation and Feeling Defective in Relationships

I = I am capable of developing secure, caring, supportive relationships.

A = I will proactively act to be emotionally available to growing and developing relationships socially, romantically, and at work. I say yes to relationships.

M = I have the ability to create situations and opportunities where I can meet and connect with colleagues, peers, and new friends. I choose not to withdraw from people and social activities.

Your Self-Accepting Dialogue about Shaming Isolation

5. Feeling Suspicious: Untrusting of People and Authority

Dread of Life, Authority, Feeling Small, and Powerless Shaming Inner Belief Dialogue

I have no control of my life. I don't trust people. I feel my job has power over me. I fight to be independent from everyone. I don't like change. Everyone is out for themselves; no one cares about anyone. I have been on my own since sixteen, and I resent it. Nothing ever goes my way at work. My father was a loser. My mom was a cold, icy bitch. People can't handle my truth or past. No one will ever disrespect me. I am paranoid of everyone. The world is an awful place.

Relationships aren't necessary. I don't take risks. I don't understand why people are so emotional; I am fine. My childhood is in the past; it's not relevant to my trust issues. Everyone secretly resents me even when they are nice. Being honest is dangerous. I am not going to live very long. I like to use drugs to have some fun. I don't talk to my family. I don't believe in psychology or therapy; its unnecessary—just don't get close to people.

Self-Acceptance Trusting and Embracing Inner Dialogue

I trust myself to make good choices. Relationships are important to me. I choose to stop abusing myself and others. I choose to be physically and emotionally sober. Trust takes time to develop and is worth the effort. I have psychological boundaries that allow me to stay emotionally connected to people. I forgive myself for acting out when I am scared. I understand my past trauma and no longer need to keep reliving it. I am trustworthy friend, supervisor, parent, and partner. I enjoy my life today. I live in the present not the future. I can have safe, secure, and trusting relationships in my life. I embrace my desires to grow and fulfill my dreams. I trust my colleagues, supervisors, and people to support my life. I allow myself to emotionally connect with different social groups.

Your I AM Rebuttal to Paranoia, Fear of Authority, and Fear of Living

I = I can trust myself and the people in my life today. I embrace the uncertainty in my life.

A = I choose wisely the people I allow into my life. People aren't perfect. My life is my responsibility, and no one controls it.

M = I have the option to change any situation, environment, or circumstance I don't feel safe in or like. I have the ability to trust and have close relationships.

Your Self-Accepting Dialogue about Having
Trusting, Supportive, Caring Relationships

6. Fear of Intimacy: Feeling Like
Damaged Goods and Unlovable

Fear of Intimacy Shaming Inner Belief Dialogue

People don't like me. I have a lot of problems. I feel isolated and lonely. I can't be too close to people. Men always leave me. Women don't find me interesting. I can't keep a relationship for more than three months. Intimacy is overrated. I can't be in relationships. I don't want people to see me up close. I keep things very superficial with my friends. No one knows me. I can't handle rejection. I never had a close family growing up. I don't date. I haven't had a romantic partner in years. I don't let anyone see my true self. I don't like deep discussions. People are phony. I have a public image that no one sees past. I control my family with money. I feel like damaged goods since my divorce. All the good partners are taken. I will live alone forever. I feel scared if someone spends too much time with me; they will not like me. I have an ice cold marriage. My wife stays with me because of the money not me. My husband married me to have kids, not to be with me. I feel invisible to the opposite sex. I can't perform sexually. My family will reject my sexual orientation. No one is gay in our extended family. I don't communicate my feelings to anyone; they would be overwhelmed. I cover myself up in tattoos. I am overweight, so no one will be with me. I think of dying. I feel worthless most of the time. I failed my parents, family, and colleagues. No one thinks I am any good or valuable.

Self-Acceptance Secure Relationship Inner Dialogue

I can have loving, caring intimate relationships. Men and women find me interesting and fun to be around. I have the ability to develop secure relationships socially, professionally, and personally. I accept my sexual orientation. Sex is safe and intimate. I don't have to hide my core self. I like my body and looks. I can emotionally bond and be transparent with my friends. My family cares about me. I care about myself and my choices. I am enough for myself. My opinion matters to my partner. I enjoy socializing and being alone. I accept my challenges and allow people to support me. I accept and forgive my parents. I can say no when needed. I don't numb myself out with drugs, alcohol, or self-defeating addictive behaviors. I make choices that empower me. I don't save people, I support people. My relationships are mutual and caring. I love to do new things and see other perspectives. I am a great partner. I am honest and emotionally sober. Conflicts are normal and it is possible to resolve them. I respect myself and others.

Your I AM Rebuttal to Fear of Intimacy

I = I choose to be open and vulnerable in my relationships. I accept my life with gratitude and compassion.

A = I will act to foster and develop secure intimate relationships. I can have positive communication without judgment and anger.

M = I am good enough for myself and the people in my world. I have the ability to be vulnerable, open-minded, and to create important emotional bonds.

Your Self-Accepting Dialogue about All the Relationships in Your Life

7. Fear of Criticism: Placating, People Pleasing, and the Inability to Tolerate Feedback

Shaming Fear of Being Exposed, Inferior and Inadequate Inner Belief Dialogue

People only like me because I can help them. I avoid conflict at all costs. I can't mentally handle people being upset with me. I need the approval of others. I need constant reassurance about my life and choices. I am anxious about not pleasing my clients, supervisor, children, and partner; My parents still don't approve of me. I can't ever please the people in my life. No one cares about me or my needs. I was always told to do better as a child. I feel bad when people aren't happy with me. I don't like feedback about myself. I emotionally hide so my partner doesn't get mad at me. I never feel competent or loved. I hate that I seek the approval of my friends. I will leave a relationship when I can't face myself. I let people take advantage of me. I try to help everyone so no one is upset with me. I hate conflict. I don't argue or fight for my opinion. I feel stupid most of the time. I can't say no. People only like me because I make them feel good. I solve everyone's problems.

Self-Acceptance Feedback and Feeling Competent Inner Dialogue

I am open and receptive to learning about myself. I have personal boundaries. I evaluate any feedback for my greater good. I approve of myself. I support my colleagues for their personal growth. Disapproval doesn't control my life, relationships. and choices. I accept disagreements as natural events. My life is my responsibility. I accept my life today. My own approval is the most important in my life. I have nothing to hide or avoid in my past or present today. I make choices that empower me. I am capable of taking risks outside my comfort zone. Failure is a learning tool. I gain competence from experience. I choose to be around positive-minded people. I forgive my past. My wounded child is healing, and I am the only one responsible for him or her. My life will not end if someone is rude, critical, or mean to me. My life is bigger than any mistake, fear, or misunderstanding.

Your I AM Rebuttal to Criticism and People Pleasing

I = I choose who has input into my life. I can evaluate any relationship or situation for myself.

A = I will take action to have mutually beneficial relationships in every area of my life.

M = I can change, adjust, and create situations that are supportive and loving for myself and others.

Your Self-Accepting Dialogue about Fear of Criticism

CLOSING THOUGHTS

> *If there is anything that we wish to change in the child, we should first examine it and see whether it is not something that could better be changed in ourselves.*
> —Carl Jung, *Integration of the Personality*, 1939

The child within us is the child that is craving and needing our full attention and time. Changing our emotional wiring, healing from old traumas, and unplugging from our old cycles of shame is personal mastery. Carl Jung's quote is very powerful for both a child and parent. I am interpreting the quote to also refer to the child inside of the adult who is intimately bonded to them. The inner child isn't separate from the adult woman or man. The idea that our inner child needs to change starts with our best adult-self changing, which is our process of personal growth. Individuating from your Mother Factor and your Father Factor is the start of a very exciting trip of self-discovery and healing. The four steps to furthering your identity formation are ongoing tasks with a lasting personal benefit: peace of mind, stable relationships, less psychological anxiety, and less worry about the past, present, and future. Emotional freedom allows you to stay present and experience your life moment to moment. The absence of the repetitive cycles of shame covered in fear, anxiety, and terror allows you to think, feel, and act for yourself. Creating personal space creates your new identity regardless of your trauma and past struggles. Individuating forms and shapes how to live your life on your terms.

Unplugging from Your Shame Factor Triggers

The following are some things to consider immediately removing from your life. These are only a few of the negative beliefs, behaviors, and fears provoking your shaming emotional and psychological triggers.

Fear of embarrassment, and fear of being vulnerable

Anger and raging outbursts brought on by feeling powerless

Anxiety about the past and the future and feelings of dread and impending doom

Change is always traumatic

Imposter syndrome and feeling defective

Isolation and fear of intimacy and being exposed

Mistrust of others, authority, and yourself; having no respect for leadership or mentors in your life

Don't let anyone see your weaknesses

Feeling inadequate as an employee, partner, parent, and friend.

Plugging into Your Self-Acceptance Potential via Individuating

The following is a list of self-accepting beliefs and actions that will help you to discover your core self and change the course of your life. Each sentence starts with *I*, followed by the new action, a commitment to change, and your courage to remove shame from your life.

I can be honest with myself, being transparent to others and making secure emotional connections.

I am choosing to be more emotionally flexible rather than always trying to be right.

I no longer need to abuse myself or others (self-loathing vs. self-acceptance).

I am capable and willing to express my thoughts, feelings, and emotions in a productive manner.

I have the courage to pursue my goals and dreams.

I can ask for support and guidance in my life.

I am capable of having loving, caring, and mutually supportive relationships in every area of my life.

I am committed to the process of healing my trauma, abuse, and childhood neglect.

I am emotionally open to uncovering old wounds and embracing my wounded and scared inner child.

I accept and will make the necessary changes in life, which are positive
    and productive for my personal healing and transformation.
I trust my ability to make informed decisions regardless of outside
    pressures.
I embrace my life—all of its parts!
I take full responsibility for all my choices, past, present, and future.
I can "save" myself—no one else can or will.
I choose who can support my healing.
No one's opinion of me is more important than my own.

Unplugging from the treacherous shame triggers that we all
struggle with brings emotional freedom and personal mastery. You
are beginning to see that the insidious secret nature of shame, once
exposed, can't exist in your life. Finally, the hunter is no longer
hunting you with your deepest fears and terrors. Exposing the distortions, trauma, self-neglect, and self-abuse is a major step forward in
becoming the person you have always wanted to be but didn't know
how to access. In the next chapter, we are going to discuss how to
connect all the different parts of your life to your core self. We will
talk about how to integrate self-acceptance into the fabric of your
life while addressing your avoidance, denial, and emotional amnesia.
Remember that how you feel about yourself is what people will
remember about how you made them feel. This is a great reminder
of the influence you have and will have for many years to come.

> *They may forget what you said—but they will never forget how
> you made them feel.*
> —Carl Buehner, *Richard Evans' Quote Book*, 1971

CHAPTER 11

THREE BIG-TIME CHANGES: ACCEPTANCE, EMPATHY, AND UNDERSTANDING— IT'S ALL WITHIN YOU

In the process of letting go you will lose many things from the past, but you will find yourself.
—Deepak Chopra, *The Path to Love*, 1997

Never be afraid to fall apart because it is an opportunity to rebuild yourself the way you wish you had been all along.
—Unknown

What lies behind us and what lies before us are tiny matters compared to what lies within us.
—Henry Stanley Haskins, *Meditations in Wall Street*, 1940

LOOKING INSIDE FOR YOUR HAPPINESS AND HEALING

All great discussions, theories, and healing techniques lead to one place—you. All rivers lead to the ocean, and so do all healing paths lead to you. We know that shame thrives and bullies its victims from within, while always threatening destruction, embarrassment, and despair. The haunting fear of being completely exposed as something horrible is shame's unspoken control of you and your happiness. The brute force of our paralyzing trauma, avoidance of our private issues, and emotional amnesia of the past acts as a greenhouse that nurtures our shame factor year after year. One of the best-kept secrets is that we can resolve all of our fears, despair, dread, impending doom, and anxiety. No one truly believes in the power of their core self until they experience it and discover its endless potential. The quotes above remind us that the road to recovery, healing, and lasting inner peace starts within us. Ultimately, your path inward is your pathway to everything you want, desire, and ever dreamed.

Throughout the book, we have discussed the many different facets of your shame factors—such as seven emotional shame triggers, six life challenges covered with the mud of shame, your individuation process, and your self-acceptance discovery. Now we are going to talk about the removal of shame's bodyguards: avoidance, denial, and amnesia. These three highly sophisticated psychological defenses wrap themselves around the three most common elements of shame: anger, embarrassment, and self-loathing. We discussed the ongoing interplay of these shame factors in chapter 1 and at various points in the book. Now we are going to discuss the emotional medicine, cognitive rebuttal, psychological cure, and lasting resolution to deal with these outdated beliefs. Shame can't withstand insight, happiness, and exposure. The parable below will lend some clarity to the already brewing personal process you have embarked on.

Look Inside for Happiness: It's All There

From Glenn Van Ekeren, *Words for All Occasions* (Paramus, NJ: Prentice Hall, 1998), pp. 207–208.

There is an ancient Indian legend about a little-know tribe that was constantly at war with other Indian tribes. They abused their religion and their families, had no morals or feelings for others, and laughed at wisdom or any kind of order. Murder, theft, and plundering were a daily occurrence. This violent Indian tribe seemed doomed to wipe themselves off the face of the earth. Finally, an old chief gathered together a few of the least violent of the braves and held a council to discuss how they could save their tribe from themselves. The wise old chief decided that the only thing to do was to take the secret of happiness and success away from those who abused it. They would take their secret and hide it where no one would ever find it, so it could not be abused again. The big question was, where should they hide it?

One Indian brave suggested they bury the secret of happiness and success deep in the earth. But the chief said, "That will never do, for man will dig deep down into the earth and find it."

Another brave said to sink the secret into the darkness of the deepest ocean. Again, the chief replied, "No, not there, for man will learn to dive into the depths of the ocean to find it."

A third brave thought they should hide the secret at the top of the very highest mountain. But again, the chief said, "No, for man will climb even the highest of mountains to find it, and again take it for himself."

Finally, the old chief had the answer, "Here is what we will do with the secret of happiness. We will hide it deep inside of man himself, for he will never think to look for it there."

To this day, according to the Indian legend, man has been running all over the earth, digging, diving, climbing, and searching for something he already possesses within himself!

Insight into Your Healing

Your childhood sexual abuse, physical trauma, emotional neglect, loneliness, depression, insidious shame cycles, despair, and lack of self-worth can't block your journey inward. Remember, water is strong because it is flexible and wears away the inflexible rock. Shame is inflexible, rigid, and unforgiving, while your healing efforts are flexible and fluid to cure, remove, and resolve your past and present emotional pain. What is flexible (you) is strong, and what is rigid is weak (shame). The only thing that blocks and keeps you away from your own happiness, healing, and peace of mind is when you look everywhere but at the source—which lies inside of you. Your ever-increasing self-awareness of your happiness within is indispensable to your entire life. All the different psychological techniques, theories, and mindfulness tools of healing all point to one thing: you. Please forgive my emphasis on your inner healing, but it's a tremendous barrier that isn't fully understood.

Your ego will argue that all this self-help stuff is garbage and that things never change. The years upon years of avoidance, denial, and rejecting your innate abilities as the solution to your issues is the toughest challenge in removing shame from your life. The distortions of shame will neutralize your emotional strength, hope, and compassion. Many people will argue about their limitations and their inability to change, and they blame their past for their present-day struggles. I completely understand the frustration, fear, and avoidance associated with changing and exposing trauma that seems immovable. The insular self-preservation that you constructed many years ago isn't going away without your permission and full attention. Psychological paradigms, defenses, and personality styles are all amenable to change and updates.

Personal Question: What unspoken shaming fear/belief is keeping you from you?

Take another look inward, as the wise old Indian chief suggests in the above parable. Sincerely answer the question above. Don't allow yourself to say, "I don't know." The phrase "I don't know" really means "I do know, and I would prefer to keep my denial in place and not feel any discomfort." Remember, denial is a brilliant ally for keeping shame powerful and untouchable. What seems impossible to address, heal, and recover from is possible with your steady methodical honesty, exposure, and vulnerability to yourself. The seemingly illusionary smoke and mirrors of failure, self-loathing, heartbreak, career frustration, and despair serve as shaming roadblocks to your happiness and healing. The journey to expand your core self foundation and learn to experience self-love, self-worth, self-forgiveness, self-image, and self-acceptance happens within you. Experiencing self-compassion and empathy for yourself and others transcends all the old issues of self-doubt and the critical voices in your head and heart. The Indian legend is a timeless metaphor for the crazy, frantic, and desperate need to find what you already possess.

> *Shame can't exist or function with your insight into your own healing.*

Shame has all of us running like our hair is on fire, down the dead-end street of despair and hopelessness. The ups and downs of feeling humiliated, terrorized, and anxious keep reoccurring within your old closed system of avoidance, with no outlet for permanent relief. The short-term outlet from the terrorism of shame is how addictions are created. We discussed in chapter 6 the super-glue bond of shame and addictions—the short-term relief from shame that creates long-term life-threatening addiction problems. We have a chronic need to find the "next best thing" that will solve all of our problems, although that solution is something we already possess. The emotional and psychological exhaustion of codependent relationships, placating everyone in your life, and hiding your vulnerabilities is no longer necessary. Accepting that you no longer need to avoid, deny, or turn a blind eye to your past and present is a game changer.

> *Looking into yourself is an acquired art that is available with patience and self-acceptance.*

The idea that you can be cured of the incurable dis-ease of shame if you are only good enough at work, wealthy enough, thin enough, and doing enough good for others is all wrong and a myth. The cure is within you, which is the last place anyone ever thinks to look, consider, or seek out. The answers to your questions about your life, relationships, childhood, trauma, and insights on all the different events that have happened to you lie right inside of your heart and soul—within your core self.

We have all been trained to believe that we can achieve lasting happiness and fulfillment through hard work, persistence, and being "good." This is a truism if we start from the correct place (our core self) and then live our life from the inside going to the outside. Our core self is the doorway to our outward journey, not the other way around. We know from our discussion throughout the book how shame keeps us forever outside of our life, away from our happiness, and paralyzed and unable to access our dreams and potential. Shame is a glass wall and a major mudslide of distortion inside us. Shame forces our inner child to stand outside of our life with their nose pressed up against the window of our house, looking inside. The scared inner child wonders why they aren't "good enough," "lucky enough," or "pretty enough" to be inside at the party.

CHANGING OF THE GUARD: REMOVING YOUR PSYCHOLOGICAL, EMOTIONAL, AND BODY GUARDS

We only think when we are confronted with a problem.
—attributed to John Dewey, *I'm OK—You're OK,*
by Thomas A. Harris, 1969

It's important to remember that learning a new personal narrative is possible and doable. The philosopher John Dewey knew the lasting value of thinking outside of our old shame habits. Rethinking your life will only enhance and bring about positive lasting changes for you and your circle of influence. Shame is a lethal cancerous emotional habit, reaction, and avoidance of pain and discomfort. The step for internal change starts with questioning old repetitive patterns and self-defeating familiar emotional habits.

I can't tell you how many people ask me about this book and say, "That's interesting, I don't have any shame." Without fail, I have found that ten times out of ten this is because of classic denial. Upon closer examination, the person claiming "no shame" is carrying it around in their life like a hundred-pound brick on their back. The misperception of shame is why so many people struggle with feelings of dread, anxiety, depression, and self-doubt. They assume the feelings are normal because of the years of denial and avoidance without addressing the underlying problem. Living superficially on the periphery of your life becomes a very difficult task when your life demands you go inside and take care of your business. Because something is comfortable and familiar does not mean it has benefit and purposefulness. The three psychological roadblocks have served a defensive purpose, but their services are no longer needed. The lure of the familiar is how addictions and personality disorders become part of one's life, regardless of the potential dangers and self-destructive outcomes.

The phrase "I don't know what shame is" really means "I don't want to deal with it." Everyone knows what their challenges are but addressing them is another matter.

It's never too early or the wrong time in life to heal, change, or resolve your past and present challenges. Your new shame-free ways of feeling and thinking will be your starting point every day. The purpose of avoidance, denial, and emotional amnesia (being forgetful about your past and present trauma) needs to be reevaluated in order to allow yourself to reconnect to all the forgotten areas of your life. The big three defenses of your shame fabric maintain your wounded inner child, keeping the terrorized and anxious adult from changing or attempting any changes. However, your defensive wall has three assertive psychological rebuttals that directly contrast to the old automatic shame defenses: approach behavior, self-acceptance, and engagement. Your inward journey is made up of many parts, and these are three parts that will begin to reacquaint you with your newly found core self.

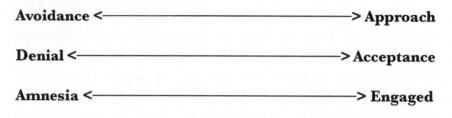

If an egg is broken by outside force, life ends. If broken by inside force, life begins. Great things always begin from the inside.
—Unknown

All lasting personal change starts within you and your desire to stop your suffering. The above quote describes the analogy of the egg and our transformation as one and the same. The psychological approach of Internal Family Systems Therapy is the theoretical foundation for helping you cohesively reconnect the disowned parts of yourself. The most productive and curative approach to lasting peace of mind and healing is to crack from the inside out the hard shell of shame surrounding your heart. The all-important psychological process of replacing your old rigid habits, your anxious beliefs, and your automatic reactions start with these three antidotes to shame: approach, acceptance, and engagement.

> **Fragmentation happens when the pieces of our core self are disconnected from each other by the distortion of fear and shame.**

Shame continually causes us to disown, create distance, and avoid parts of our core self. Psychologically speaking, our disowning process is called "fragmentation" of the self. The term implies the splintering of our core personality.[1] It's as if all the pieces of our self are scattered around our life like pieces of notebook paper, with no order or sense of connection. As much as we can consolidate these fragmented parts of our personality is the same amount that we will be able to experience cohesive stable relationships and emotional stability. The conquer and divide mentality of shame becomes the emotional mud that distorts who and what we are. The three new psychological building blocks are invaluable for reconnecting the untouchable, off-limits, traumatized, and avoided parts hidden within all of us. Unifying your personality means that your shame factor won't be the team captain any longer. Yes, we are now poking the toothless tiger with a red-hot iron rod. You are cracking the self-absorbed ego and shame-cemented walls of your life from the inside out.

The operating premise of Internal Family Systems Therapy is that all the different parts of yourself that have been alienated by the dominant role shame has had in your life up to this point will be reintroduced. Your inner feelings have been fragmented and walled off from the healing, compassionate, and self-accepting parts of you. In sports, shame would be considered a selfish "ball hog," with no regard for the other players on the team. This selfish player, colleague, friend, or partner divides the team (you) and doesn't build unity or care about winning. Shame can also be likened to a "mean girl" who is dismissive, abusive, and alienating to anyone she chooses. Shame is critical of everyone else, and it cannot be supportive or believe in someone.

The movie Inside Out *is a 3D example of the Internal Family Systems Therapy in action.*

The Pixar animated movie *Inside Out* (2015) is a fabulous illustration of how Internal Family Systems Therapy works to unify all the parts of a person. The story is based on adorable young girl, Riley, who is struggling with being a preteen, having parents, and being forced to move to a new city. Her internal emotions—Joy, Fear, Anger, Disgust, and Sadness—all live in the cognitive headquarters of Riley's head. The integration and interplay of these different emotions makes up the movie's challenge and theme. Within her core self, Riley's primary emotion of Joy tries to manage the other headstrong emotions in a productive manner. The movie beautifully demonstrates the inherent challenges that the conflicting emotions have with each other. Riley's emotions each have their own distinct personality, their own opinions, and their own controlling natures. Joy—her primary emotional ally—tries to manage the other emotions without causing Riley too much trouble. The movie is a wonderful metaphor for how each of our emotional shame variables interact with each other in our emotional headquarters. Meanwhile, our hope and joy within our core self tries to manage the unruly demands and the controlling nature of shame, fear, anger, sadness, and despair. The animation and voices of the various emotions shows the power and influence they have in all of our lives.

Your Shaming Internal Voice

Please note that initially these critical feelings, negative thoughts, and traumatic experiences were outside of you. Over time, we begin to incorporate these voices into our own voice. Now these voices are in your adult voice, but where did they originate from, when, and with whom?

Whose is the voice of shame in your head?

What does the voice of denial, avoidance, and amnesia sound like?

Whose critical voice do you hear or feel during a shame cycle?

Whose is the self-doubting voice in your head?

Your First Memory of Shame

Think about the first time you felt embarrassed, shamed, or scared of getting in trouble. These early experiences are defining moments in the formation of your sensitive core self. The terror you felt and remember was a scratch on your emotional being that began your shame experience and belief.

What was your first shaming experience?

What age were you?

Where did it happen?

Who was involved in the incident?

Did anyone know how shaming the event was to you?

What and how did you physically feel?

My first shaming experience was at the beach on the swing set. We were all about five or six years old and pushing each other on the swings to see who could go the highest. I pushed a kid too high and he jumped off and hit the sand face first. No one was hurt, just a lot of crying and yelling. Everyone ran away, and the kid I pushed said he was going to tell on me to the lifeguard on duty that day. I spent the rest of that day and the entire summer waiting for the lifeguard to come and "get" me. The lifeguard never came, but that began my first conscious experience of that sickening feeling of "being bad," "not good enough," and scared of authority. I could still see the beach, the lifeguard tower, and all of us playing on the swings. I spent so much energy watching the different lifeguards each day, knowing this might be my day of reckoning. The feeling in my gut that day is the same all-too-familiar and terrifying sense of dread, impending doom, and cognitive paralysis I feel now when shame tries to control me.

Your inner voice has a personality, particular style, and mood. The movie *Inside Out* takes our abstract emotions and makes them into three-dimensional lively characters. What's interesting is how we experience joy, hope, anger, shame, fear, and the rest of our feelings as individual parts of our personality. Your beliefs, fears, and shame triggers all have a particular role in your emotional headquarters. You have the innate ability and responsibility to reassign, terminate, retire, and hire new "people" to be inside your emotional headquarters (your core self). Your core self is designed to help you to live and experience your life. No one, and no emotion or belief, can dominate or control your life unless you give it permission. For example, Riley, the main character in the animated movie, learns that she ultimately has control of her emotions and choices.

Introducing positive new actions and beliefs can help you connect to your core self, which is becoming more and more influential in your life. The questions below will help guide you through the courageous exposure process of issues that are under the water, underground, or hidden in your private closet of shame. The old story of monsters in your closet always turns out to be a battered raincoat hanging there when you push the door open all the way and turn on the lights. Let's open the doors and windows of your life, allowing fresh ideas to create your next chapter in life.

Answer the following questions, or finish the sentences with your own answers—take your time and don't edit or "candy-coat" the truth. Write your answers in the book; this is for you and no one else. Sentence completion allows you to consciously begin to access your unconscious blocks, unspoken reasons for hiding, and the terror associated with exposing these vulnerable parts of your life. Integrating the lost parts of yourself begins with uncovering the person who has been imprisoned with shame. The ironic part of healing and releasing yourself from shame's imprisoning power *is that you always possessed the key to open the unlocked prison door.* No one ever considers the inward option until all the external options have been exhausted to no avail.

Your Avoidance Questions

When do I avoid emotional issues with myself and others?

What is one issue, topic, or relationship that I knowingly avoid?

Why do I avoid things in my life that are scary?

When did I first start avoiding emotional issues in my family, life, career, friendships, health, and marriage?

Your Denial Questions

What am I in denial about?

What do I knowingly refuse to accept in my relationships, family, and friendships?

What am I choosing to tolerate that is "crazy-making" for fear of a confrontation or abandonment?

What do I intentionally overlook in my personal life?

Your Amnesia Questions

I keep myself safe by not remembering or feeling my trauma because:

Why do I remember some things in my past but blank out the rest?

I deliberately don't recall my past or present struggles because:

I don't remember the conflict in my marriage, relationships, or child-hood because:

I don't remember when I drink too much because:

Replacing these three primitive psychological blocks with three new psychological action beliefs is a major step forward in your healing. Updating your internal emotional narrative is doable, powerful, and transformational. The questions above step into, around, and over the power shame has had on you since an early age, and begin to wash it away. The three common emotions of shame—anger, embarrassment, and self-loathing—operate within your intellectual and emotional core self paradigm to keep you imprisoned. Regardless of how long and how deeply you have feared your fear, it's absolutely within your power to change and heal. Denial, avoidance, and amnesia will no longer work or hide you from you any longer. The iron door of shame can only be opened by you with your self-accepting choices.

Kind words will unlock an iron door.
—Kurdish Proverb

Internal Family Systems Therapy has a phrase: *transformation of the parts of the self-energy.* The term implies that the energy and power of our core self is the connective emotional tissue of our life.[2] All the pieces of your life are connected to your internal hub. Everyone has a core self, the self-energy that must internalize and integrate all the parts and pieces of a person. Recovering your shamed self and discovering your core self is a never-ending journey into who, what, and why you are the way you are.

Action Belief Questions

Answer these questions with the idea of merely exposing the monster of shame in your private closet. You have the choice to create, heal, and be the person you choose. President Lincoln's statement is as timeless today as it was in the 1860s:

> *Folks are usually about as happy as they make up their minds to be.*
> —attributed to Abraham Lincoln
> by Frank Crane, 1914

Approaching Your Life

What would approaching and opening my emotional private closet look like?

What is one issue that I want to approach, address, and consider in the next few months?

What keeps me from incorporating self-love, self-acceptance, and self-forgiveness in my life?

What is the primary shame issue that I want to expose and remove?

Accepting Your Life

What am I embarrassed about in my life?

What do I refuse to accept or understand in my life?

What do I choose to forgive myself for?

What about me feels too damaged, too much for people, and/or scares my family?

Engaging in the Present

When do I leave my "numb out"?

What scares me about me?

If I am emotionally present, what will I feel and see in my life?

When I engage myself and others, how do I feel?

Shame-Free Questions of the Day

Who or what do I want to approach in my life?

What does empathy mean to me?

What does understanding and forgiveness mean to me?

What have I chosen to take action regarding?

What do you believe could emotionally "kill" or destroy you if confronted or addressed in your marriage/divorce?

Where in your life are you reluctant and scared to stand up or take action for yourself?

What is something you no longer choose to selectively forget?

These shame-free probing questions are emotional teasers for starting to see how all the different parts of your core self are related, connected, and can function together. Meeting and connecting the fragmented, wounded, and lost pieces of your life starts with realizing you can reconnect and create a unified and complete you. It takes courage to start peeling away the layers of mud and actively work on your own healing. I love this quote by Carl Sagan because it is the doorway to you and your emotional freedom and potential.

> *We can judge our progress by the courage of our questions and the depth of our answers, our willingness to embrace what is true rather than what feels good.*
> —Carl Sagan, *Carl Sagan's Universe*, 1997

TWO STORIES OF APPROACH, ACCEPTANCE, AND ENGAGEMENT: JON AND LYNN

Jon from Chapter 7: "I Am Never Leaving My Patio"

Jon started to address in therapy his dread of the future and his free-floating anxiety. He began peeling away the layers of denial formed by years of avoiding his childhood terror of being verbally and physically abused. He had been in denial and had forgotten (amnesia) his childhood experiences until his divorce ten years earlier. At that point, these repressed shaming feelings and fears started to reemerge.

Jon related the following during our therapy sessions:

> I placated my ex-wife with all my decisions hoping that she would eventually be happy and content with me and our life. When she divorced me, I felt like a complete failure because I had invested all of my self-worth in her opinions, moods, and thoughts about me. I was in a chronic state of anxiety and worry for being "wrong." I remarried quickly to feel loved and accepted for the first time in my life. What has happened is my old anxieties and fears of being not "good enough" all started coming back. I now realize that I never really resolved or grieved my marriage and my mother's verbal and physical abuse. I am now approaching issues at my company, with my wife, and my family that I have never done or even considered. Unfortunately, I think I have hidden behind my money to stay away from my sadness. My wife was going to leave me if I didn't stop drinking and start therapy.

Dr. P: "Do you feel relieved to let go of your childhood abuse?"

Jon: "It is so embarrassing and humiliating to tell you. I never acknowledged it until now, how I have avoided all my feelings of exposing my secret. You know this secret has always haunted me. Its irrational but it has controlled my life until now."

Dr. P: "What did you do to keep it buried all these years?"

Jon: "You have no idea how hard I tried to pretend everything was perfect in my childhood and my parents were just emotionally distant 1950s-style parents. I knew deep down when my ex-wife divorced me, it was only a matter of time before this bomb was coming out. I just couldn't hide anymore. My new wife wasn't going to let me drink myself to an early death. That's why I am in your office. I do feel calmer, less anxious, and not so worried about keeping my life hidden. My denial was literally killing me with my increased drinking and cigarette smoking."

Lynn from Chapter 7: "I Am Moving Away"

Lynn began to address her sense of abandonment by her father in therapy. Lynn's parents got divorced when she was three years old, and she saw her father on a regular basis until about age ten. Then her father moved across the country. Lynn said that while she was growing up her father was always "yelling" and "raging" at her. Lynn began to see the psychological connection between her father and why she has a history of distant emotional attachments with men. The hidden fear of re-experiencing a man's anger kept Lynn on the periphery of intimate loving relationships. In fact, Lynn knew she tended to keep both men and women at an emotionally safe distance, away from her terror of conflict.

Lynn told me the following during the course of her therapy:

I have had an inherent fear of upsetting people, and especially men. My fear of disapproval by a man feels paralyzing and terrorizing to me. I don't think I have ever confronted or truly stood up for myself in a relationship. This may sound weird, but I think I will die if I confront a man. I fear being emotionally annihilated, which keeps me away from any disagreements or upsets with men. My mom was very passive, and she never argued with anyone. I think I have taken on her passivity with men.

Dr. P: "Can you voice your opinion about anything with your partner?"
Lynn: "If it's something important or could lead to argument, I will acquiesce without being aware of it. I am scared of a man's anger!"
Dr. P: "What might happen to you if your partner or a man gets mad at you?"
Lynn: "I know it's not rational, but I think I am going to die. I placate and people please men so I never get in trouble or yelled at. I have never been physically abused by a man. It's a man's yelling or anger that triggers my father stuff. I always blame myself if my partner gets mad or upset about anything."
Dr. P: "Could you explain your history of abuse and fear of men to your partner?"
Lynn: "I have to, or I am going to break up with him and move out of town. I am going to stop hiding and speak up. I have broken up

with every boyfriend I have had since high school. My reflex is to always leave before there is a conflict or major blowup. I know it's messed up!"

EXPOSING YOUR SECRET: NO MORE EMOTIONAL TERRORISM

There is no greater agony than bearing an untold story inside of you.
　　—Zora Neale Hurston, *Dust Tracks on a Road*, 1942

NO *is a complete sentence*

The single biggest block to healing your shame factor and connecting to your core self is the fear of the word *No*. The word *No* is your starting point to changing your life narrative, developing self-acceptance, completing the individuating process, recovering from addiction, stopping your codependent and placating people-pleasing habits, and becoming shame free. *No* creates boundaries, and without boundaries there is no *You*. Zora Neale Hurston's quote is a reminder of the necessity of telling our story. We can't fully tell our story until we say *No* to the people, events, and decisions in our life that psychologically imprison us in the house of shame and fear.

The courage to start saying *No* to your suffering requires you to start developing your core emotional strength of self. There is a psychological truism that until a person learns how to say *No*, they don't truly have the ability to say, *Yes*. People who automatically say, *Yes* to everyone, every suggestion, and every situation are feeling powerless. The use of *No* creates personal boundaries, identity, emotional sobriety, clarity, secure relationships, and the healing of your shame factor. It's impossible to be in a codependent, shame-driven relationship when you start saying *No*. This single action word becomes the foundation to build your entire life on and around. A baby's first word is *No* as a means of having control in her world. In adult life, the purpose of the word is the same, and it is necessary for any lasting personality change.

> ### *Using the word* **No** *creates personal space for your identity to grow.*

Lynn took a break from therapy after we started to explore her fear of men. Approximately four months later, she came in to see me to continue her discussion about men and her difficulty in saying *No*. Lynn related the following:

> I have avoided for years my innate fear of saying *No* to anyone. Women aren't usually a problem for me. My boyfriend isn't a bully, but I have never voiced a difference of opinion on anything with him. It could be what to eat, what to drink, having or not having sex, and hanging out. Whatever he wanted, I automatically wanted, without even thinking about it. My codependency and shame always made me feel like a second-class partner, and I didn't have any respect for myself in the relationship. I finally told my partner that I didn't like his lack of communication, lack of affection, and indifference toward me. He got so upset and broke up with me on the spot. The relief I now feel two months later, not having to hide all my feelings and thoughts for fear of being a "bad person." I didn't really like my last boyfriend. I wanted a boyfriend because it made me feel normal, like my girlfriends who have one. I was just checking my box of being okay. I am now dating a guy who talks to me and listens to my needs and wants. I am not going to avoid any conflicts or be in denial about what is really going on in my love life.

> ### *Saying* **No** *and making your own choices is living shame free.*

The terrorizing fear of being unable to express yourself will create nonstop problems in every relationship in your life. Women tend to be victimized when they feel unable to express their opinion. The word *No* creates boundaries that are very important with regard sexuality, date rape, and sexual harassment. Fear of upsetting someone, causing a conflict, and having a difference of opinion are all features of emotional enmeshment combined with self-loathing. Learning how to tolerate your partner's anger, moods, and their arguing with you for using the word *No* is a very important step.

What are five things you want to say *No* to in your life starting right now?

1.

2.

3.

4.

5.

In my clinical practice, the power of *No* elicits a stronger negative response and more instantaneous terror than any other word. Incorporating the use of this two-letter word into your communication is solid evidence of your new personal boundaries, emotional sobriety, frustration tolerance, individuation, and self-care and acceptance.

People ask me all the time about shame and how they might know if they have any shame issues. I ask them this simple question: In what situations in your life, or to whom, do you have difficulty saying *No*? The answers are usually very surprising—"My husband," "Saying *No* to my children," "I can't say *No* to my eighty-eight-year-old mother," or "I don't say *No* to anyone." All these responses are dripping wet with shame, self-doubt, people pleasing, fear of rejection, and self-loathing. The process of setting psychological boundaries allows you to have mutually supportive relationships in every area of your life. The emotional freedom that comes from your core self-acceptance gives you the courage, strength, and clarity to say *No*.

When feeling a relapse of shame, ask yourself this question to regain your emotional balance and perspective:

Who or what am I afraid of expressing my opinion to or about?

Saying *No* will always serve your highest and best good, particularly when feeling your old shame triggers and self-doubts. The three old psychological defenses are rendered powerless when you start to enlist your ability to make empowered choices about your life. In a moment, we will look at a list of positive personality traits that stand in opposition to shame-based personality traits.

NEW COLLECTIVE QUALITIES OF YOU

Internal Family Systems Therapy is the psychological process of reconciling the disowned parts of your core self. The fifteen positive aspects of yourself listed below are contrasted against fifteen common fragmented and shaming pieces of you. All fifteen positive empowering core self traits have a role, purpose, and meaning in your life. You can see from the list that the shaming parts of you also had a purpose and role. We have discussed throughout the book the purpose of shame. Now it's time to visualize and think about what parts of you, your life, and your past and present feel uncomfortable, dismissed, and difficult to discuss. Avoidance, denial, and amnesia are no longer viable options for your growth and development. Your new narrative is shifting the rigid and despairing behaviors, placating and abusive relationships, and self-defeating choices out of your life.

Three practical steps for integrating your newly forming self are:

- Exposure—Approach Behavior
- Blending—Empathy and Acceptance
- Direct Access—Courage and Understanding

What Is Exposure?

Exposing your wounded and disowned shame-laden self starts with approaching the wound under the mud of your avoidance and denial. Your suffering will ultimately motivate you to expose and approach your outdated beliefs. Acknowledging your particular shame beliefs, triggers, and fears leads to psychological freedom. Shame can't exist when you uncover it. Shame can only continue in your relationships if you deny it, avoid it, and numb out to keep it going. The questions we talked about to expose avoidance, denial, and amnesia are designed to wash the mud off your core self. Approaching, accepting, and feeling empathy allows you to embrace your core and reconnect to your lost parts.

What Is Blending?

Blending your old beliefs with your positive core self allows you to develop an emotional and psychological balance within yourself. No more polarizing feelings of dread and despair, exaggerated reactions, or distorted personal perceptions and beliefs. For example, when you feel frustrated about your partner, you don't immediately tell yourself that you need to get a divorce and move away. Blending requires your new insight to look below the surface of your anger, embarrassment, and self-loathing. Blending involves rescuing your inner child, while exposing the trauma and terror. Going beyond your blame, despair, and rage allows you to blend and incorporate new parts of yourself.

Many times, the fear of connecting to your trauma and your past or present-day struggles can slip into your body. Somatic reactions keep you away from the source of your pain and suffering. Your body can be a barometer for your level of fear. Your body can't handle or tolerate long-term emotional denial. Eventually, your unresolved fragments, your pieces of pain and despair, will spill out into your physical body (i.e., as psychosomatic illnesses). Embracing the rejected, abandoned, and scared child within stops your search for seeking approval. Developing your positive core self can help to heal you physically as well as emotionally.

What Is Direct Access?

Direct access means speaking to the scared parts of you that are resistant to becoming incorporated into your loving, understanding, and empathetic self. For instance, you might explicitly talk to the part of you that feels like an imposter at work. The talk is in third person, and you are asking yourself, "Dave, why do you hide and feel scared that your colleagues don't like or respect you?" The imposter voice might respond, "You know that everyone secretly knows you are a fraud. Don't let anyone know or find out." Your first-person core self might say, "I am capable. This fear is from my childhood and it no longer applies to my life." The purpose of such a dialogue is to create new insights and increased clarity about the psychological distortions that control and guide your choices and core beliefs.

The *You* list is below: Consider the following two questions when reading these emotional and psychological contrasts of your shaming self compared to your positive core self.

1. What parts of you do you reject, disown, deny, or find make you anxious?
2. What parts of you do you want to embrace, develop, and experience?

Saying *Yes*, Codependency	<——You——>	Saying *No*, Self-Respect
Body Hatred	<——You——>	Self-Care
Wounded Child, Self-Doubt	<——You——>	Self-Acceptance
Abuse History	<——You——>	Self-Forgiveness
Anger and Rage	<——You——>	Self-Compassion
Anxiety	<——You——>	Self-Control
Imposter, Fraud	<——You——>	Self-Love
Fear of Embarrassment	<——You——>	Self-Worth
Isolation	<——You——>	Self-Engagement
Suspiciousness	<——You——>	Self-Confidence
Damaged Goods	<——You——>	Self-Awareness
People Pleasing	<——You——>	Self-Boundaries
Emotional Terror	<——You——>	Self-Perspective
Denial	<——You——>	Self-Motivation
Emotional Avoidance	<——You——>	Self-Direction

Every flower must grow through dirt.

—Unknown

You and Only You Hold the Keys to Your Life!

CLOSING THOUGHTS

There are better things ahead than any we leave behind.
—C. S. Lewis, June 17, 1963,
The Collected Letters of C. S. Lewis, vol. 3, 2007

Atelophobia: The fear of imperfection; the fear of never being good enough.

Living without the hundred-pound ball and chain of shame is possible. Saying *No* stops the cycle of shame like an emergency brake stops the runaway train from going off the tracks and heading for a cliff. The fearful self-loathing momentum of your life is suddenly halted and challenged from within by you. The ability to put your life on the fast track to your potential and happiness is within you. Your old shame buddies are now getting pushed off the cliff into nonexistence. The ability to approach, accept, and remain in the present moment is your pathway to healing. Learning to tolerate and withstand your old self-doubts begins to allow all the tools inside of you to emerge. C. S. Lewis, in the above quote, is encouraging us about the hope that is waiting on the other side of our old familiar comfort zone. The word *You* will always stand between your shame and your core self. No one else can be in the center of your core. Many people will tell you that they know better than you do about who and what should be in your core. Enmeshed relationships, codependent lovers, and fused identities can't survive the developing personal boundaries of a core self. Innately, you know from the inside out that your emotional headquarters can be your command center for love, acceptance, and understanding. It's very interesting that self-empowering traits start with you and your core self. The need for perfection and not being good enough—atelophobia—is an ego-driven shaming myth. Self-acceptance wipes out all the myths and fears of rejection.

The untapped treasures inside of you can only be assessed by you and no one else. The defensive posturing of our wounded, fragile self can't be the last chapter in our life. The self-empowered empathetic, compassionate, and loving self takes you to the hidden treasures you have been carrying all your life and never knew you possessed. Let's end our discussion with the reminder that going within is where you will find your greatest assets.

> *The mule that carries a bag of gold on its back doesn't know the value of that load. Likewise, man is so absorbed in toting the burdens of life, hoping for some happiness at the end of the trail, that he does not realize he carries within him. Because he*

looks for happiness in "things" he doesn't know he already possesses a wealth of happiness within himself.

—Paramahansa Yogananda,
as quoted in *Divine Will Healing*, 2013

The world breaks every one and many are strong in the broken places.

—Ernest Hemingway, *A Farewell to Arms*, 1929

CHAPTER 12

DEVELOPING YOUR OWN EAGLE MINDSET: YOUR ENDLESS RESOURCE

The self is not something ready-made, but something in continuous formation through choice of action.
—John Dewey, *Democracy and Education*, 1916

Don't let the noise of others' opinions drown out your inner voice.
—Steve Jobs, commencement address at Stanford University, June 12, 2005

Peace is the result of retraining your mind to process life as it is, rather than as you think it should be.
—Wayne Dyer, *There's a Spiritual Solution to Every Problem*, 2001

The healing process is simple and complicated simultaneously. Retraining your mind and letting go of your old issues seems endless, like it will go on forever, and then, all of sudden, it happens. There is an old adage that overnight success takes fifteen years. The practice, insight, openness, and self-awareness that allows you to create inner peace and a better quality of life starts with you. The frustration of continually feeling "bad" or like a "failure" comes from old distortions and old patterns of distraction created during your life. You are now in a position of emotional clarity to shift your life into the place of empowerment, insight, and contentment. We have discussed throughout the book the inception of shame, your family influence, your childhood trauma, addictions, six basic life challenges, seven emotional triggers, relationships, individuation, and your self-acceptance development. All your struggles and successes up to this point in your life have occurred with shame as a lurking terrorist. We are going to discuss now how your cognitive self can operate at a fuller capacity. There are three distinct parts of your cognitive self that operate within you. Let's call these three parts your lizard mindset, your owl middle mindset, and your eagle fullest-capacity mindset. Each of these mindsets are affected by your choices, psychological insights, and increased practice of loving self-acceptance and empathy. Having peaceful, calm, and stable relationships with yourself and with others is achieved through your higher mindset brain, as we will discuss further later in the chapter.

Before we explore this very interesting topic of cognitive mindset healing, let's revisit our working definition of shame from chapter 1 with some additional insights:

> Shame is a primary emotional wound, not a secondary belief; not based on a particular action; a paralyzing free-floating emotional, mental, and psychological state of mind that distorts a person's view of themselves in their world and with others; preventing them from developing a loving sense of self and impairing the individual from developing trusting, secure, safe relationships that are based on mutual respect and understanding; a chronic state of fear of feeling inadequate and/or not good enough; constant emotional terror of being discovered as a phony, a fraud, and an imposter.

This definition was expanded with our discussion of toxic families and codependent shame. The bottom line of shame in all its various permutations is that it has negative long-term, far-reaching consequences for the victim.

Every area of the victim's life is damaged and tortured by this growing emotional cancer of the heart and soul. During our journey through the valley of shame and dread, the various hiding spots of the shame terrorist have been revealed as outdated fragments of your past, no longer valuable or useful. We now know that shame is rendered completely powerless when its psychological defenses of avoidance, denial, and amnesia are no longer options. Your new psychological and emotional tools of approach, acceptance, and mindfulness are shame resistant. The ability to live shame free is emotional freedom and allows for the full expression of your core self. All the loving, self-directed actions of empathy, compassion, understanding, and forgiveness are a result of your best self-expression. Your newfound personal boundaries, both within and without, allow you endless options of who and what you can become. Experiencing the freedom of new options, choices, and insight is a function of your mindset awareness. Emerson's quote below is a gentle reminder that your life is completely under your control and up to you to direct. You have worked very hard, confronted your terror, and resolved your shame in order to arrive at this point in your life.

> *The only person you are destined to become is the person you decide to be.*
> —attributed to Ralph Waldo Emerson

THE THREE MINDSETS WITHIN YOUR EMOTIONAL HEADQUARTERS: LIZARD, OWL, AND EAGLE

Neuropsychology is the study of how the different parts of our mind work and impact our emotions, health, relationships, and well-being. The different parts of the mind and brain all play important roles in how our life functions and interacts with the outside world. The three mindsets are Lizard, Owl, and Eagle. Each mindset has its own set of characteristics, which can be understood, controlled, and productively managed. Creating your own mindset is another part of your core self, self-acceptance, and identity.

> ***The "lizard mindset" is reactive, defensive, and protective while facing real or imagined threats.***

Lizard Mindset

The most primitive part of your brain is located at the base, near the neck. This part is often called the "lizard" mind. The reason is that this part of your brain controls your automatic physical functioning, survival instincts, and emotional reactions and movements. This part of the mind reacts to survival threats real or imagined, and involves reflexes, instincts, emotional reactions, and automatic responses. The emotional part of the lizard mind isn't sophisticated or calm. It functions with aggression, anger, survival, and a hunting mentality. Reasoning isn't used when the lizard mind is engaged, since it is reaction based, not rationality based. It simply reacts with whatever force, energy, or action it deems necessary or needed. Often, alcohol, drugs, and anger will negatively impair and exaggerate its reaction. The low-level of self-control in the lizard mind is the perfect "fight or flight" environment for shame's terrorizing fears and controlling reactions. Shame lives in the lizard mindset for its survival and functioning.[1]

Owl Mindset

The middle mindset is more rational, knowledgeable, and intellectually based. The middle mindset is often referred to as the "owl brain." It has the capacity to think through situations logically without the adrenaline rush of the lizard mindset. The owl mindset is very calm, emotionally detached, and lives in the world of logic. Reason, scientific facts, and predictable outcomes are the mainstays of this mindset operation. Often, a person who operates mainly according to the owl mindset is described as being "in their head" and not seeing or experiencing the three-dimensional parts of life. Prior experiences form the owl mindset, without a person making emotional connections or psychological insights into their life based on those experiences. Their life experience stays within the strict parameters of logic, reason, and cognitive focus. For those who live in this mindset, going outside the "owl" comfort zone is cognitively forbidden and can't be emotionally tolerated or processed. Cognitive dissonance is the disagreement between the logical self and the insightful heart self for this person. Facts, research, linear thinking, and planning are the strengths of the owl mindset. The "owl brain" is what neurologists know as the midbrain, which doesn't process emotional issues or feelings.[2]

Logic, reason, and the absence of emotion or feeling is the owl mindset function.

Eagle Mindset

The full-capacity "eagle mindset" has the acquired ability to balance emotional feelings with cognitive reason and insight. This part of the brain is located in the frontal lobe (i.e., the forehead area). This is the highest functioning area of the brain. The experience of love and empathy for yourself and others is a major feature and function of the full-capacity eagle mindset adult. Creating emotional space for yourself with wisdom, insight, and reason when you are feeling strong feelings is this mindset's primary function. The ability to have emotional hindsight, foresight, and present moment insight into any situation is what it means to live and operate at your fullest capacity. We can call this your "eagle mindset" because of its ability to assimilate information without reacting to or recreating old self-defeating patterns. Developing perspective in your life allows you to consider reason, emotion, and possible solutions. The lower two mindsets don't have the capacity to process your higher-level needs, desires, and everyday emotional challenges.

The eagle mindset can experience the emotions and feelings of the moment and respond appropriately. The lizard mindset is impulsively driven without thinking or considering the consequences of its actions. The owl mindset has to think through life before it allows itself to experience life. Additionally, the middle brain, the owl mindset, is cognitively insulated and psychologically guarded from the lurking terror of the hunter shame. The owl mindset is hyper-vigilant about any perceived fear, risks, and mental or emotional vulnerability. Both the lizard and owl mindsets are psychologically and emotionally exhausting and tortured by their past shame, trauma, and present-day denial, avoidance, and amnesia.

> *Change your thoughts and you change your world.*
> —Dr. Norman Vincent Peale, as quoted in
> *Back on Track: How to Straighten Out Your Life When It*
> *Throws You a Curve,* by Deborah Norville, 1997

The full capacity of the eagle mindset has the intellectual patience, intuitive wisdom, and psychological balance to incorporate change. We can all learn to function and live our lives from our eagle mindset regardless of where we started from or have operated within. Dr. Peale, who was starting his career during the Great Depression of the 1930s, was one of the first advocates of the idea that everyone had an innate power to embrace personal change and happiness. Changing your mindset and accessing your potential will change your entire life. This isn't a rainbow-and-unicorns hyperbolic statement but rather the result of doing the emotional and psychological work of becoming your highest and best self.

The pathway to accessing your fullest capacity eagle mindset brain begins with learning to sit with yourself. I know this idea sounds terribly simple and elementary. The term "sitting with yourself" is the learned practice of stepping back from your reactions, feelings, and fears in any given moment. The art of stepping back, pausing your emotions, and saying *No* to your automatic emotional reactions allows for mental space. Creating personal emotional room allows you to access your innate wisdom and knowledge. It's possible, regardless of prior impulse control issues, addictive behaviors, drug use, and avoidance, to stop running away from your feelings. Pausing, feeling, and thinking is an important habit to develop, which is shame proof, calming, and powerful. Cognitively and emotionally controlling your responses to anything that comes across your path is considered mastery of life in both Eastern and Western psychology.

> *You cannot always control what goes on outside, but you can always control what goes on inside.*
> —attributed to Wayne Dyer

Your fullest capacity eagle mindset accesses your full potential.

Your highest and fullest mindset is a sustainable long-term strategy for living your life to its potential. The psychological, emotional, relational, financial, personal, and health benefits are incredible when living with your eagle mindset. It's worth mentioning that the three animal references to our brain are very appropriate for their symbolism. The lizard is a reptile with limited functions and options in life. The lizard is a basic creature with impulse and survival reactions. Living in our "lizard mindset" limits the opportunities in our life for fulfillment and happiness. The owl is a mysterious creature that hides in the trees of life and is difficult to see and relate to. The owl stays in its tree to avoid any degree of vulnerability and participation with other creatures or birds—in other words, it avoids relationships. The owl mindset does not allow you to come out of your head to engage and experience life in the moment. You can't think through love, happiness, or sadness; you must feel and experience it. Neither the lizard nor the owl mindset are equipped to address the complicated psychological mess that shame creates in an individual's life and relationships. The eagle mindset has the big picture perspective and understanding of the environment—in other words, your life. The eagle knows where it's going and how to manage its life without having to be grounded or hidden like the other two mindsets. Let's explore how to access your eagle mindset of personal wisdom and healing.

EAGLE MINDFULNESS MINDSET: PRESENCE OF YOUR MIND

Your higher fullest cognitive "eagle" mindset has the capacity, patience and insight to develop new responses for your life going forward. Your higher mindset responds rather than reacts to conflicts and personal issues from your lizard survival mindset. Peace of mind is an emotional and psychological state that we all desire and want to foster in our day-to-day life. Shame is the opposite of peace. Shame is founded on fear and internal conflict. It's psychologically impossible to have any lasting peace of mind when shame is terrorizing you with fear and self-doubt. Conflict consumes our ability to have insight and clarity, and this is shame's primary operating procedure.

> *Shame and inner peace are incompatible— shame operates through fear, threats, and internal conflict. Peace of mind operates through acceptance, love, and understanding.*

The residual influence of shame is constant, internal, and outward conflict and self-doubt, and, in severe cases, suicide. Unbridled shame over time will become toxic, increasingly aggressive, and fatal if you do not interrupt it. Shame is emotionally debilitating, especially when it is coupled with anxiety and all of its different expressions of living in the future with dread and impending doom. Shame combined with depression means living in the past with regret and self-loathing. Anxiety and depression are symptoms of shame's ability to keep our mindset in perpetual turmoil and dis-ease. Your highest and best self will always live in the present moment. The power of the present is a popular concept and for good reason. Being present means being calm. Your eagle mindset, which keeps your life in perspective, allows you to come up with new ideas and solutions. The quote below is a reminder of the insidious nature and control shame exerts in our past, present, and future.

> *If you are depressed, you are living in the past.*
> *If you are anxious you are living in the future.*
> *If you are at peace you are living in the present.*
> —Unknown

One of the goals in healing your shame factor is to create inner peace and calmness within you. None of your relationship conflicts, challenges, or misunderstandings can be solved when you are in any type of shame cycle. The degree to which you feel calm and peaceful will be the same degree to which your relationship world will reflect peace and harmony. Relationship challenges don't have to be shame challenges but rather opportunities for healing. Secure and stable relationships are possible in any area of your life when living shame free. The absence of inner conflict allows for your higher mindset to function at its full capacity.

FULL-CAPACITY EAGLE MINDSET BENEFITS

When you begin to respond to your life from a place of internal self-confidence rather than dread, you begin to cultivate emotional freedom, peace of mind, and emotional clarity. Responsiveness is an acquired skill that is developed through your practice, learning, and tolerating the emotional experience of suffering. The contrast of suffering versus peace of mind is glaring. The idea of being emotionally, psychologically, and physically present when stressed is often referred to as mindfulness. The eagle mindset embraces and includes all these aspects of mindfulness. When we are emotionally suffering, psychologically avoiding our trauma, and forgetting our core self we are sleepwalking through life.

> *People only change when the pain of not changing is greater than the pain of changing.*
> —attributed to Dr. Albert Ellis

The lizard and owl brains keep the defensive walls up and guarded against loss of control. It's impossible to relax and silence the shame terror when you are in the midst of reacting to it. Mindfulness is a higher-level eagle mindset functioning that takes you out of the grind of minute-to-minute activity. Stepping back from the stress of the day and staying emotionally connected to yourself is the purpose of any mindfulness practice. The opposite of being peaceful is sleepwalking, numbing out, being in denial, reacting with fear and anger, or retreating to addictive or compulsive behaviors.

Yoga, meditation, guided imagery, deep breathing, and any technique that quiets the noise in our head is valuable. Some of the benefits of mindfulness are as follows:

- Improved mental clarity
- Reinforcement of a healthy lifestyle
- Increased energy
- Decreased stress (i.e., shame) and slowed down aging
- Increased blood and oxygen circulation
- Reduced pain
- Increased self-awareness
- Increased happiness and peace

These are just a few of the many internal physical, emotional, and psychological benefits of living from your peaceful core self. The alternative is to live with your chronic fear reaction to embarrassment, fear, and self-loathing. Living with your mindset of competence, courage, and insight increases your ability to enjoy your life in the present moment.

> **All mindfulness practices are shame resistant. Shame can't exist in a calm mind.**

The reason for discussing the different cognitive mindsets coupled with shame-resistant mindfulness practices is to give you tools that will help you to remain shame free. Cancer survivors will make drastic life changes to enhance their health and remain cancer free. No one wants their cancer coming back in another part of their body. Shame requires the same level of commitment and self-discipline for your psychological health. You have worked very hard to begin the process of living shame free. The eagle mindset along with mindfulness practice will help keep shame and its insidious friends out of the garden of your heart and soul. Your ability to experience a peaceful and productive life is directly correlated with your ability to remain calm and peaceful. Your eagle full-capacity mindset is your path to healing and happiness.

> *Buddha was asked, "What have you gained from meditation?" He replied, "Nothing!"*
> *"However," Buddha said, "let me tell you what I have lost: Anger, Anxiety, Depression, Insecurity, Fear of Old Age and Death."*
>
> —Unknown

I love this response that shows the value of mindfulness, the eagle mindset, meditation, and any type of self-soothing practice. Developing the ability to be silent, putting all electronics down for five minutes, is the beginning of a wonderful self-exploration into the depths of your heart and soul. Meditation involves simply becoming more self-aware of your thoughts, feelings, and responses. Meditation, mindfulness, and self-awareness are all designed to help you discover your mind-body connection. There is no wrong way to meditate or quiet your mind. Any introspective habit that slows down your brain—keeping you on your side of the relationship tennis court and out of other people's personal storms—is valuable. There is no religious connotation that comes with meditation and mindfulness practices. I highly recommend whatever calms you down, gives you more clarity, and improves the quality of your life. A calm mind allows you to process your self-realization of your innate gifts and talents. Learning how to sit silently for five minutes, breathing slowly and clearing out all the clutter in your mind, is a great beginning point. I love this reminder by Thich Nhat Hanh that sometimes life is this simple.

> *Life is available only in the present moment.*
> —Thich Nhat Hanh, *True Love:*
> *A Practice for Awakening the Heart*, 2006

YOUR QUICK SELF-CHECK HEALING GUIDE

The list below is specifically designed as reminder to you to remain shame free and courageous and operate from your highest mindset perspective. Your innate abilities, self-empowered resources, and core emotional strengths are all part of the process of changing. Writing your new narrative will incorporate your core-self gifts, updated psychological tools, and your emotional mindfulness, which have all been untapped sources up until now. Remember, your story has never been written before, and it's not complete. Many stories have been written, but no one will write your story except you.

Staying on your life track is a day-to-day process. Feeling overwhelmed and momentarily defeated, and repeating old emotional shame habits is understandable and to be expected. This condensed, quick self-check guide can help you regain and maintain your inner focus and inner connection. Let's review twenty-five daily reminders for reinforcing and strengthening your peace of mind and expanding your psychological insight. Staying shame free is possible with your new emotional choices and psychological clarity. Have patience and understanding with your imperfections, accepting their existence, which will go a long way in reducing the role and influence of shame inside of you and in all your relationships.

> *No matter how great the talent or effort, some things just take time. You can't produce a baby in one month by getting nine women pregnant.*
> —Warren Buffett, chairman's letter to shareholders of Berkshire Hathaway Inc., March 4, 1986

Your Personal List:

1. **There are no losses in your life. No one is a loser—never!** It's through your evolving insights of pain and suffering that you found the courage to change. Your new awareness and empathetic understanding has created emotional space for you to stop your self-loathing and self-doubt. You're healing your inner child with acceptance, self-love, and understanding. Being patient and understanding is your self-acceptance in action.
2. **When feeling worthless and scared, ask this question: What would self-love do?** This question pulls you out of the past and immediately into the moment. Your secure emotional perspective widens with your clarity of the situation. Asking yourself insightful questions will calm you, ease your panic, and reduce your fear. Questioning your old reactions helps you to keep developing the responsiveness of your eagle mindset.
3. **Cognitive dissonance will become cognitive acceptance.** Replacing the old self-doubts with self-acceptance

will become automatic over time. Your self-loathing isn't quick to release its position of power, handing over the reins to your loving self-worth. The gap between your emotional healing and your shame self will ultimately be resolved with your self-accepting actions, beliefs, and choices.

4. **Emotional sobriety creates emotional and psychological space for new responses and new actions**. Addictive and compulsive behaviors can't function when you are responsive and thoughtful. Pausing, breathing, and thinking creates clarity and new opportunities and solutions. Staying in your eagle mindset expands your ability to be responsive rather than reactive.

5. **Emotional regression is a shaming fear reaction**. Learn to recognize the emotional age you become when feeling scared, embarrassed, or angry? The key is to be self-aware when you are feeling old shame triggers, which is a regression and a pathway to feeling powerless. Staying in your adult eagle mindset allows you full access to any and all solutions.

> *Don't get upset with people or situations, both are powerless without your reaction.*
>
> —Unknown

6. **Emotional boundaries are necessary in any relationship.** Forming psychological limits with yourself and your partner, family, children, and colleagues allows for your individuality to emerge in the relationship. Losing yourself or trying to find yourself in another person is a formula for disaster and heartbreak (stemming from shaming codependence). You can't save or fix anyone. Empathy doesn't mean taking responsibility for another person.

7. **Expanding your comfort zone is necessary for your healing.** Living courageously means pursuing your per-

sonal dreams. Self-acceptance is the foundation from which to step beyond your critical voice and into your own life. Discomfort and fear of the future is resolved by staying present with your choices and self-approval. Feelings of safety and familiarity aren't always in your best interest; change requires the momentary suspension of your comfort zone in order to move forward.

8. **Tennis takes two players—and requires staying on your own side of the court.** You can't play both sides of the court in your relationships; allow the other person to hit the ball back to you. Your new sense of self-respect means you no longer need to seek approval from another person. Codependent and placating behaviors shame you and frustrate the other person. No one can accept and love you until you do it for yourself. Self-acceptance is your sole responsibility, not that of your partners or parents. You can't outsource your personal responsibility in a relationship. Relationships require two participants to have a mutually beneficial connection.

9. *No* **is a complete sentence.** Resisting old shame feelings can be very scary, but this is necessary for your healing and personal transformation. The practice of asserting your boundaries isn't being self-centered, mean, or rude. Creating your own identity starts with your ability to not to placate, people please, or seek to find yourself in your partner. You can stop your abusive behaviors. Practice saying *No* at least once a day to develop and strengthen your core self-muscles and clarity. Living shame free involves staying out of other people's drama and emotional storms.

Peace cannot be kept by force, it can only be achieved by understanding.

—Albert Einstein, speech to the
New History Society, December 14, 1930

10. **Your core self is always growing and expanding**. All the aspects of your self-acceptance, self-worth, self-confidence, and positive personal traits come from you! Everything you need or want is inside of you, along with all the tools to solve whatever challenges you may face. Positive qualities of empathy, compassion, and self-forgiveness are all within us to discover. Looking inward allows you to find solutions that will help you live your life to its fullest. Learn to listen to your intuition.

11. **Good shame is a moral compass.** Feeling ashamed of something you did is valuable. Having ethics, morals, and integrity are all roles of good shame. Bad shame is feeling defective and like a bad person. Good shame is related to actions or behavior. Considering your influence and impact on others is wise and helps you care for yourself and others. Listening to your positive inner voice will guide you in making good decisions.

12. **Everyone has challenges in the six areas of life**. Money, relationships, career, family, children, and your health and body can create many challenges and demands. You aren't defective or bad if you are struggling in one or two, or even in all of these areas at any given time. Learn your life lessons from these challenges and use them in your future. No one is exempt from growing, changing, and learning. Focus on the three psychological tools in every situation: approach behavior, acceptance, and staying present. Shame personalizes your challenges as negative and creates self-loathing.

13. **Permission isn't necessary for your individuation process and identity formation**. You have the right to pursue your life and not be psychologically responsible for the identities of others. Enmeshed relationships resist your autonomy. Having your own opinions, thoughts, and choices means you are functioning shame free. Forming a sense of

yourself in your family and relationships shows that you are developing your core self strengths. Shame plays the guilt card, but having your own life is nothing to feel guilty about.

14. **Taking personal responsibility for your life is a game changer**. No one can control you with shame when you take the reins of your past, present, and future. This action step is very powerful and immediately neutralizes shame's hold on your life. Asking yourself what your responsibility is in any situation is a very important emotional technique to find insight, maintain your boundaries, and keep your emotional sobriety. Acceptance removes blame and resentment from your life. Your eagle mindset functions at its fullest capacity with responsible actions and choices.

15. **Your childhood and family is your starting line, not your finish line**. Your upbringing is part of your history, but it doesn't define you. You are in control of your life narrative going forward. Shame imprisons us with the distorted belief that because of our chaotic, unstable family background we are "damaged goods" and "not good enough." You are bigger than your history or any abuse that you have experienced. Families are a launching point for your development and adult life. The key to living shame free is separating your past from your present-day challenges. Reliving your old shame cycles can be resolved with your approach behavior and staying present. You are in charge of your destiny regardless of where you started in life. You aren't a prisoner of your past.

The person who ultimately knows what's best for you is you!

16. **Relationships matter and so do you!** Every aspect of your life is a relationship. Your most important relationship is the one you are fostering with yourself. Removing the mud

of shame from your core self will change your view of relationships. Fulfilling emotional connections stop and start with you, and you are in control of the barriers standing in your way. Shaming, codependency, placating, addiction, people pleasing, and approval seeking are nonstarters to your identity and highest best self. All your relationship styles and patterns start with your shame-free approach. It's possible to update your relationship style to bring secure, mutually supportive people into your life. Relationships are a classroom for learning about yourself. Your life's healing progress is always reflected in your relationship world. Embrace your individuality so others in your life can also.

17. **Mutually supportive relationships are shame resistant.** The ability to be honest, open, and transparent builds your self-worth. Creating your own support system is liberating. Addiction and trauma recovery are reasons to allow people to know your story. The ability to accept and receive love, empathy, and compassion from others is critical to healing your wounded inner child. Being able to accept compliments and love is a form of self-love. Seeing your personal worth allows you to develop safe, secure connections. Mutual relationships have boundaries and respect for each other's needs. Individuals have healthy relationships that are productive for all parties involved. Guilt and shame are not factors in mutually functional relationships.

18. **Developing frustration tolerance.** There is a cognitive art to self-acceptance and understanding others. Learn to emotionally step back from your desire to have the world and other people work the way you want (i.e., your control issues). Emotional tolerance of disappointment, shame, and fear unhooks you from your lizard brain anger and reactions. Your eagle mindset helps you to keep a wider perspective about people. Responding to challenges allows you to pursue new options and solutions. Accepting your life and its

circumstances breeds confidence and reduces your anxiety. Feeling powerless is a primary source of shame, rage, and despair. Empathy and compassion for others is a form of developing tolerance and understanding in your life.

Accepting your past and present "shame"
lets you out of emotional hell.

19. **No secrets—exposing your shame.** Shame can't exist when it is exposed as a lie. The only power that shame comes through threatening you with your unspoken secrets, self-doubt, and self-loathing. Exposing and accepting your deepest weaknesses, flaws, and traumas lets you out of psychological hell. The fear of revealing your repressed memories and history is no longer necessary. Allowing your soul and heart to breathe without the gorilla of shame sitting on your chest is liberating. Facing your trauma and abuse is the pathway to your healing and to living emotionally free from your inner terrorist. Confronting your inner demons is necessary for your well-being and future. You no longer need to live in the shadow of embarrassment and self-loathing.

> *I knew that if I failed, I wouldn't regret that, but I knew the one thing I might regret is not trying.*
> —Jeff Bezos, Academy of Achievement interview,
> May 4, 2001

20. **Taking courageous steps—exposing the imposter syndrome.** Feeling competent and capable are habits that can be acquired and developed. Allowing yourself to learn and make mistakes reduces the paralyzing fear of being discovered. There is nothing to hide from or avoid about yourself. Permission to continually learn wipes out the old fears of incompetence. Perfectionism is a form of self-loathing. Self-

acceptance is a process, not a destination in your career or life. Allowing yourself to take new jobs and embrace new opportunities is empowering. When in doubt do something courageous to expand your personal and professional foundation.

21. **Living inside out**. Your life paradigm has shifted from external influences to internal influences. Your vast tools, talents, gifts, and abilities are all within and waiting for your self-discovery. The emotional headquarters of your life is located inside of your core self. You—and not the other people in your life—are making all the choices and decisions. You are fully in control of your emotional responses and your interactions with people. No one other than you controls your life. The happiness, peace of mind, and ability to live calmly are found by looking within yourself, and they cannot be affected by the outside world. Your internal feelings of love, acceptance, belonging, and forgiveness are yours to share with the people in your life. Your identity, destiny, and dreams are all contained inside of you. It's your job to uncover them. Your personal success comes through connecting to your dreams and turning them into reality.

22. **Individuation is a life-saving process.** People will continually tell you what to do and how you should act and live. Creating your own separate identity is a necessary step for having a peaceful and fulfilling life. You don't have to apologize for being a self-sufficient, high-functioning adult. Separating from your family isn't abandonment, but, rather, it's an act of psychological necessity. Enmeshed relationships resist individual identities for fear of being lost.

23. **Pulling the roots of shame out of your addictions.** Living shame free is one of the best ways to live addiction free. Psychological clarity and emotional balance allow you to heal the horrors of past and present traumas. No addictive behavior is beyond the reach of healing and self-love. Self-loathing and shame can't exist when you begin to allow your hidden pain

to become visible to you. The power of feeling embarrassed, defective, and damaged has over you can be healed with your self-acceptance, understanding, and empathy.

24. **You and your eagle mindset control your destiny.** No one holds the keys to your present or future except you! It's a powerful responsibility of adulthood to take complete ownership of your life for today, tomorrow, and all the days ahead. Your past disappointments aren't a reason to stop your personal growth or stop walking along your path of healing. Taking time to find "you" within "you" allows you to live at your fullest with the best version of yourself. Eagles soar and never worry about where they are going to land next. Living in the present means living shame free and expanding your life vision. Meditation, mindfulness, and being quiet are all inward tools for living peacefully in the outside world. When you are panicking or feeling fearful, take a five-minute timeout to check in with yourself. You will be continually surprised about the wisdom contained inside of your heart and soul.

25. *Yes*, **you have permission to do the impossible.** Developing all your newly acquired skills, tools, and core strengths might seem overwhelming at times. Living without the black cloud of shame hanging over you will take some time to fully appreciate and get used to. It is liberating to constantly not feel inadequate, inferior, and insecure. The idea that you know what you want to do, that you can decide to move, change careers, or have a relationship, is a byproduct of your personal growth. You no longer have to hide your sexual orientation, family secrets, or dreams from anyone. You do not have to look for the approval of others or pay attention to those who tell you how to behave. You have won the emotional lottery of unlimited resources and hope. The next chapter in your book of life will now be all about how you want to live according to your innate self.

FURTHER THOUGHTS

> **Challenge**: *When a fearful thought enters your mind, pause and think of three positive thoughts. Practice flipping your old script over to your new self-accepting script. You have that much personal power!*
>
> —Stephan B. Poulter

> *I find it extremely liberating to see that I was the cause of all my problems. With this realization I have also learned that I am my own solution. This is the great big gift of personal accountability. When we stop blaming external forces and own up to our responsibility we become the ultimate creators of our destiny.*
>
> —Jenna Galbut

Remaining calm and centered when having a shaming moment and re-experiencing a paralyzing wave of despair is all part of the process. This quote by Jenna Galbut is one of the themes of your healing and your new normal. The personal power of accepting who and what you are is psychological freedom. Regardless of past experiences, you have the personal power to flip your shame script to a shame-free life. The twenty-five shame-free reminders above all point to one thing: you. Your new eagle mindset with which you respond to your day-to-day experiences is adding energy to your life. The insight and wisdom to stay out of the personal storms of your friends and family will serve you well. Everyone has to save and heal themselves. Being supportive isn't doing the other person's healing. Disconnecting from codependent placating relationships will, in itself, change your life. Giving yourself approval, understanding, and forgiveness is taking full control of your life. Unless someone is willing and open to healing, you can't do anything for them. Continue to embrace your new insights and your expanded emotional base.

WHEN AND WHY SHOULD I GET
PROFESSIONAL SUPPORT—NO STIGMA

> *Never let someone who has done nothing tell you how to do anything.*
>
> —attributed to Al Pacino

I love this quote by Al Pacino. People who don't understand or know shame, a traumatic childhood, or the internal struggle of despair aren't a good resource. Friends, family, and partners can be fabulous emotional supports. The delicate art of processing one's terror, trauma, and hidden shame, however, requires someone who is trained as a mental health provider. We all have blind spots, and a therapist can help expose those hard-to-find places. Finding a therapist you feel comfortable with is critical, regardless of their degrees. I know, professionally and personally, that parts of our healing can be expedited with the compassionate support of a trained professional. If money and resources are a problem, there are many different options, such as reduced fee clinics, twelve-step codependents anonymous groups, and various other support groups throughout the country. Additionally, there are online therapists who can support your healing process and provide cost-effective access to therapeutic support. There is no wrong way to heal. When in doubt about whether or not you need a therapist, choose therapy. If you don't need that level of support, it will become apparent before long.

There is no stigma or judgment attached to seeking out therapy. I do it myself, and I know the freedom and relief that comes from having a neutral third party hear my story. The empathy, compassion, and insight you can gain from having an understanding person in the room with you is, in itself, a profound curative experience. It takes incredible courage to sit down weekly to discuss your story. The self-caring intention of taking the responsibility of removing the mud of shame and trauma from your life is transformational. It is classic denial, avoidance, and emotional amnesia to think that your trauma will simply fade over time. If hiding from our problems worked, none of us would need to advocate for the value of healing. The only thing that will fade is your clarity and your ability to keep your shame buried and out of sight. Sweeping your past under the carpet is not a viable option or a good long-term healing strategy.

CLOSING THOUGHTS: MY THOUGHTS FOR YOU

> *If someone offers you an amazing opportunity but you're not sure you can do it, say yes—then learn how to do it later.*
> —Richard Branson, "Y Is for Yes,"
> *Virgin* (blog), December 18, 2017

The amazing opportunity awaiting you is your personal self-realization, self-awakening, and healing. The quote above is universal in its application and purpose. Mr. Branson is absolutely correct about saying *yes* to continuing on your journey to living shame free. You will figure out how to navigate the next chapter of your life with clarity and purpose.

I want to thank you for taking time to read *The Shame Factor*. As I wrote this book, I imagined what you, the reader, might say or think. I hope I was able to help you expose your inner terrorist. We are all working to heal ourselves, which in turn heals the greater good in our world. Living shame free is the opportunity I want all of us to take, even if we don't know what the road of life ahead looks like. You have the tools, persistence, and ability to figure out your own emotional geography and life map. No one has to vote on or approve of the way you are processing and healing your deepest wounds. There isn't a subject, theory, or item of shame in this book that I am not personally acquainted with or don't understand. The subject of shame has been only scratched in this book. You will write your own internal story about how you pulled shame out of your life by the roots.

I mentioned in the preface that my struggle with shame started early on. It was not anyone's fault; I had many personal challenges. When shame was formally defined for me, it was relief to finally name it. Not knowing what was wrong with me had been torture itself. It's been a bumpy road of healing and becoming less and less controlled by my inner terrorist. If I can overcome my shame-laden life, I know that you have the innate wisdom to do it as well.

The breadth and depth of unresolved trauma, abuse, and self-loathing is serious issue. Refer back to the relevant parts of the book as you go on, for ideas about your healing and your continued personal evolution. Your healing and the exposure of shame is transformational and profound. The deep healing work of growing your inner core strength will never be popular, but it will leave you feeling valuable (giving you a sense of self-worth) and loved (allowing you to embrace self-acceptance). Your entire world, from the inside out, will be positively impacted, and that's a priceless legacy.

The one enduring gift that everyone can develop through their healing process is persistence. Having persistence for your healing creates patience, understanding, self-acceptance, love, empathy, compassion, and self-awareness, which will serve you well in any situation. Healing your inner child is liberating and involves a courageous process. The persistence that allows you to push beyond your old self-doubts and heartbreak is your greatest asset. No amount of crippling shame or personal torture can withstand your commitment to living a healthy, whole, peaceful, and fulfilling life. Reread the list of the twenty-five core strengths and new abilities whenever your heart feels weak or scared. The opportunity to write a new narrative about yourself is worth it. Your persistence is omnipotent! I want to leave you with my all-time favorite quote to hold onto and take with you going forward.

Persistence . . .

Nothing in the world can take the place of persistence. Talent will not; nothing is more common than unsuccessful men with talent. Genius will not; unrewarded genius is almost a proverb. Education will not; the world is full educated derelicts. Persistence and determination alone are omnipotent.

—attributed to Calvin Coolidge in the
Dallas Morning News, August 16, 1929

NOTES

Chapter 1. The Shame Factor: What Is It, Doctor? Exposing the Big Secret

1. C. G. Jung, *The Archetypes and the Collective Unconscious*, 2nd ed., trans. R. F. C. Hull (Princeton, NJ: Princeton University Press, 1968), pp. 42–54.

2. D. W. Winnicott, *The Collected Works of D. W. Winnicott*, ed. Lesley Caldwell and Helen Taylor Robinson, 12 vols. (Oxford: Oxford University Press, 2016); Simon Grolnick, *The Work and Play of Winnicott* (Northvale, NJ: Jason Aronson, 1990), p. 44.

3. Shelly A. Wiechelt, "The Specter of Shame in Substance Misuse," *Substance Use and Misuse* 42, no. 2–3 (2007): 399–409.

4. Shahida Arabi, *Becoming the Narcissist's Nightmare: How to Devalue and Discard the Narcissist While Supplying Yourself* (New York: SCW Archer, 2016), chapter 1.

5. Neema Trivedi-Bateman, "The Roles of Empathy, Shame, and Guilt in Violence Decision-Making" (PhD diss., Institute of Criminology, Cambridge University, 2015), pp. 18–25.

6. Carl R. Rogers, *A Way of Being* (New York: Houghton Mifflin, 1980), pp. 27–40.

Chapter 2. Your Early Years and Your Personal Shame Beginnings: Five Common Shaming Parenting Styles

1. Sigmund Freud, "Psychopathology of Everyday Life," in *The Basic Writings of Sigmund Freud* (New York: Modern Library, 1995), pp. 3–148.

2. Benjamin Spock, *The Common Sense Book of Baby and Child Care* (New York: Duell, Sloan, and Pearce, 1946), pp. 44–70. (Note: Since the original publication in 1946 there have been ten more editions printed.)

3. Dorothy Corkille Briggs, *Your Child's Self-Esteem: Step-by-Step Guidelines for Raising Responsible, Productive, Happy Children* (New York: Broadway Books, 1988), pp. 72–120.

4. Darius Cikanavicius, "A Brief Guide to Unprocessed Childhood Toxic Shame," *Psychology of the Self* (blog), October 17, 2018, https://blogs.psychcentral.com/psychology-self/2018/09/childhood-toxic-shame/.

Daniela F. Sieff, "Uncovering the Secrets of the Traumatised Psyche: The Life-Saving Inner Protector Who Is also a Persecutor," in *Understanding and Healing Emotional Trauma: Conversations with Pioneering Clinicians and Researchers* (London: Routledge, 2015), pp. 11–24.

5. Michael Windle, "Substance Use and Abuse among Adolescent Runaway: A Four-Year Follow-Up Study," *Journal of Youth and Adolescence* 18, no. 4 (August 1988): 331–44.

"Runaway Youth," DomesticShelters.org, January 4, 2016, https://www.domesticshelters.org/articles/children-and-domestic-violence/runaway-youth.

Jody M. Greene et al., *Sexual Abuse among Homeless Adolescents: Prevalence, Correlates, and Sequelae* (Washington, DC: US Department of Health and Human Services, November 2002).

6. Susan Forward, *Toxic Parents: Overcoming Their Hurtful Legacy and Reclaiming Your Life*, with Craig Buck (New York: Bantam Books, 1989), pp. 75–125.

Martha Vannicelli, *Group Psychotherapy with Adult Children of Alcoholics: Treatment Techniques and Countertransference Considerations* (New York: Guilford, 1989), pp. 12–150.

Bente Storm Mowatt Haugland, "Recurrent Disruptions and Routines in Families with Paternal Alcohol Abuse," *Family Relations* 54, no. 2 (April 2005): 225–41.

Basem Abbas Al Ubaidi, "Cost of Growing Up in Dysfunctional Family," *Journal of Family Medicine and Disease Prevention* 3, no. 3 (2017).

7. Marika Lindholm, "8 Mental Health Challenges Single Moms Face," Talkspace, November 23, 2016, https://www.talkspace.com/blog/2016/11/8-mental-health-challenges-single-moms-face/.

8. Rachel A. Haine, Tim S. Ayers, Irwin N. Sandler, and Sharlene A. Wolchik, "Evidence-Based Practices for Parentally Bereaved Children and Their Families," *Professional Psychology, Research and Practice* 39, no. 2 (April 2008): 113–21; Thomas Crook and John Eliot, "Parental Death during Childhood and Adult Depression: A Critical Review of the Literature," *Psychological Bulletin* 87, no. 2 (1980): 252–59; Margaret S. Stroebe, "Coping with Bereavement: A Review of the Grief Work Hypothesis," *OMEGA: Journal of Death and Dying* 26, no. 1 (February 1993): 19–42; Irwin N. Sandler et al., "Linking Empirically Based Theory and Evaluation: The Family Bereavement Program," *American Journal of Community Psychology* 20, no. 4 (August 1992): 491–521; "Losing a Parent, 'Take-Aways' from Research That Can Make a Difference," Sympathy Solutions, August 25, 2014, https://www.sympathysolutions.com/losing-a-parent,-"take-aways"-from-research-that-can-make-a-difference.html.

9. Pamela S, Webster, Terri L. Orbuch, and James S. House, "Effects of Childhood Family Background on Adult Marital Quality and Perceived Stability," *American Journal of Sociology* 101, no. 2 (September 1995): 404–32; Galena K. Rhoades, Scott M. Stanley, Howard J. Markman, and Erica P. Ragan, "Parents' Marital Status, Conflict, and Role Modeling: Links with Adult Romantic Relationship Quality," *Journal of Divorce and Remarriage* 53, no 5 (2012): 348–58.

10. Andrew J, Cherlin et al., "Longitudinal Studies of Effects of Divorce on children in Great Britain and the United States," *Science* 252, no. 5011 (June 7, 1991): 1386–89.

Andrew J. Cherlin, P. Lindsay Chase-Lansdale, and Christine McRae, "Effects of Parental Divorce on Mental Health throughout the Life Course," *American Sociological Review* 63, no. 2 (April 1998): 239–49.

11. Les B. Whitbeck et al., "Intergenerational Continuity of Parental Rejection and Depressed Affect," *Journal of Personality and Social Psychology* 63, no. 6 (December 1992): 1036–45.

Chapter 3. How Shame Plays Out for the Sexes: Toxic Male and Female Shame

1. Dane Archer, *Gender and Relationships: Male-Female Differences in Love and Marriage* (Berkeley, CA: Berkeley Media, 2002), film, 42 min.; Allan G. Johnson, *The Blackwell Dictionary of Sociology: A User's Guide Sociological Language*, 2nd ed. (Malden, MA: Blackwell, 2000).

2. Lisa Ferentz, *Letting Go of Self-Destructive Behaviors: A Workbook of Hope and Healing* (New York: Routledge, 2014), chap. 5.

3. Devona Gruber, Lauren Hansen, Katrina Soaper, and Aaron J. Kivisto, "The Role of Shame in General, Intimate and Sexual Violence Perpetration," in *Psychology of Shame: New Research*, ed. Kevin G. Lockhart (New York: Nova Science, 2014), pp. 39–62.

4. Suzanne Degges-White, "Battered Men: Shame May Keep Them Silent," *Psychology Today*, November 28, 2017, https://www.psychologytoday.com/us/blog/lifetime-connections/201711/battered-men-shame-may-keep-them-silent.

5. David Eagleman, "The Mystery of Stephen Paddock's Brain," CNN, October 5, 2017, https://www.cnn.com/2017/10/05/opinions/mystery-of-stephen-paddocks-brain-opinion

-eagleman/index.html; Dave Philipps and Matthew Haag, "Las Vegas Gunman's Criminal Father Vanished from Sons' Lives," *New York Times*, October 2, 2017, https://www.nytimes.com/2017/10/02/us/benjamin-paddock-stephen-paddock.html.

6. Christine Hauser, "Gun Death Rate Rose Again in 2016, CDC Says," *New York Times*, November 4, 2017, https://www.nytimes.com/2017/11/04/us/gun-death-rates.html.

7. "Men and Suicide," Centre for Suicide Prevention, https://www.suicideinfo.ca/resource/men-and-suicide/; Thomas Joiner, *Lonely at the Top: The High Cost of Men's Success* (New York: Palgrave Macmillan, 2011), pp. 266–70.

8. Dana Crowley Jack, *Silencing the Self: Women and Depression* (Cambridge, MA: Harvard University Press, 1991); Ronald C. Kessler, "Epidemiology of Women and Depression," *Journal of Affective Disorders* 74, no. 1 (March 2003): 5–13.

9. "Domestic or Intimate Partner Violence," Office on Women's Health, US Department of Health & Human Services, https://www.womenshealth.gov/relationships-and-safety/domestic-violence; "Get the Fact and Figures," The National Domestic Violence Hotline, https://www.thehotline.org/resources/statistics/.

10. "Eating Disorder Statistics," National Association of Anorexia Nervosa and Associated Disorders, https://anad.org/education-and-awareness/about-eating-disorders/eating-disorders-statistics/; Danielle A. Gagne et al., "Eating Disorder Symptoms and Weight and Shape Concerns in a Large Web-Based Convenience Sample of Women Ages 50 and Above: Results of the Gender and Body Image (GABI) Study," *International Journal of Eating Disorders* 45, no. 7 (November 2012): 832–34; Elizabeth W. Diemer et al., "Gender Identity, Sexual Orientation, and Eating-Related Pathology in a National Sample of College Students," *Journal of Adolescent Health* 57, no. 2 (August 2015): 144–49.

11. Amir A. Mufaddel, Ossama T. Osman, Fadwa Almugaddam, and Mohammad Jafferany, "A Review of Body Dysmorphic Disorder and Its Presentation in Different Clinical Settings," *The Primary Care Companion for CNS Disorders* 15, no. 4 (2013).

12. Eric Levenson and Brynn Gingras, "Kate Spade, Fashion Designer, Found Dead in Apparent Suicide," CNN, June 6, 2018, https://www.cnn.com/2018/06/05/us/kate-spade-dead/index.html; Katie Kindelan, "Kate Spade's 'Sounded Happy' before Her Suicide: How Depression Can Be so Hidden and What Loved Ones Can Do," *Good Morning America*, June 7, 2018, https://www.goodmorningamerica.com/wellness/story/kate-spade-sounded-happy-suicide-depression-hidden-loved-55718387.

Chapter 4. The Daily Functioning of Shame: Seven Common Emotional Cycles

1. Donald Winnicott, MD, a pediatrician and psychoanalyst, developed the concepts of True Self, Fake/False Self in 1960 and used these terms in connection to narcissism and other personality disorders (e.g., borderline, dependent). He wrote many works on topics such as stages of development, holding environment, subjective omnipotence, objective reality, transitional experience, good enough parent, and true vs. false self. See D. W. Winnicott, *Maturational Processes and the Facilitating Environment: Studies in the Theory of Emotional Development* (London: Hogarth, 1965); *The Collected Works of D. W. Winnicott*, ed. Lesley Caldwell and Helen Taylor Robinson, vol. 6, *1960–1963* (Oxford: Oxford University Press, 2017), chapter 1.

Chapter 5. Where Shame Hides and Terrorizes: Your Money, Your Love Life, Your Family Past and Present, Your Health/Body, and Dying

1. Conrad W. Baars and Anna A. Terruwe, *Healing the Unaffirmed: Recognizing Emotional Deprivation Disorder*, rev. and updated ed. (New York: Alba House, 2001).

2. Erik Erikson's eight stages of development are considered universal challenges. Each stage is a contrast between two competing psychological issues that everyone has to address during the course of their lifetime. The stages are, in order of appearance in a person's life: 1. trust vs. mistrust; 2. autonomy vs. shame; 3. initiative vs. guilt; 4. industry vs. inferiority; 5. ego identity vs. role confusion; 6. intimacy vs. isolation; 7. generativity vs. stagnation; 8. ego integrity vs. despair. See Saul McLeod, "Developmental Psychology," *Simply Psychology*, January 14, 2017, https://www .simplypsychology.org/developmental -psychology.html; Michael Rutter, "Stress, Coping, and Development: Some Issues and Some Questions," *Journal of Child Psychology and Psychiatry* 22, no. 4 (October 1981): 323–56.

3. Enmeshment is a description of a relationship between two or more people in which personal boundaries are permeable and unclear, This often happens on an emotional level in which two people (parent-child) "feel" each other's emotions, or when one person becomes emotionally escalated and the other family member does as well. See "Understanding Enmeshment: Definition, Causes, & Signs You May Need Help," New Haven Residential Treatment Center (blog), https:// www.newhavenrtc.com/parenting-teens/understanding-enmeshment/.

4. Sharon K. Farber, "Self-Mutilation, Eating Disorders, and Suicide," *The Mind-Body Connection* (blog), *Psychology Today*, November 12, 2014, https://www.psychologytoday.com/us/blog/ the-mind-body-connection/201411/self-mutilation-eating-disorders-and -suicide. See also Sharon K. Farber, *When the Body Is the Target: Self-Harm, Pain, and Traumatic Attachments* Lanham, MD: Jason Aronson, 2002).

Chapter 6. The Big Cover Up, Super Glue: Addictions and Shame

1. Luna Dolezal and Barry Lyons, "Shaming People about Their Lifestyle Habits Does Nothing to Improve Their Health," *The Conversation*, December 5, 2017, http://theconversation .com/shaming-people-about-their-lifestyle-habits-does-nothing-to-improve-their-health-88427.

2. Sigmund Freud, *Introductory Lectures on Psychoanalysis*, trans. James Strachey (New York: Penguin), pp. 383. According to Freud, regression is a psychological defense mechanism in which a person abandons age-appropriate coping skills in favor of earlier more childlike patterns of behavior.

3. Christopher Ingraham, "One in Eight Americans Is an Alcoholic, Study Says," *Washington Post*, August 11, 2017, https://www.washingtonpost.com/news/wonk/wp/2017/08/11/study-one -in-eight-american-adults-are-alcoholics/?noredirect=on&utm_term=.546fff067a3e. This article is based on this research by Bridget F. Grant et al., "Prevalence of 12-Month Alcohol Use, High-Risk Drinking, and *DSM-IV* Alcohol Use Disorder in the United States, 2001–2002 to 2012–2013: Results from the National Epidemiologic Survey on Alcohol and Related Conditions," *JAMA Psychiatry* 74, no. 9 (September 2017): 911–23.

4. According to the CDC, cigarette smoking causes more than 480,000 deaths each year in the United States. This means nearly one in five deaths is smoking related. "Smoking and Tobacco Use: Fast Facts," Centers for Disease Control and Prevention, 2018, https://www.cdc.gov/tobacco/ data_statistics/fact_sheets/fast_facts/index.htm See the website; cdc.gov for complete life-threatening impact of cigarette smoking.

5. "Global Information System on Alcohol and Health," World Health Organization, https://www.who.int/gho/alcohol/en/.

6. Commonly known as : The Big Book. The actual title is *Alcoholics Anonymous: The Story of How Many Thousands of Men and Women Have Recovered from Alcoholism* (New York: AA World Services, 1939). The book is one of the bestselling books of all time, with over 30 million copies.

7. "Compulsive Gambling," Mayo Clinic, https://www.mayoclinic.org/diseases-conditions/compulsive-gambling/symptoms-causes/syc-20355178.

8. Marie Wilson, "Creativity and Shame Reduction in Sex Addiction Treatment," *Sexual Addiction and Compulsivity: The Journal of Treatment and Prevention* 7, no. 4 (2000): 229–48.

Rory C. Reid, James M. Harper, and Emily H. Anderson, "Coping Strategies Used by Hypersexual Patients to Defend Against the Painful Effects of Shame," *Clinical Psychology & Psychotherapy: An International Journal of Theory & Practice* 16, no. 2 (March/April 2009): 125–38.

9. Sex trafficking is human trafficking for the purposes of sexual exploitation, including sexual slavery. See Siddharth Kara, *Sex Trafficking: Inside the Business of Modern Slavery* (New York: Columbia University Press, 2010).

Chapter 7. Your Personal Brand of Shame: Fear, Avoidance, and Emotional Terrorism

1. Ernest Wolf, *Treating the Self: Elements of Clinical Self-Psychology* (New York: Guilford Press, 2002).

John R. Ogawa, L. Alan Sroufe, Nancy S. Weinfield, and Elizabeth A. Carlson, "Development and the Fragmented Self; Longitudinal study of Dissociative Symptomatology in a Nonclinical Sample," *Development and Psychopathology* 9, no. 4 (December 1997): 855–79.

2. Egil W. Martinsen, "Physical Activity in the Prevention and Treatment of Anxiety and Depression," *Nordic Journal of Psychiatry* 62, sup. 47 (2008): 25–29.

Chantal Henry et al., "Anxiety Disorders in 318 Bipolar Patients: Prevalence and Impact on Illness Severity and Response to Mood Stabilizer," *Journal of Clinical Psychiatry* 64, no. 3 (2003): 331–35.

3. Susan Gordon, "Eastern versus Western Psychology," *Unbound* (blog), Saybrook University, April 20, 2015, https://www.saybrook.edu/unbound/eastern-western-psychology/.

Yozan Dirk Mosig, "Conceptions of the Self in Western and Eastern Psychology," *Journal of Theoretical and Philosophical Psychology* 26 (1–2), pp. 39–50, 2006.

Chapter 9. No More Secrets: Your Own Healing Exposure Process—Viewing All the Parts of Your Life from 10,000 Feet

1. Erik Erikson's eight stages of development and his landmark work on human development makes him the pioneer in developmental psychology. His classic book is Erik Erikson, *Childhood and Society* (1950; New York: W. W. Norton, 1993).

2. Jan E. Stets and Peter J. Burke, "Self-Esteem and Identities," *Sociological Perspectives* 57, no. 4 (December 2014): 409–33; Steven Stosny, "Recovering More of the Core-Self," *Anger in the Age of Entitlement* (blog), *Psychology Today*, March 18, 2011, https://www.psychologytoday.com/us/blog/anger-in-the-age-entitlement/201103/recovering-more-the-core-self.

3. Stephanie Scheck, *The Stages of Psychosocial Development According to Erik H. Erikson* (New York: Open Publishing Group, 2005); William Damon and Richard M. Lerner, eds., *Handbook of Child Psychology*, vol. 4, *Child Psychology in Practice*, ed. K. Ann Renninger and Irving E. Sigel, 6th ed.

(Hoboken, NJ: Wiley, 2006); Urie Bronfenbrenner, *The Ecology of Human Development: Experiments by Nature and Design* (Cambridge, MA: Harvard University Press, 1979).

4. Timothy A. Judge and Joyce E. Bono, "Relationship of Core Self-Evaluations Traits—Self-Esteem, Generalized Self-Efficacy, Locus of Control, and Emotional Stability—with Job Satisfaction and Job Performance: A Meta-Analysis," *Journal of Applied Psychology* 86, no. 1 (February 2001): 80; *Core self* is defined in an article by Margarita Tartakovsky, "Connecting to Your Core Self," *World of Psychology* (blog), July 8, 2018, https://psychcentral.com/blog/connecting-to-your-core-self/.

Chapter 10. Rewriting and Rewiring Your Emotional Triggers

1. Kathy Hardie-Williams, "Emotional Incest: When Parents Make Their Kids Partners," GoodTherapy, September 14, 2016, https://www.goodtherapy.org/blog/emotional-covert-incest-when-parents-make-their-kids-partners-0914165; Kenneth M. Adams, *Silently Seduced: When Parents Make Their Children Partners*, rev. and updated ed. (Deerfield Beach, FL: Health Communications, 2011); Kenneth M. Adams, *When He's Married to Mom: How to Help Mother-Enmeshed Men Open Their Hearts to True Love and Commitment* (New York: Touchstone Books, 2007).

2. Jim Orford, *Excessive Appetites: A Psychological View of Addictions*, 2nd ed. (Chichester, UK: John Wiley and Sons, 2001); Jon Elster, *Strong Feelings: Emotion, Addiction, and Human Behavior* (Cambridge, MA: MIT Press, 1999); John Bradshaw, *Healing the Shame That Binds You* (Deerfield Beach, FL: Health Communications, 1988); John Bradshaw, *Homecoming: Reclaiming and Championing Your Inner Child* (New York: Bantam Books, 1990).

Chapter 11. Three Big-Time Changes: Acceptance, Empathy, and Understanding—It's All within You

1. Fabiana Franco, "Complex Trauma: Dissociation, Fragmentation, and Self-Understanding," Psych Central, October 8, 2018, https://psychcentral.com/lib/dissociation-fragmentation-and-self-understanding/; Janina Fisher, *Healing the Fragmented Selves of Trauma Survivors* (New York: Routledge, 2017), chap. 4.

2. Richard C. Schwartz, *Internal Family Systems Therapy*, rev. ed. (New York: Guilford, 1997), chap. 1; Frank Anderson, Martha Sweezy, and Richard C. Schwartz, *Internal Family Systems Skills Training Manual: Trauma-Informed Treatment for Anxiety, Depression, PTSD, and Substance Abuse* (New York: PESI, 2017), sect. 1.

Chapter 12. Developing Your Own Eagle Mindset: Your Endless Resource

1. Seth Godin, *Linchpin: Are You Indispensable?* (New York: Portfolio, 2010), chap. 2. This book wonderfully describes how our lizard brain functions in a day-to-day setting. The automatic reactions we sometimes have aren't always our best response. This a non-scientific look at our brain's functioning.

2. David G. Andrewes, *Neuropsychology: From Theory to Practice* (New York: Taylor and Francis, 2001). This is an excellent introduction to the way all the different areas of the brain interact and function. The three parts of the brain we are discussing—lizard, owl, and eagle—are explained in excellent detail. The complexity of the brain and its impact on a person's life is the scope of this book. The field of neuropsychology focuses on all the different relationships between brain functioning and its emotional and psychological impact on us.

BIBLIOGRAPHY

Allen, Patricia, and Sandra Harmon. *Getting to "I Do": The Secret to Doing Relationships Right.* New York: William Morrow, 1994.

American Psychiatric Association. *Diagnostic and Statistical Manual of Mental Disorders, Fifth Edition.* Washington, DC: American Psychiatric Association, 2013.

Angelou, Maya. *Rainbow in the Cloud: The Wisdom and Spirit of Maya Angelou.* New York: Random House, 2014.

Beattie, Melody. *Codependent No More: How to Stop Controlling Others and Start Caring for Yourself.* Center City, MN: Hazelden, 1986.

Bowen, Murray. *Family Therapy in Clinical Practice.* Northvale, NJ: Jason Aronson, 1988.

Bowlby, John. *A Secure Base: Parent-Child Attachment and Healthy Human Development.* New York: Basic Books, 1988.

Bradshaw, John. *Healing the Shame That Binds You.* Deerfield Beach, FL: Health Communications, 1988.

———. *Homecoming: Reclaiming and Championing Your Inner Child.* New York, Bantam Books, 1990.

Brazelton, T. Berry. *Working and Caring.* Reading, MA: Addison-Wesley, 1985.

Briggs, Dorothy Corkille. *Your Child's Self-Esteem: Step-by-Step Guidelines for Raising Responsible, Productive, Happy Children.* New York: Broadway Books, 1975.

Brown, Brené. *The Gifts of Imperfection: Let Go of Who You Think You're Supposed to Be and Embrace Who You Are.* Center City, MN: Hazelden, 2010.

———. *I Thought It Was Just Me (But It Isn't): Making the Journey from "What Will People Think?" to "I Am Enough."* New York: Avery, 2007.

Brown, Byron. *Soul without Shame: A Guide to Liberating Yourself from the Judge Within.* Boston, Shambhala, 1999.

Bryan, Mark. *Codes of Love: How to Rethink Your Family and Remake Your Life.* New York: Simon and Schuster, 1999.

Canfield, Jack. *The Success Principles: How to Get From Where You Are to Where You Want to Be.* New York: Harper Resource, 2005.

Carter, Elizabeth A., and Monica McGoldrick, eds. *The Family Life Cycle: A Framework for Family Therapy.* New York: Gardner, 1980.

Chapman, Gary. *The Five Love Languages: How to Express Heartfelt Commitment to Your Mate.* Chicago: Northfield, 1992.

Chödrön, Pema. *Comfortable with Uncertainty: 108 Teachings.* Compiled and edited by Emily Hilburn Sell. Boston: Shambhala, 2002.

Chopra, Deepak, and Leonard Mlodinow. *War of the Worldviews: Science vs. Spirituality.* New York: Harmony Books, 2011.

Dass, Ram. *Still Here: Embracing Aging, Changing, and Dying.* New York: Riverhead Books, 2000.

Dyer, Wayne W. *There's a Spiritual Solution to Every Problem.* New York: HarperCollins, 2001.

————. *Wishes Fulfilled: Mastering the Art of Manifesting.* Carlsbad, CA: Hay House, 2012.

Eden, Donna, and David Feinstein. *Energy Medicine for Women: Aligning Your Body's Energies to Boost Your Health and Vitality.* New York: Jeremy P. Tarcher/Penguin, 2008.

Ellis, Albert, and Harper, Robert. *A Guide to Rational Living.* Englewood Cliffs, NJ: Prentice-Hall, 1961.

Glasser, William. *Choice Theory: A New Psychology of Personal Freedom.* New York: HarperCollins, 1998.

————. *Reality Therapy: A New Approach to Psychiatry.* New York: Harper and Row, 1965.

Hay, Louise L. *You Can Heal Your Life.* Santa Monica, CA: Hay House, 1984.

Hay, Louise L., and Robert Holden. *Life Loves You: 7 Spiritual Practices to Heal Your Life.* Carlsbad, CA: Hay House, 2015.

Holden, Robert. *Happiness Now! Timeless Wisdom for Feeling Good Fast.* London, UK: Hodder Mobius, 1998.

Hollis, James. *Swamplands of the Soul: New Life in Dismal Places.* Toronto, ON: Inner City Books, 1996.

Jung, C. G. *Memories, Dreams, Reflections.* Recorded and edited by Aniela Jaffé. Translated by Richard and Clara Winston. New York: Pantheon Books, 1961.

————. *Symbols of Transformation: An Analysis of the Prelude to a Case of Schizophrenia.* Translated by R. F. C. Hull. 2nd ed. Princeton, NJ: Princeton University Press, 1967.

Kabat-Zinn, Jon. *Wherever You Go, There You Are: Mindfulness Meditation in Everyday Life.* New York: Hyperion, 1994.

Karen, Robert. "Shame." *Atlantic Monthly*, February 1992, pp. 40–70.

Kübler-Ross, Elisabeth. *Working It Through: An Elisabeth Kübler-Ross Workshop on Life, Death, and Transition.* New York: Macmillan, 1982.

Millman, Dan. *Way of the Peaceful Warrior: A Book That Changes Lives.* New rev. ed. Tiburon, CA: H. J. Kramer, 2000.

Myss, Caroline. *Defy Gravity: Healing beyond the Bounds of Reason.* Carlsbad, CA: Hay House, 2009.

Nhat Hanh, Thich. *True Love: A Practice for Awakening the Heart.* Translated by Sherab Chödzin Kohn. Boston: Shambhala, 2004.

Peck, Scott M. *The Road Less Traveled, 25th Anniversary Edition: A New Psychology of Love, Traditional Values, and Spiritual Growth.* New York: Simon and Schuster, 2002.

Poulter, Stephan B. *The Art of Successful Failure.* Bloomington, IN: Hay House, 2016.

———. *The Father Factor: How Your Father's Legacy Impacts Your Career.* Amherst, NY: Prometheus Books, 2006.

———. *Father Your Son: How to Become the Father You've Always Wanted to Be.* New York: McGraw-Hill, 2004.

———. *The Mother Factor: How Your Mother's Emotional Legacy Impacts Your Life.* Amherst, NY: Prometheus Books, 2008.

———. *Your Ex-Factor: Overcome Heartbreak and Build a Better Life.* Amherst, NY: Prometheus Books, 2009.

Rinpoche, Sogyal. *The Tibetan Book of Living and Dying: A New Spiritual Classic from One of the Foremost Interpreters of Tibetan Buddhism to the West.* San Francisco: Harper, 1992.

Ruiz, Don Miguel. *The Four Agreements: A Practical Guide to Personal Freedom.* San Rafael, CA: Amber-Allen, 1997.

Sheehy, Gail. *Passages: Predictable Crises of Adult Life.* New York: E. P. Dutton, 1976.

Spock, Benjamin. *The Common Sense Book of Baby and Child Care.* New York: Duell, Sloan, and Pearce, 1946.

Strong, Mary. *Letters of the Scattered Brotherhood.* New York: Harper, 1948.

Tolle, Eckhart. *A New Earth: Awakening to Your Life's Purpose.* New York: Dutton, 2005.

Van Praagh, James. *Adventures of the Soul: Journeys Through the Physical and Spiritual Dimensions.* Carlsbad, CA: Hay House, 2014.

Zax, Barbara, and Stephan B. Poulter. *Mending the Broken Bough: Restoring the Promise of the Mother-Daughter Relationship.* New York: Penguin, 1998.

RESOURCE GUIDE

The listings below are for your assistance in navigating the process of finding the proper treatment, psychological information, crisis support, self-care, and information to direct you to whatever next steps you may need to take. This is a starting point for many different concerns and interests that you might have. Please explore all the professional options listed below that may be necessary for your well-being and health.

Assistance in finding a mental health professional (e.g., psychiatrist, psychologist, or licensed clinical social worker)

- Psychology Today: www.psychologytoday.com
- Find a Psychologist: www.findapsychologist.org
- American Psychological Association: www.apa.org
- American Psychiatric Association: www.psychiatry.org
- Referrals from family or friends
- Referral from a primary care physician
- Referrals from a local university's psychiatry or psychology department
- Employee assistance programs or helpline supported by your employer

Support groups to find general information or local groups in your area

- Alcoholics Anonymous: www.aa.org
- Co-Dependents Anonymous: www.coda.org
- American Addiction Centers: www.recovery.org
- American Addiction Centers: Drug Abuse: www.drugabuse .com
- Sex Addicts Anonymous: www.saa-recovery.org
- National Domestic Violence Hotline: www.thehotline.org
- National Drug Helpline: www.drughelpline.org
- National Suicide Prevention Lifeline: www.suicideprevention lifeline.org
- National Runaway Safeline: www.1800runaway.org

Guided meditation and mindfulness support, apps, and workshops

- The Mindfulness App: themindfulnessapp.com
- Calm: www.calm.com
- Headspace: www.headspace.com
- Buddhify: www.buddhify.com
- Gaiam: www.gaiam.com
- mindbodygreen: www.mindbodygreen.com
- Local temples, churches, or centers sponsoring meditation classes, workshops, and retreats
- Yoga classes and retreats

General information and resources on various mental health topics for day-to-day emotional issues

- Psychology Today: www.psychologytoday.com
- American Addiction Centers: Mental Help: www.mentalhelp.net
- Psych Central: www.psychcentral.com